A L[ ]

o*f*

OLD BALLS

James Harkin and Anna Ptaszynski are senior researchers, writers and script editors for the BBC's *QI* and two-fourths of the award-winning podcast *No Such Thing As A Fish*. Between them, they have authored thirteen books with the QI Elves and toured sell-out shows across the world, from the London Palladium to the Sydney Opera House.

They are long-suffering fans of Jacksonville Jaguars and Charlton Athletic, respectively.

Also from QI

Funny You Should Ask . . .
222 QI Answers to Your Quite Ingenious Questions

QI FACTS SERIES

1,227 QI Facts To Blow Your Socks Off
1,339 QI Facts To Make Your Jaw Drop
1,411 QI Facts To Knock You Sideways
1,234 QI Facts To Leave You Speechless
1,342 QI Facts To Leave You Flabbergasted
1,423 QI Facts To Bowl You Over
2,024 QI Facts To Stop You In Your Tracks

GENERAL IGNORANCE SERIES

The Book of General Ignorance
The Second Book of General Ignorance
The Third Book of General Ignorance
The Book of Animal Ignorance
Advanced Banter: The QI Book of Quotations
The QI Book of The Dead

BY NO SUCH THING AS A FISH

The Book of the Year 2017
The Book of the Year 2018
The Book of the Year 2019

A LOAD
of
OLD BALLS

The QI *History of Sport*

James Harkin and
Anna Ptaszynski

faber

First published in 2023
by Faber & Faber Ltd
The Bindery, 51 Hatton Garden
London EC1N 8HN
This paperback edition published in 2024

Typeset by Ian Bahrami
Printed and bound in England by CPI Group (UK) Ltd, Croydon CR0 4YY

A CIP record for this book
is available from the British Library

ISBN 978–0–571–37254–6

Printed and bound in the UK on FSC® certified paper in line with our continuing
commitment to ethical business practices, sustainability and the environment.
For further information see faber.co.uk/environmental-policy

2 4 6 8 10 9 7 5 3 1

For Jelly and Bean

CONTENTS

INTRODUCTION

At quarter to midnight on Sunday 28 May 2023, Latvia's parliament was called for an unscheduled, urgent meeting. At the hastily convened session, it was declared that the following day would be a national public holiday. The reason? The country's success at the Ice Hockey World Championships.

Latvia hadn't actually won the competition – that honour had gone to Canada. Nor had they come second – the silver medal went to Germany. But they had unexpectedly beaten the USA to claim third place, in by far their best-ever showing at the tournament.* The game itself had tested the nerves of fans, with the USA ahead 3–2 until five minutes before the final whistle. A last-minute equaliser from Latvian defenceman Kristians Rubins pushed the match into overtime, before Rubins again found the net to complete a stunning comeback.

....

* Better to be Latvia than Germany under the circumstances. Studies of athletes' facial expressions on the podium have repeatedly found that bronze-medal-winners appear happier than silver-medal-winners. The former are just happy to have a medal at all, but the latter will always wish they'd won gold. As psychologist William James put it in 1892: 'That he is able to beat the whole population of the globe minus one is nothing; he has "pitted" himself to beat that one; and as long as he doesn't do that nothing else counts.'

As Latvia's entire population woke up to their surprise holiday the next morning, 50,000 of them took to the streets of the capital to celebrate. The plane carrying the team flew low over the city centre to greet the crowds on its way home.

As popular as ice hockey is in Latvia, it's unlikely that all 1.9 million Latvians are avid fans. But it's also unlikely that many of them were unaffected by the communal sense of joy that day – and not just because they didn't have to go to work.

That feeling of shared elation might well be familiar to you, if you picked up this book because you're the type of person who flips straight to the back pages of the newspaper or watches replays of games where you already know the score. But this is also a book for people who don't consider themselves sports fans, or 'sporty' more generally. It aims to show that far from being an exclusive bubble, sport is for everyone – as the Latvian parliament recognised. And far from being an inconsequential trifle, sport is fundamental to being human.

Even if you'd rather pull out your own toenails (see p. 192) than sit through a rugby match or snooker tournament, we hope you'll be entertained by the stories that have emerged out of millennia of people trying to be the fastest, strongest, most skilful or, indeed, the most determined. We defy anyone not to feel invested in the adventures of Dick-a-Dick the Aboriginal cricketer, who rescued three lost children from the outback and fell in love with an Englishwoman; or in the pioneering swimmer who had bagpipes serenade her across the English Channel. And most readers, surely, will struggle not to take sides in the ongoing saga of golfers vs rabbits, which once almost resulted in murder.

Alongside compelling narratives, all sports throw up a wealth of unexpected trivia. If you're intrigued by capuchin monkeys' attitude towards cheating, the final resting place of Mary Queen of Scots' football or the activity that links actor David Arquette and baseball legend Babe Ruth (hint: it's not baseball), read on. These facts and stories help illustrate the enduring appeal of sport throughout human history: fundamentally, it's not really about sport at all, but about human beings (or, occasionally, monkeys), in all their glory and absurdity.

Sport permeates every part of life: history, politics, technology, mythology, psychology, medicine, art and philosophy to name a few. Looking at it from any one of these perspectives reveals fresh truths and fascinating tales. Indeed, ask any number of people what it is that sport means to them – as we did in the process of writing this book – and you will very rarely hear the same answer twice.

Some of those we spoke to were drawn to the element of play and fun; others loved the camaraderie and team spirit involved. Some enjoyed the discipline of playing within the rules or the intellectual challenge of analysing a game; others pointed to the satisfaction of facing and overcoming mental and physical challenges. Several mentioned the joy of being able to lose yourself in a sport, while the subject of narrative and drama also came up repeatedly, applying both to matches, races and events as they happen in real time, and to the wider context in which they take place. In this great range of themes, one thing was clear: sport offers something for everyone.

We set out to write a book that did the same. Nothing here requires prior knowledge about, or even interest in, a particular sport. However, we are hugely indebted to those who possess knowledge and interest in spades: the devotees and experts whose works we mined along the way. One of the great things about humankind's obsession with sport is that there is some delightfully obscure and niche literature out there. We had the pleasure of reading whole books dedicated to crown green bowling, Afghan goat polo, women's competitive multi-day race-walking and dozens of other arcane forms of entertainment. We also scoured as many contemporary sources as we could find, so that even if some stories are familiar to you, they should still feature details that are new to every reader.

Our research revealed that at its best, sport can be truly democratic, regardless of age, experience or physical ability: just ask the thirteen- and fourteen-year old girls who represented England in the 1971 football World Cup; American Robert Garrett, who won gold in the first Olympic discus event, despite having never seen one before; or Matt Stutzman, the world-record-holding archer who was born with no arms. And this inclusivity applies to the endless variety of sports on offer, too. If you're bored senseless by cricket, tennis or football, the final chapter of this book gives plenty of niche sports that are just waiting to be tried (we wouldn't suggest everyone goes out looking for a game of 17th-century goose-pulling, but there's always professional pillow fighting or international 'keeping the balloon in the air').

Sport can be divisive, as we'll see at various moments in this book, but more often it brings millions of people together like nothing else on earth. That power to connect is what drew 50,000 Latvians to the streets as they greeted a low-flying plane in Riga during their impromptu public holiday. It's what had us cheering for coach Pop Warner's wily college football underdogs; Collingwood's eternally underperforming Aussie-rules side; and the incredible Taiwanese women's tug-of-war team. Whether you find yourself rooting for Shoeless Joe, Paula the Crawler or the Secret Squirrel Club, we hope you enjoy hearing about their stories just as much as we did.

James & Anna

1

WRESTLING FOR THE PHARAOHS

WHY THE ORIGINS OF SPORT ARE SO HARD TO PIN DOWN

Life without sport is not life.
Mary Breese
(18th-century equestrian)

You have small feet and long legs. You have good balance. You have large buttocks. We're not just dishing out compliments here – these are traits shared by almost all humans, and they're what make us such exceptional runners. Our ancient ancestors had much longer toes, which are great for climbing trees but not so good for jogging: if your toes were just 20% longer, running would take twice as much energy.[*]

You also have a strong jawline. By and large, men have stronger jaws than women. It was long thought that these evolved because early hominids ate lots of nuts, seeds and tough meat. But this theory cannot explain the difference between the sexes, nor why strong jaws are also found in a human ancestor called *Australopithecus*, a species that mostly ate soft fruits. The most recent theory is that we evolved strong jaws in order to become good fighters, since they can take a

....

[*] This is because your feet act like the gears on a bike. When you run flat-footedly, the speed at which you can run depends on the ratio between the length of your lower leg and the length of your foot. When you run on your toes, it's the ratio between the length of your foot and that of your toes. That's a steeper ratio, thanks to our short toes, meaning if you go from foot-running to toe-running, it's like going up a gear.

punch. It could also explain why our hands have evolved in the way they have – they make such a good fist.

Humans, in short, are built for running and fighting. Martial arts and foot races are usually considered to be the first sports that we invented, but why did we go from running and fighting just to stay alive to doing so for recreation? What made our early ancestors, fleeing predators on the savannah or battling for survival, stop and think: 'Hang on, this is actually quite fun'?

It all comes down to our love of play, and the reason why we play at all is almost certainly because it helps children practise adulting. There's plenty of evidence for this. For instance, archaeologists in North America have found many smaller, children's versions of hunting implements that date back 2,000 years; they reason that by throwing a small spear or rock, a child would develop hand–eye co-ordination skills that would be vital in later life.* It's not a huge leap to go from there to throwing a dart at a board or a basketball through a hoop.

Practising sport has other benefits, too, which explains why humans continue to do it into adulthood. Of course, it would have made our ancestors healthier, and so more attractive to the opposite sex and more likely to live longer (survival of the 'fittest' in both meanings of the word). But it goes beyond this: working as a team can help mental health, and pushing the body to its limits can produce incredible highs. Watching

---

* Among the Sirionó people of Bolivia, who subsist on hunted game, boys receive their first tiny bow and arrow when they're just three months old. Girls are given miniature spindles to play with.

sport can give you a feeling of belonging. Winning can give you a drug-like high. Even cheating can make you feel better.

These facts help to explain how sport went from being a necessary part of growing up to an integral, species-defining aspect of human culture. It takes a similar role to ritual and religion, to such an extent that the Mayans actually believed there were sporting clashes before the Sun and the Moon existed (presumably they had very good floodlights) . . .

A WHOLE DIFFERENT BALL GAME

The *Popol Vuh*, the sacred book of the K'iche' people (a Mayan group), features the story of the twins Hunahpú and Xbalanqué. According to the legend, as punishment for disturbing the inhabitants of the underworld with their noisy ball games the twins were summoned to play a match of their favourite sport against the gods of death. The two teams would compete to see who could get a rubber ball into their opponent's goal.

The gods were confident of victory. The twins' journey to the chosen venue required them to pass through the House of Gloom, the House of Knives, the House of Cold, the House of Jaguars, the House of Bats and the House of Fire. All of these buildings were aptly named, so it was likely that they would arrive at the match a little worse for wear. And, of course, their opponents were gods and, therefore, omnipotent beings, which is likely to be a clincher in any sporting event.*

---

* Though it's not always quite so simple: in the Bible (Genesis 32:24–25), Jacob wrestles with God. The omnipotent one was victorious – but

To make matters worse for the twins, their pre-match build-up was disrupted by Hunahpú having been decapitated by a killer bat in the aforementioned House of Bats. So it was something of a surprise when he and Xbalanqué nonetheless took to the pitch at the allotted hour. The gods, represented by two of their number known simply as One death and Seven death, arrived with the match ball – which was in fact the recently severed head of Hunahpú. This surely gave them a psychological edge.

The brothers had a trick up their sleeves, however, which was their special relationship with the animals of the earth. A friendly raccoon had found a squash and offered it to Hunahpú as a replacement for his head. And then, mid-game, when Hunahpú's actual head was kicked into a tomato patch, it was hidden by a rabbit, who then bounced out of the vegetation and onto the pitch, pretending to be the ball. As the gods chased the rabbit, Xbalanqué retrieved his brother's head and returned it to him, swapping it for the squash. The referee seemed happy enough that the vegetable could now be used as the match ball (no VAR in those days), and Xbalanqué punted it into the goal. It smashed on impact with the ground, its seeds flying everywhere. With no more ball, the game was over. The twins had won 1–0.

The tale continues with the brothers running away from the angry gods, before being caught and burnt to death, and having their ashes scattered into a river, where they

only after he 'touched the hollow of his [Jacob's] thigh', which many people take to mean that Jacob suffered a blow 'below the belt'.

reconstituted into catfish and finally turned back into humans. After several other scrapes with the gods of death, they eventually climbed into the heavens, where they became the Sun and the Moon.

In Mayan society, the game that the twins played against the gods was regularly re-enacted, and this became one of the most important rituals in ancient American culture. The ceremony, known to us as the Mesoamerican Ballgame, is believed by many to be the oldest-known team sport. For at least three millennia, Americans from Nicaragua in the South to Arizona in the North played various iterations of the game, with names such as *tlachtli*, *ullamaliztli*, *pok-ta-pok* and *pitz*. The exact rules of each version are unclear, since most of what we know comes from artistic depictions, archaeological remains and fantastical stories about rabbits and gods. But the aim was probably to propel the ball with your hips, upper arms or sometimes a bat to the opponent's end of the pitch, where hoops were used as goals.

Mesoamerican carvings and mythology suggest matches would often end with a human sacrifice, but if that's true, we're not sure who was sacrificed. Some academics think it was the losing team; others believe it was the winners. You might think that if it was the latter, it would result in teams throwing games, though the Mayans would consider that impossible, since it was the gods who decided the result. The general consensus among historians is that it would be a bit daft to sacrifice your best sportspeople – win or lose – and that if any sacrifices did occur, it would have been prisoners who were killed.

The association of violence with sport is not confined to the Mayans. Novelist George Orwell referred to sport as 'war minus the shooting', and many cultures have used play as a way to prepare for battle. Just as sport has long helped children to learn adult skills, so it has been used to help young men and women prepare for combat. Ironically, since sport has united people on so many occasions, a lot of modern sports have in fact been born out of classic human belligerence.

PLAY-FIGHTING

Polo is an ancient sport, but the first match played in Britain took place in 1869, after an army officer called Edward 'Chicken' Hartopp (whose nickname appears to have been an ironic reference to his size and bravery) read about a modern version of an ancient Persian game that was being played in India. He organised a match with fellow officers, initially calling it 'hockey on horseback'. Players in those early games usually used a cricket ball, which they hit with walking sticks rather than mallets (although one early match was said to have used golf clubs and a snooker ball*).

The game took off among the British military, who formulated the modern rules and spread their version around the

---

* Such was the claim of Colonel Robert S. Liddell, who watched and recorded the earliest games. None of his fellow officers corroborate this, however, and if it were indeed the case, most of the game would in all likelihood have been spent looking for the snooker ball, rather than hitting it towards the goal (especially if they chose to play with the green one).

world – appropriately perhaps, since the Persian original was invented to prepare men for war.* In fact, the Persian game was effectively a battle in miniature. Unlike the modern game of polo, which is four-a-side, the Persian version could have up to a hundred riders on each team. The sport clearly extended beyond its military purpose, though, since women often played, despite almost never having a role on the battlefield. In one of the most influential works of medieval Persian literature, the romantic tragedy of *Khosrow and Shirin*, the lovers and their attendants play each other in games of polo, apparently equally matched.

Many of the ancient Greek Olympic events also had military roots. Throwing the javelin and the 'footrace in armour'† self-evidently aped skills required in battle; the race in which participants had to jump off a chariot moving at full speed, run alongside the horses and then jump back onto the vehicle perhaps not so obviously – but this came from the fact that Greek soldiers were often transported to the battlefield

---

* The British military still likes to use sports to wind down. The Royal Navy plays a game called 'deck hockey' aboard its ships. Rather than a ball or a puck, they use a coiled piece of rope, which they try to hit with sticks into an improvised goal. A typical game goes through a lot of rope, since the 'ball' regularly finds its way overboard. The rules tend to be lax; anything you can do to score a goal is seen as fair play.
† This appeared in the 6th century BC and, unlike in other races, which were run naked, competitors had to wear bronze shinpads and a metal helmet and carry a large shield, which weighed around 6kg. Presumably affronted by all that clothing, in later versions they did away with the helmets and shinpads.

Shirin and Khosrow's polo match. Foreshadowing the nickname of the England women's football team almost a millennium later, the story reads: 'Seventy maidens like lionesses presented themselves before Shirin, all blazing with ardour.'

in a chariot and needed to be ready to fight immediately. Once they had won a battle (or were forced to retreat) they would leave the site the same way.

News of the Greek victory at the Battle of Marathon was famously reported by a long-distance runner – hence the name of the modern-day race. But according to the teacher Philostratus (writing more than 200 years later), it was the wrestling the Greeks did in training that made all the difference on that day, as it rendered them expert in hand-to-hand combat.

Wrestling has been prized as a training method for soldiers since the time of China's semi-mythical Yellow Emperor's army (2700 BC),* and to this day is still used by the US Air Force. And some of the oldest depictions of wrestling known to man were created to demonstrate the dominance of the ancient Egyptians over their vanquished foes.

GRAPPLING WITH HISTORY

The American National Wrestling Hall of Fame says that their sport is the oldest in the world, and frankly we're not going to argue with them – though we may nit-pick. Their website, like many other sources, claims that there are cave

----

* Chinese scholars long treated the Yellow Emperor as a historical figure, but most now see him as a legend. However, many of the details of his stories do stand up to historical scrutiny, including the existence of this early form of wrestling, known as *jiao di*, or 'horn-butting', since opponents would don horned helmets and use them to headbutt and gore each other. Ancient texts show that the martial art is certainly more than 3,000 years old.

paintings from more than 10,000 years ago that show wrestling matches and foot races, but any claims of ancient Hulk Hogans should be taken with a pinch of salt. Apart from the lack of bulging muscles, skimpy trunks and over-the-top storylines in ancient art, a still image of two interlocked humans could just as easily be a dance or embrace as a wrestling bout. And a depiction of a foot race could just as easily be hunters running towards their prey as an early 100m race.

However, if we go back to the earliest examples of human writing, it becomes clear that wrestling is as old as civilisation itself. Our oldest example of literature, *The Epic of Gilgamesh*, was written 4,000 years ago in Mesopotamia, at a time when agriculture, mathematics and the wheel were all new ideas, and it begins with the title character taking on a wild man sent by the gods in a physical fight. Like a couple of modern-day Marvel superheroes, the two wrestle together, causing nearby buildings to shake on their foundations, before gaining each other's respect and becoming firm friends.

Outside of fiction, we know that the ancient Egyptians loved wrestling. Detailed paintings and murals show the sport being practised, with one famous example, on the walls of the tomb of a high-ranking official called Baqet, depicting no fewer than 400 figures grappling, each wearing nothing but a belt. The figures are in pairs, and in every example one combatant is pale-skinned, the other dark; it seems possible that the mural depicts the same two people in a series of different poses. It could be a kind of comic strip showing all of the moves used in a particular fight, or it could be a training manual outlining every possible hold and throw used at the time. Interestingly, many of the images show grappling positions that are still used in modern wrestling.

If the mural is in fact a comic strip of a bout, then since one of the images shows the pale figure holding the dark-skinned figure's belt aloft, it could be that the aim of the contest was to strip off the opponent's belt. Wrestling belts appear to have been worn with pride by characters in other murals, and heroes were often depicted holding one, so the item could also have been a prize. It's similar to pro wrestling today, where athletes 'fight' to win a belt. An even more striking similarity is that these earliest wrestling matches may have been entirely choreographed.

If you remember anything from your history lessons, it might be that much of life in ancient Egypt revolved around the River Nile. If you followed the river southwards, you would eventually get to a set of rapids, through which boats struggled to pass. This was the natural barrier that brought you to the border between Egypt and its neighbour to the south, Nubia. The relationship between Nubia and Egypt was a complicated one. The former was extremely rich in resources, containing much of the gold that had been discovered by that time. While the Egyptians often traded with Nubia, they would also send out military expeditions to expand their borders and enslave the Nubian people. Despite this, a number of Egyptian pharaohs are known to have had Nubian blood, and even Nefertiti – one of ancient history's most prominent women – is thought by some to have been at least part Nubian, as evidenced by the fact that she is often depicted with dark skin. It could also be the case that the black figure in the wrestling cartoon in Baqet's tomb was Nubian, and that he was defeated by an Egyptian athlete.

Baqet died as many years before the birth of Jesus as we exist after it. It was a time when Egypt was advancing into Nubia, and Egypt demanded tributes from their vanquished foes in the form of minerals, animals and slaves. They also brought wrestlers from the south to take part in sporting events that would see high diplomats from both countries watching as Egyptians fought Nubians. In all known depictions of Nubian–Egyptian bouts, the northerners won – a symbol of their country's dominance. This, along with the fact that fights were often attended by the pharaoh, nobles and the royal court, suggests that upsets weren't allowed. It's fair to assume that they were choreographed in some way, just like modern pro wrestling.

Another depiction of wrestling, in the tomb of Rameses III, dating a little later (in ancient Egyptian terms), to around 1200 BC, shows a third similarity to the pro wrestling of today. As the Egyptian champion grapples with his defeated Nubian opponent, he is shown saying: 'Woe to you, oh Nubian enemy! I will make you take a helpless fall in the presence of the pharaoh!' It's a 3,200-year-old example of 'smack talk'.

TEEING OFF?

The origins of most other modern sports are significantly harder to nail down. There's no evidence for the oft-repeated tale that a public schoolboy picked up a soccer ball and created rugby, for instance; and the idea that baseball was invented by a famous American Civil War general was itself invented to hide the fact that it probably evolved from the English game of rounders.* Even two of the world's most popular sports – football and golf, the first of which is often said to be 'coming home' to England; the second of which has a famous 'home' at St Andrews in Scotland – have uncertain origins.†

The modern rules of golf were certainly written down in Scotland, though the event actually occurred about 50 miles down the coast from St Andrews. On 7 March 1744, a group of men who called themselves The Gentlemen Golfers of Leith

....

* In 1905, the National Baseball League appointed an official task force to investigate the origin of baseball, which famously concluded it was conceived by Civil War general Abner Doubleday. The evidence was based on testimony from a 'reputable source', Abner Graves (apparently the name Abner was at peak popularity around this time). Graves went on to murder his wife at the age of ninety and was committed to an institution for the criminally insane for the rest of his life, which frankly raises questions about his reliability as a source. The Doubleday story is probably more well known in America now as a myth than a fact. Even the National Baseball Hall of Fame, situated in Cooperstown, New York (because that's where Doubleday supposedly invented the game), treats the story as a fabrication.
† The hybrid sport footgolf, in which players kick a football into an oversized golf hole in as few shots as possible, has much more certain beginnings, however. After retiring from professional football in 2001 due to persistent hip injuries, Tottenham Hotspur's Dutch winger Willem Korsten told his friend Michael Jansen about a game that the Spurs had played. After training they would compete to see who could get the balls back into the dressing room in the fewest kicks. Seven years later, Jansen created footgolf, which today is one of the fastest-growing sports, with around 35,000 players worldwide.

met at their clubhouse in Edinburgh and agreed on 13 laws that would form the basis of their club championship. To begin with, only that group could take part in the tournament, but it would eventually become 'open' to everyone, and today it is called The Open Championship – the oldest golf tournament in the world, and arguably still the most prestigious.

The Gentlemen Golfers of Leith continued to golf in the Edinburgh area and changed their name to the Company of Edinburgh Golfers. They founded a new course called Muirfield, which is today feted as the oldest continually running golf club in the world. Muirfield has hosted six Open Championships, but in 2017 it had its right to host the world's oldest tournament revoked after members failed to vote to allow women to join the club. After a public backlash, the club held a second vote and women were finally allowed in. In 2022, the course hosted the Women's British Open.

Back in the late 19th century, responsibility for the laws of golf passed from the Edinburgh group to the Royal & Ancient Golf Club in St Andrews; they are still in charge today, alongside the United States Golf Association. St Andrews is, therefore, known as the 'home of golf', and a visit is seen by amateur golfers from all around the world as almost a pilgrimage. However, many people believe that the game of golf is much older than the Scottish iteration and that its origins lie further east than the east coast of Scotland.

A painting by a Chinese artist called Du Jin, created sometime around AD 1500, shows three women holding sticks with long shafts and paddles at the end. The objects look almost identical to modern golf clubs. The women are looking at

A work by Du Jin (c.1465–1509), showing Ming Dynasty women playing golf. By coincidence, the artist shares a name with (at time of writing) the number-one female golfer in the world, Jin Young Ko.

a small ball on the ground, and behind them are two 'caddies', holding the clubs they are not using. A slightly earlier painting shows the emperor Xuanzong, complete with similar equipment and surrounded by five holes, each of which contains a flag. He appears to be getting ready to take a shot. All these people are playing *chui wan* (literally, 'hitting a little ball with a stick'), an ancient sport that has incredible similarities to modern-day golf – albeit with a much more forward-thinking approach to the inclusion of women than has recently been seen at Muirfield.

The game of *chui wan* was played with bamboo clubs, whose length varied depending on the height of the player, and with balls that were a little larger than a walnut, sometimes with dimples on them. The game would begin with players placing the ball on the *ji* – a small boxed area – and they would have to hit it into a hole, which was marked with a flag. Everyone would play towards the same hole, and whoever landed furthest from the hole would go first on the next turn. The aim was to get it into the hole in as few shots as possible. You would have a caddy (or sometimes a couple) to carry your clubs. The distance from the starting point to the hole would vary, though not between around 100m and 600m like a modern golf course – the lengths ranged between a more modest 3m and 150m.

Another similarity, perhaps, is that both *chui wan* and golf began as games of the upper class. All of the poems and paintings that describe the Chinese game refer to nobles, and it could be that this was the reason it disappeared in the East. The fashions of the upper class often changed, and when the Qing Dynasty arrived in the 17th century, *chui wan* went out of vogue. Without a large population of ordinary people to keep it going, the sport completely died out. Indeed, when the modern Western version of the game was introduced in the 1980s (it had been banned by the Chinese Communist Party as too bourgeois before that), only a few historians knew that an extremely similar sport had been popular in the country 500 years earlier.

The most striking similarity of all was in the etiquette. Modern golf prides itself on its unwritten rules, which shape the game. It is also supposed to be self-policed, and the worst thing a golfer can be accused of is cheating.* The same

* The final straw for many golfers who might otherwise have supported

was true of *chui wan*. Early texts describing the game are very clear that players shouldn't brag about winning or be upset by losing. They also list methods of cheating that are strictly forbidden. It was meant to be played in the spirit of Confucianism, whereby inner virtue and respect, as well as a love of nature, were more important than the result of the game. Players were expected to play for playing's sake.

Aside from its inherent classism, one of the other reasons *chui wan* died out was that successive Qing emperors favoured other sports, such as ice skating. They would organise festivals in which skaters performed acrobatics and archery on Beijing's frozen lakes. Subsequent foreign invaders also brought their own games. But that hasn't stopped some historians from speculating that golf may have come to Scotland from China via mainland Europe. It wouldn't be so surprising, since multiple Chinese inventions, such as paper and gunpowder, made their way to Europe and became entrenched in society. But the evidence is scant, and it seems that the two sports evolved independently.

WHICH WAY HOME?

If the original home of modern golf is uncertain, that of modern football is even more murky. The rules of association football

....

President Donald Trump was his attitude on the golf course: opponents have reported that he cheats so regularly – by kicking his ball into better positions – that caddies nicknamed him Pelé, after the legendary Brazilian footballer.

were definitely written up in England, in London in 1863. But the first mention of a ball game in Britain comes from Wales. Nennius, a 9th-century monk,[*] wrote that a local king called Vortigern had been told by his advisors that he needed to build a castle in a particular place. Vortigern assembled a team of workers and materials, but one night the equipment disappeared. He collected the materials again, and again they were taken. When it happened for a third time, he sought help from his advisors, who (somewhat bloodthirstily) said that the only way to stop the thefts was to find a child who had been born without a father and sacrifice them. The king sent out some messengers to find such a kid, and they came across a group of boys arguing over a ball game. Overhearing one of the children say to another, 'O boy without a father, no good will ever happen to you,' the messengers kidnapped the boy in question and took him to the king, who . . . Well, we won't spoil the rest of the story.[†]

We don't know what ball game the boys were playing, or indeed what roles the boys had in the game. Perhaps the fatherless boy was being insulted on the playing field because he was acting as the traditional recipient of on-pitch abuse – the referee – and hence was the first ever 'bastard in the black'.[‡] But either

....

[*] He was also the first person to have written anything about the mythical King Arthur. Perhaps he had a predilection for round things.
[†] OK, we will. Long story short, instead of getting himself killed, the boy manages to convince the king to hand control of the region over to him, and he goes on to rule it and 'all the western provinces of Britain'. In later stories, his identity is conflated with that of Merlin.
[‡] An insult today, but a matter-of-fact description of the referee in the

way, the fact that Nennius doesn't tell us any more about the game suggests that playing ball was such a common occurrence in 9th-century Britain that no more explanation was needed.

A few hundred years later comes the first mention of a ball game taking place in London. In 1174, one of Thomas Becket's clerics, William Fitzstephen, wrote:

After the midday meal the entire youth of the city of London goes to the fields for the famous game of ball. The students of the several branches of study have their ball; and the followers of the several trades of the City have a ball in their hands. The elders, the fathers, and men of wealth come on horseback to view the contests of their juniors.

This is often taken to be the first mention of football in Britain, although it never specifically mentions playing with the feet. In fact, the hand is the only body part that gets a namecheck, and in other early mentions hands often have as much of a role as feet during play. You might, for instance, carry the ball over the goal line rather than kick it.

It does seem strange for a game that involved as much throwing and catching as it did kicking to be named after the foot, but the horses mentioned in the passage above might help point us towards another theory as to why it got the name 'football': it was a game that is played 'on foot' as opposed to a sport played 'on a horse', like polo. But there were a number of other ball games played on foot, such as

first international between England and Wales in 1879 and also the previous year's FA Cup final. His name was Segar Bastard.

early versions of golf or tennis; why would you call one of the games 'football' above the others?

A newspaper article of 1845 gives a third possibility. It describes 'football' as a term 'used by metonymy for the diversion of driving the ball itself'. A metonym is a word that is used as a substitute for something it is closely related to, like saying 'Westminster' when you mean the House of Commons. So the idea here is that the name 'football' originally just referred to the ball itself, and evolved later to mean 'the game that you play with such a ball'. Of course, the problem is now just transferred – where does the name of the ball come from? Because it was easily kicked? Or perhaps because it was about one foot in diameter?* We might never know.

Another piece of evidence for the metonym theory is that the first reference to 'football' in England referred to the balls themselves. Specifically, it referred to them being banned. In 1314, the mayor of London, Nicholas de Farndone, wrote on behalf of Edward II, who had sallied up to Scotland for a battle, that:

> *Whereas there is great uproar in the City, through certain tumults arising from the striking of great footballs in the fields of the public, from which many evils perchance may arise, which may God forbid, we do command and do forbid, on the King's behalf, on pain of imprisonment, that such game be practiced from henceforth within the City . . .*

Edward III and Edward IV both issued laws against football during their reigns, and Henry IV also tried to ban it,

....

* The modern ball is 22cm in diameter, roughly three-quarters of a foot.

alongside another sport called cock-threshing.* Richard II and Henry V also requested football be banned because it stopped people practising their archery, and in 1424, James I of Scotland decreed that 'na man play at the Fute-ball'. Henry VIII of England definitely played the game, though, and owned the first pair of football boots we know of.†

That's the evidence for Britain being the home of football, but just as with golf, China also has a decent claim, which depends on how you define the invention of a sport.

In 2014, FIFA president Sepp Blatter announced that a 2,300-year-old Chinese ball game called *cuju* was the first kind of football played anywhere in the world, much to the chagrin of English football fans. The word '*cuju*' literally means 'kick ball' and it has many similarities to modern football. Games took place between two teams, and the aim was to get a ball made from an animal's bladder between goalposts built with bamboo. As with the early English game of football, *cuju* was banned by the authorities after it became too popular. Hongwu, the first emperor of the Ming Dynasty,

* Cock-threshing, also known as cock-running and 'throwing at cocks', was a popular game played on Shrove Tuesday, in which a rooster was tied to the ground and people threw stones at it until it fell over. The cocks must have been mightily relieved when we invented pancakes.

† Mention of Henry VIII's boots was discovered by historian Dr Maria Hayward as she looked through the Great Wardrobe – the list of clothing bought for the King. Along with the football boots, he also ordered two pairs of fencing shoes, and 37 pairs of velvet shoes, which were presumably not sport-related.

considered it to be a distraction from military training, and the punishment for playing was to have your foot cut off.

Cuju was another sport that owed its origin to warfare. According to one story, the game began when the Yellow Emperor defeated a dangerous enemy called Chiyou and had his vanquished opponent's stomach removed, filled with hay and turned into a ball. The first *historical* evidence of the sport comes from the 'Warring States' period of Chinese history (475–221 BC), when multiple states battled for supremacy, with writers of the era describing the sport as a type of fitness training for soldiers. But like *chui wan*, by the 17th century *cuju* had all but disappeared from China, and despite the startling similarities, there's no direct link between ancient Chinese *cuju* and the modern game of football.

The fact that such sports can be invented completely independently is arguably evidence that taking part in sport is an inherent human trait. Humans are unusual among animals in that we have very long childhoods – gorillas, for instance, are adults by the time they're 12 years old – during which we are dependent on our parents, and we're also one of the few creatures to engage in organised warfare between groups of the same species. Other animals play with and fight each other, and yet they don't take part in sport. Dolphins don't turn their love of ball play into games of netball, any more than chimpanzees adapt their turf warfare into feisty rugby matches. To do so would require a capacity and appetite for social coordination and teamwork that seems to be uniquely human.

2

THE DAREDEVIL INNKEEPER OF GARMISCH

HOW TO SERVE UP A WINNING TEAM

> One man alone can be pretty dumb sometimes,
> but for real bona fide stupidity, there ain't
> nothin' can beat teamwork.
> **Edward Abbey**

Baby kangaroos play-fight with their mothers; killer whales will deliberately move objects around just to annoy researchers; kestrels attack pine cones as though they were mice; chimps sometimes play with dolls; and elephants slide down mud chutes for fun. Squid don't bother with games at all – despite what Netflix might have you believe.[*] Overall, it's fair to say that play is very common in the animal kingdom. Humans, though, are the only species that we know for certain plays in teams, and plays to win at that.[†]

That's not to say animals don't form like-minded groups. Locusts can form swarms of up to a billion at a time, all descending on an unfortunate farmer's fields to feed. And animals such as wolves, dolphins and even birds of prey will often get together to hunt their quarry. But this is co-operation in

---

[*] Oddly enough, despite being closely related to squid, octopuses do play. And it can be almost as dangerous as the Netflix show *Squid Game*: they like to mischievously wrestle the breathing masks off scuba divers.

[†] Dolphins sometimes swim and leap in groups, though most researchers think that rather than it being purely for leisure, they're practising for future fighting or mating events.

order to survive. It is only humans who are willing to work together as part of their play.

One reason for this is that team sports require large amounts of brain power. Not only do you need to have good co-ordination within your own body, you need to be able to co-ordinate with your teammates, judge what they will do and act accordingly, all the time anticipating what your opponents might do. If you put 22 dogs on a football field, they may well chase the ball, but they won't know why they're doing it and they certainly don't have a concept of being in a team or beating the opposition. Still, upwards of 10 million Americans tune in every year for the Puppy Bowl, which takes place on the same day as the Super Bowl and is televised on the Animal Planet cable channel. The two-hour event purports to show an American football match between two teams of canines, in which the aim for each player is to get a 'ball' (a plush toy) over the goal line. In fact, it's filmed over two days and involves over 70 dogs from shelters and rescue organisations, who are constantly swapped in and out to avoid any animals becoming overly exhausted. Viewers get to see only the very best action, which, as far as the producers are concerned, consists of the cutest moments. It's a very different attitude to that taken with the human Super Bowl, where 40% of fans say that heavy tackles are integral to their enjoyment of the game.

Since the dogs don't know that there is a match going on, they tend to run around aimlessly. It's only the inspired editing and the commentary by presenter and 'referee' Dan Schachner that creates the illusion of a team sport. Schachner claims (with tongue very much in cheek) that the dogs some-times use complex trick plays and co-operation in order to get the toys over the line,* but the 20-plus bags of (thankfully untelevised) poop that the participating animals produce every year (and the fact that participants have been known to get rather too familiar with each other mid-match) certainly betrays the fact that they're just dogs being dogs. After the game, viewers are able to adopt their favourite players.

Unlike non-human animals, artificial intelligence can understand the concept of team sports, but it also struggles to comprehend the ideas of co-operation and teamwork. When a team at Google's DeepMind programmed four robots to play a two-a-side soccer match, they tended to run directly towards the ball, like a team of five-year-old humans might. The machines took their cues from watching humans playing the game, but even so, it took 30 years' worth of simulated learning even to get to the stage where the program realised its players could kick the ball into space to get around an opponent.[†]

Though perhaps we should cut the robots some slack, since it took decades for humans to work out that the best

---

* One trick play that Schachner pointed viewers towards was the 'locker-room loophole', in which a dog called Aberdeen pretended to leave the pitch but brought the 'ball' with him, and then sneaked a touchdown. Whether it was a genius scheme or a happy accident, given that the exit and the end zone were in the same place, only Aberdeen can truly know.
† In fairness, this 30 years' worth of computing time took only two to three days in the real world.

way to play soccer was for team members to have specific positions, to exploit spaces and outmanoeuvre their opponents. We fans often complain that our favourite teams still haven't grasped this.

THE BEAUTIFUL GAME

In the 1860s, football was far from a beautiful game. The rules hadn't been completely ironed out,* but most matches involved a mass of brawny men guarding the ball as they marched to their opponent's goal, the other team trying all the while to barge them out of the way so they could retrieve the ball and start their own attack in the opposite direction.

That's the style of game that the England men's football team expected for their match against Scotland in Glasgow in 1874. It was the third game ever to take place between the two teams, and after the first two ended in a 0–0 draw and a 4–2 win, England had the upper hand. They had a team of stars, including their captain Cuthbert Ottaway, who was expert at dribbling. He would often be the one to run with the ball, while his teammates guarded him from tacklers.†

. . . .

* Newspapers reported that one 1864 match between Clapham Common Club (CCC) and Blackheath was spoiled because CCC couldn't understand the rules. And an 1866 game between Crystal Palace and Barnes was described as being 'much improved' because both teams had agreed to do away with the confusing offside law.
† Ottaway was also a trained barrister, and practised law until he died of a chill caught while spending the night dancing.

The weather was fine, and there was a crowd of 8,000 spectators as the teams arrived on the pitch at exactly 3.30 p.m. The two sides would be recognisable to today's fans: Scotland in their familiar dark blue shirts and white shorts; England all in white. The only differences were that the English wore blue caps throughout the game, and every player on the pitch had differently coloured socks. The organisers handed out leaflets that listed the players and their sock colours so that you could identify them.

The game began as everyone imagined it would. The English forwards powered their way into Scottish territory, while the Scottish players attempted to repel them. After 22 minutes, there was an almighty scramble in front of the Scottish goal, somebody kicked the ball and it rebounded off the chest of English attacker Robert Kingsford and into the goal. 1–0 to the Three Lions.

The opening goal served only to get the Scottish fans going, and that in turn inspired the Scottish players. Suddenly, they adopted a tactic that the English had never seen before: they started to pass the ball. The English sporting newspaper *Bell's Life* reported the new tactics:

> *What the Scotch lacked in weight was amply made up in swiftness and playing-together power – a course which was splendidly illustrated during the game, and there can only be one opinion about the manner in which they profited by each other's play, passing the ball, in several instances, in a way that completely astonished their opponents.*

After 42 minutes, the passing Picts had equalised, and three minutes later, striker Angus MacKinnon shot through the English goalkeeper's legs to put his team into the lead. For all their effort and bluster, England were unable to come back, and so Scotland inflicted England's first-ever international defeat. But more importantly, they had invented a new way of playing that would change the game forever. It would evolve into the passing and moving that the great Brazilian forward Pelé was referring to when he named his autobiography *The Beautiful Game*, thus popularising the term.[*]

It's arguable that this match was the first true example of the game of football as we know it today. Before 1874, the tactics used by most teams resulted in a game that would be quite alien to modern fans. In the Scotland match, for instance, the England coach positioned three defenders at the back, seven forwards right at the front, and no one in the middle. The reason this tactic is rarely used today is that with a well-organised series of passes, the entire pitch comes into play, so players need to spread out into distinct positions. The Scottish innovation also changed the way that players tackled. No longer were interceptions made exclusively by barging an opponent off the ball; a sliding tackle could not only win possession but allow the player to simultaneously pass the ball to a teammate.

The Scottish passing tactic was a classic example of necessity being the mother of invention. While England's players before the 1870s largely came from its public schools, Scotland's team

* Billiards, lacrosse and cricket were all known as the 'beautiful game' at various times in the 19th century.

was plucked from the factories and shipyards. On average, Scottish players were of smaller stature, due in part to the lack of nutrition suffered by the working-class population of the time. There was no way for them to outmuscle their opponents, and so they had to come up with something different.

It was obviously a huge improvement in strategy. Football, it turns out, is a sport that is particularly suited to teams in which players know their separate roles within the unit, rather than one where all the other players support a single dribbler. Everyone who played against the Scots could see that immediately. When a team from Sheffield played a combined Glasgow XI in 1876, they lost so heavily that they decided to host a series of trial matches in the city with the sole purpose of finding 'the best passing players' and dropping 'any of the players exhibiting selfishness'.

DREAM TEAMS

Teamwork makes the dream work. There's no 'I' in 'team'. The group is greater than the sum of its parts. Such clichés exist for a reason: when teams work well together, success often follows. Gestures of mutual support and camaraderie are essential to this. Today, these often come in the form of bum-slapping, especially in American sports, and statistics have shown that teams who engage in more congratulatory bum-slapping tend to see better results.* And basketball teams in which every player

---

* Nobody knows where the sporting bum-slap originated. It seems it may have been in baseball: the earliest mention we've found is from

gets a similar number of touches (of the ball) outperform those with a single stand-out player who hogs the limelight. Things can change quickly, though: the basketball study found that when these successful teams got to the finals (the climactic series of games that end the playing season), the level of team-work decreased, as players began to focus on their personal performance. They knew that a good run in the finals could lead to a lucrative contract. Co-operative play tends to spread through a team, as you might have guessed, but researchers have found that selfish play spreads much more quickly. When one player stopped playing for the team in these important matches, the rest tended to follow suit.

In fact, our more selfish instincts mean that teams are not *always* greater than the sum of their parts. Asking a group to perform a task previously carried out by an individual doesn't automatically mean it gets done better. This was shown by a Frenchman called Maximilien Ringelmann, who was in charge of testing farming machinery in France in the 1880s. He wanted to work out the most efficient way to plough fields, and so measured how much weight a single horse would pull, and then how much a group of four could manage. He expected the four horses to pull four times as strongly as the individual, but instead found that there was a shortfall. When he tried the experiment with humans pulling a rope, he found the same thing. This phenomenon is now called the Ringelmann Effect, or 'social loafing'. The idea is that if you're

1959, when a New York reporter complained that his team lacked spirit because they didn't engage in the act as much as the opposition.

in a large group, you can slack off a bit and nobody will notice, so a group naturally achieves less than the sum of its parts. At least when pulling a rope.

Although the Taipei Jingmei Girls' Senior High School tug-of-war team would probably have taken issue with Ringelmann's conclusions . . .

PULLING TOGETHER

In 1971, Taiwan lost its seat at the United Nations after pressure from the People's Republic of China, which claimed ownership over the island country. Feeling increasingly isolated on the national stage, the Taiwanese government decided that it would try to use sport to increase the country's visibility. Its National Sport Development Project looked at all the different disciplines to find those that particularly suited the Taiwanese, and one that looked promising was tug of war. The sport wasn't taken very seriously by many countries* and, like boxing, matches were organised by weight, so Taiwan would have no disadvantage against countries like the Netherlands, whose people are, on average, 10cm taller and 10kg heavier than the Taiwanese. Furthermore, unlike games such as golf, very little real estate was needed in order to practise it.

....

* Great Britain used to take it seriously, and is the reigning Olympic champion after winning the event in 1920, the last time it was contested. In 1908, Britain won gold and silver, with the latter being won by a team from the Liverpool police department, whose Swedish opponents accused them of cheating by wearing such heavy boots that they couldn't even lift their feet after the match.

By the early 1990s, the sport was being rolled out into all the schools in Taiwan. In 2004, former national tug-of-war champion Kuo Sheng got a coaching job at the Taipei Jingmei Girls' Senior High School. Six years later, he had turned his team into world champions.

Thanks to government schemes like this one, excelling at sport is one way for young people in Taiwan to rise out of poverty and get a good education. Schools scramble over the best athletes, and if players prove themselves at international level, they can be guaranteed a plum job by the government. And so most of the Jingmei tug-of-war athletes came from disadvantaged families. Unlike most students at the school, they were boarders, training before classes started and then again once everyone else had left for the day. They were coached for four hours a day, 365 days a year, pulling and lifting weights and working on mental strength and technique. They were kept on a strict diet, and romantic relationships were strictly forbidden.

Tug of war is a very technical sport that requires extreme levels of teamwork. It's not a case of everyone pulling as hard as they can at the start. Sure, that could work, but in most cases it won't, and you will have used up all of your energy in the first few seconds. Instead, competitors need to know when to tug in rhythm with the rest of the team and when to hold fast, focusing all of their strength through their feet and into the ground, making themselves virtually immovable, even by the strongest opponents.[*]

---

[*] For more on this, see the aforementioned non-squid TV show *Squid Game*.

Familiarity breeds teamwork, and day after day of training together had the Jingmei team describing themselves as
'sisters'. Together, they started to beat all-comers, but were
unable to take part in international competitions due to a
strict age limit of over-18s only. When that was lifted in 2009,
the team could finally take part in its first match outside
Taiwan: the 2010 World Indoor Championships in Italy. A
couple of older Jingmei alumni joined them to make up the
Taiwanese national team, which was entered into the 540kg
female weight category, in which the total of all eight athletes
could not go over that limit. Their sisterhood had taken them
this far, but now they sought victory on the world stage.

Switzerland and Japan were defeated in the semi-finals,
which meant the final would be between the Jingmei team, representing Taiwan, and the big favourites, China. Since China
doesn't recognise Taiwan as an independent country, in international sports the islanders play under the name Chinese
Taipei and their national flag is replaced by one featuring a
plum blossom, the country's national plant. However, nobody
had told the organisers of the tournament, and after their
semi-final win, the national flag of Taiwan was raised. The
Chinese team were incensed and protested loudly, even going
as far as grabbing the Taiwanese flag and turning it around.

If there's one thing that brings a team together, it's insults
from an adversary.

The Taiwanese team were already quietly confident, but
now they were unbeatable. According to one of the athletes, 'We
could have beaten them very quickly, but instead, we tortured
them slowly before making them lose.' They took gold, and

later that year won the World Outdoor Championships, beating a Swedish team who hadn't lost for five years. Two years later, they won both the indoor and outdoor championships again. Now retired, most of the team work as physical education teachers and tug-of-war coaches at Taiwanese schools.

The Jingmei team clearly demonstrated the importance of collective motivation to sporting success. This is backed up by research that has shown how giving players challenging but achievable goals can energise them and help them to engage. But to get those goals across you need effective communication.

IT'S GOOD TO TALK

Like many sports, American football appears impenetrable to the uninitiated. But what at first looks like a stop–start melee involving padding and helmets has been compared by more seasoned observers to a ballet, in that each of the 22 players knows exactly what route they are choreographed to run, and at what time. The game revolves around intricate individual plays, with names including the 'flea flicker', the 'fumblerooski' and the 'reverse Statue of Liberty'. It's even been suggested that teams should be able to copyright any new plays they come up with – the idea being that if they know they can profit from innovating in this way, it will encourage creativity and improve the sport.

But how does each player in the team know what to do, and when? Ultimately, it's a decision taken between the quarterback, who receives the ball at the start of each play, and the coach, who's standing on the sidelines. It's very difficult to get plans across in ear-splittingly loud venues such as Arrowhead Stadium, where in 2014 the noise peaked at 142.2 decibels – comparable with a jet engine – during the Kansas City Chiefs' pleasingly palindromic 41–14 victory over the New England Patriots, and so quarterbacks have a speaker in their helmet that is connected to their coach's microphone. This communication is considered so important that if one of the teams loses the connection, they can tell the referee, who will insist that the opposition quarterback removes their helmet speaker too.*

The Houston Texans quarterback David Carr receiving tactical tips on a landline phone, mid-match. Hopefully nobody wanted to connect to the internet at the same time.

....

* Most NFL teams have a huge team of coaches, but they can't all be at the side of the pitch. Mobile phones are banned, and so every team also has a bank of old-fashioned landline receivers located at the side of the pitch, where they can get additional tactical advice from upstairs.

Once the play is decided by the coach and the quarter-back, the latter has to get the message to the rest of his team, so they form a huddle. It seems second nature now, and the huddle is used in many, if not most, team sports. But it was unknown prior to the turn of the 20th century, when it was invented by a college football star called Paul Dillingham Hubbard.

Hubbard was the star quarterback for Gallaudet University, a specialist school for deaf and hard-of-hearing pupils in Washington DC. He was known as the 'eel' due to the fact that people found it difficult to hold on to him (some newspaper reports say it was also due to his fine strategies – though what that has to do with eels is not clear).*

In order to pass on instructions to the rest of his team, Hubbard had to use sign language, but he realised that opponents would quickly work out what each sign meant and predict his plays. Therefore, he decided that before each play, he would take the whole team to one side and get them to stand with their backs to their opponents, while he crouched down out of sight and explained his plays. Along with this unusual new pre-play ritual, Hubbard's team also became

....

* Hubbard became the coach of the first American football club west of the Mississippi, when he started a team at the Kansas State School for the Deaf in 1899. Their geographical isolation meant that players had to travel for hours to get to any match, and while their opponents would promise to pay for their transport, they would often refuse to stump up, especially if they had been beaten. Sometimes the police would have to escort the team out of town to avoid them being mobbed by irate fans.

famous for their trick plays, which required detailed choreography. Even for hearing teams, the huddle was useful to hide gestures and allow quarterbacks to give instructions in more hushed tones, and before long, all the local teams were copying Hubbard's huddle. It was popularised nationwide in the 1920s by a coach at the University of Illinois called Robert Zuppke. He is often credited as the originator of the huddle, but when asked, he openly admitted that he took the idea 'from a deaf team I saw somewhere'.

BOBBING AND WEAVING

So everyone in your team knows their job. They have a collective motivation. And they have effective communication. But none of this is useful unless you have recruited the right people to your roster.

The 1952 Winter Olympics were set to take place in Oslo, and the year before, a representative from Germany visited the organisers to decide whether or not they would send a team. Germany had not taken part in any Olympics since the Second World War, and while technically they were no longer banned, there was a worry that the Norwegian press and public would protest about their involvement by disrupting the games.

The last winter Games before the war had taken place in 1936, in the German resort of Garmisch-Partenkirchen, which lies in the shadows of famous peaks including the Alpspitze, Zugspitze and Wank mountains. Much like the more famous 1936 Summer Olympics, also in Germany, they were opened by Adolf Hitler and were an exercise in Nazi propaganda.

They were meant to showcase the fascist state's impressive facilities, including an imposing ramp, which still hosts one of the big three ski-jumping competitions every year.[*]

Inspired by those Games, and helped by the new infrastructure, a German teenager called Anderl Ostler became interested in winter sports, showing an unusual aptitude for bobsleigh. But any hopes he had of representing his country appeared to be over when the war began, bringing most sporting events to an end.

After the war, Ostler became an innkeeper and ended up with a physique not usually associated with athletes, but he kept up his sliding. Despite a reputation for enjoying his alcohol, womanising and oversleeping on race days, he was chosen to represent Germany in Oslo. His right-hand man (or, rather, his directly-behind man) would be Lorenz Nieberl, another talented bobsledder who at first glance looked like he would be more at home in a beer hall than a toboggan. The duo would take part in the two-man bobsleigh. They would also team up with another pair of strong pushers to make up one of the two German teams competing in the four-man bob.

A bobsleigh run is simply a concrete tube that winds down a hill and is covered in artificially made ice.[†] On the face of

----

[*] One of the authors once made a special trip to watch German ski jumper Andreas Wank competing against the backdrop of the Wank mountain. Listeners to our podcast *No Such Thing As A Fish* won't have much trouble working out which of us it was.

[†] Of course, the pastime originated with races on natural ice. According to the Greek historian Plutarch, writing in the first century,

it, it looks simple: you start off as fast as you can, and then you try to reach the bottom in the shortest possible time – without crashing. Basic physics will tell you that if you're looking to attain the highest speed when sliding down from the top of a mountain, you'll go faster if your mass is greater. And so, after the two German four-man bobsleighs finished in the middle of the ranking during qualifying, the team came up with a cunning plan. They would utilise their two most talented sliders, Ostler and Nieberl, who were already very hefty, and swap out their colleagues in the sleigh for the two heaviest athletes from the other team, Fritz Kuhn and Franz Kemser, who were both particularly large. They now had a super-heavyweight über-team, abandoning the second sled completely in the quest for gold.

The favourites for first place were the American team of Stanley Benham, Patrick Martin, Howard Crossett and James Atkinson. Back home, they were known as the 'Beef Trust', on account of their imposing physical presence. They weighed a total of 450kg, about the same as a large moose. But their size was no match for the Germans, who weighed as much as a moose with a fully grown British bulldog on its back.

Ostler and Nieberl already had great communication as they'd been friends since childhood, and they had also faced collective adversity in the form of the hostile Norwegian press. When extra mass was added to the mix, it made for an unbeatable team. They took top spot – Germany's first Olympic gold

---

the Cimbri were an ancient Germanic tribe who enjoyed sledging, but they always did it naked.

Anderl Ostler, the Daredevil Innkeeper from Garmisch, and his
heavyweight team.

medal in any sport since the Second World War. American
newspapers celebrated Ostler as the 'Daredevil Innkeeper
of Garmisch', but the victory resulted in the International
Bobsleigh Federation bringing in a new rule stipulating a
maximum weight for any bobsleigh team. Never again will
the Olympics see a plus-sized group such as this one hurtling
down a hill at 80mph, but if you'd like to relive the spectacle,
then you can, thanks to the 2006 German film *Schwere Jungs*
(*Heavy Boys*) – the *other* great bobsledding movie.

The weight limit was brought in to uphold the integrity
of bobsledding. Without it, the competition might have simply become a question of 'Who can put together the heaviest
team?' Rules in sport are made for other reasons, such as for

safety – of the competitors or even the crowd; they can also be brought in for practical reasons. And rules constantly have to change due to a changing world. But, essentially, every rulebook exists to define its sport – which could be described as something that comes into being when you take the human instinct for play and add rules. In the same way that a round area exists on a piece of paper, but a circle appears only when you actually draw the line, it is only when you add some boundaries that you have a sport. As much as we might bemoan the umpire's decision a lot of the time, without someone to enforce the rules it's just aimless running, jumping, kicking, hitting or throwing.

3

WHY GOLFERS HATE RABBITS

WHY THE BEST FUN IS WELL-ORGANISED FUN

If you obey all the rules, you miss all the fun.
Katharine Hepburn

Part of the purpose of rules is to tell you what you *can't* do. This is important. Without those parameters, pretty much every sport would just be *The Hunger Games*.* Even so, sometimes the restrictions imposed on players can seem arbitrarily harsh. Take netball: you can't dribble – in fact, you're barely allowed to move with the ball at all – and each player must stay in their allotted part of the court. This is even more surprising when you learn that netball was invented as a new version of basketball, which is perhaps one of the most fluid and fast-moving sports in the world. As it turns out, the restrictions that define netball, and thus the invention of netball as a sport, came about thanks to a misunderstanding over the rules.

HOOPS-A-DAISY

Basketball was invented in 1891, when James Naismith, a physical education instructor at the YMCA in Springfield, Massachusetts, decided to create a game that would maintain his students' fitness during the long winter months. He

---

* Even this series of books and movies, in which players fight each other to the death, has strict rules against a false start.

was inspired by a game he played as a child called Duck on
a Rock, in which kids used pebbles to knock a duck-shaped
stone off a large boulder. First, he took a soccer ball and asked
a janitor to find a couple of square boxes. When the search
brought only round peach baskets, Naismith decided they
would do the job just fine, so he nailed them to a balcony in
the gymnasium and practised throwing the ball into them.
That's why today's basketball hoops are round. The fact that
this balcony was 10 feet above the floor of the gym is why
baskets are placed 10 feet from the ground today. If the balcony had been a couple of feet higher or lower, then a 'slam
dunk' – where a player jumps and forces the ball down into
the basket – would have been either impossible or trivial. It
would have been a very different sport if the rules had been
only slightly different.*

At around the same time, Newcomb College in New
Orleans, the first American women's college to be linked to an
all-male university, started a physical education programme
for its students. It was a controversial decision; the college
president, Brandt Dixon, faced opposition from parents and
doctors who claimed that additional exercise would be bad

---

* There's a common myth that for the first 15 years of basketball
there was no hole in a basket, and someone had to climb up to retrieve
the ball every time. And when a hole was finally made, it was so small
that a stick had to be poked through it to retrieve the ball. In fact, by
1893, two years after the invention of the sport, there were basketball
nets for sale in US newspapers. The ball wouldn't pass through the
net, however; there was a drawstring that turned the net inside out
and released the ball.

James Naismith, the inventor of basketball, demonstrating the two crucial components of his invention.

for the health of the women or make them less feminine. One parent wrote to the school saying that he thought that his daughter had enough exercise during the summer holidays to last throughout the rest of the year. Dixon replied that by that logic, if the girl ate a hearty Thanksgiving dinner, presumably she must be excused from eating food for the rest of the year.

Dixon hired a woman called Clara Baer to take charge of the sports curriculum, and she began to look for sports that would keep the anti-exercise lobby at bay and be appropriate for female students, who were forced to play in the bulky clothing of the day. Her solution was to adapt sports played by men, and the obvious first step was to look at basketball, which was taking the country's male schools by storm. With that in mind, she wrote to Naismith and asked for a copy of his official rulebook.[*]

Her first game was a disaster. Baer herself described the

---

[*] While Baer was waiting for nets to arrive so she could get her girls playing basketball, she invented another sport to keep them fit and hone their ball-handling, which she called Newcomb (named after the school where she worked). It involved two teams throwing a ball at each other, trying to get it to hit the ground before the opposition caught or deflected it. In short, a precursor to volleyball, whose rules were drawn up a year later; it's almost certain that volleyball's inventor, William Morgan, would have encountered Baer's game. Newcomb was played by boys and girls in schools across America, and was as popular as volleyball until the 1920s. After that it disappeared entirely, but for a while the only two team sports that were officially played by women in the US, Newcomb and netball, were both invented by the same woman.

experiment as 'not entirely satisfactory', while others who attended described 'a mad game' in which the women 'grew bitter and lost control'. It only increased the number of voices that said sports were not for women. Churchmen complained that not only did the game make the women 'loud-voiced and bold', but also that basketball was a Yankee invention from the North, and therefore inappropriate to play in the South. Civil War wounds had not yet healed.

Baer initially abandoned the idea, but deep down she knew that the exercise and teamwork that basketball offered would be beneficial to her students; she just needed to temper the rules a little to make them acceptable to Southern sensibilities. And so, over the next few years, Baer set about removing the parts of Naismith's game that encouraged physical contact and disorder. There would be no dribbling in her new sport; no interference when some-one attempted a shot; and no striking, snatching or even tapping the ball. No 'needlessly rough play' was a given, but even talking during the match counted as a foul. All shots had to be taken with one hand, which Baer thought was a more graceful pose than throwing with two.* Interestingly, while the one-handed jump shot was part of netball from the off, it didn't become commonplace in basketball until the 1930s.

....

* There was also a general belief that throwing a ball with two hands flattened the chest, restricting respiration, which is another reason why the two-hander was forbidden in this early netball. The belief, and the rule, no longer persist.

But the most restrictive rule of all – one which marks probably the biggest difference between netball and basketball today – was Baer's decision that each player had to stay in a particular area of the court. Unlike the other changes, which were instigated to make the game acceptable to more conservative members of society, this was simply due to a misinterpretation of basketball's rules. Naismith's original rulebook had the court split into seven areas, but they were just guidelines, meant to help players work out where they would be best positioned at various points of the game. In his game, the players could run where they wanted. Baer thought the zones were clearly defined areas that players could not leave. Such a rule was perfect for her sport, which needed to have less body contact, and so it was one of the few laws that she decided to keep exactly as it was. Ironically, it was never a rule in basketball at all.

The new sport was a hit, and Baer sent her new rules to Naismith for his approval. He was happy with the changes, but suggested Baer changed the game's name since it was no longer very similar to basketball. Baer agreed but didn't put a great deal of effort into the new name, initially calling it basquette ball.*

Both basquette ball and basketball are relative latecomers to American sport. Many of the Founding Fathers preferred

_____

* In fact, the sport became known as 'Women's Basketball', especially in Australia and New Zealand. This became a problem when the authorities attempted to get the sport into the Olympics. The IOC said that their application had to be turned down since basketball was already an Olympic sport, and they couldn't have two sports with the same name.

cricket, and indeed, the idea of calling the leader of the new country 'president' came from the fact that cricket clubs had presidents. But by the mid-19th century, the national sport was undoubtedly baseball. North Americans had been playing games like rounders, known informally as 'town ball', for decades, but in 1845, a group from a local fire department known as the 'Knickerbocker Engine Company' decided that it was all a bit rowdy and disorganised, and that they wanted to start their own league with their own rules. They gathered together other like-minded individuals 'who were at liberty after 3 o'clock in the afternoon' and created the Knickerbocker Rules – the ones from which today's baseball laws are believed to have evolved.

FIRST BASE

The Knickerbockers* considered themselves to be 'gentlemen amateurs'. Their uniform consisted of flannel shirts and straw boaters, and they serenaded their opponents before each game. No matter the result, the match would end with

---

* The modern-day basketball team the New York Knicks are also officially known as The Knickerbockers, but the two teams are not related. Both get their names from the fact that 'Knickerbocker' was an old nickname for a New Yorker, which in itself comes from Washington Irving's first novel, *A History of New York, by Diedrich Knickerbocker* (1809). Before publication, Irving spread the rumour that an elderly man called Diedrich Knickerbocker had mysteriously disappeared, leaving behind only this manuscript, which was being published to discharge debts that he'd left behind. The PR trick worked brilliantly, drumming up public intrigue that rendered the book an immediate success.

a convivial feast. Their rules were just as you'd expect from such a gentleman's club, with rule number one being that all players must be punctual. This stipulation wasn't just for the sake of politeness; it also had some practical use. New York City was becoming much more densely populated, so there wasn't much space to play ball. As a result, players often had to schlep over to New Jersey to find a suitable area for a game. It was a real pain to go all the way over the Hudson River only to find that half the players hadn't turned up, so an emphasis on good timekeeping was vital.

Another one of the Knickerbocker Rules, and one that appears particularly odd today, stated that hitting the ball out of the stadium was a foul. Today, it's the aim of every batter to 'hit it out of the park', but in those days, the park was right next to the river. If anyone struck the ball too hard, the teams would have to fork out for some new equipment.[*]

The Knickerbockers continued to play by these rules, but as other New York teams formed, they came up with their own variations. Just as with early soccer games, when two codes collided, the teams would begin each game with a meeting, deciding on which rules to play.[†] In the 10 years after the original Knickerbocker Rules, at least six clubs published

---

[*] A rule which lives on in back-garden cricket games: hit the ball into a neighbour's back garden and it's usually 'six and out'. This phrase is also the name of an Australian rock band starring former cricketer Brett Lee.
[†] The first officially recognised game involving the Knickerbockers came when they played against a group known as the New York Club. Intriguingly, the Knicks lost 23–1, and the New York Club then disappeared from history.

their 'constitutions' in various newspapers, along with their own versions of the rules. It seemed as if everyone in New England had their own idea of what constituted a game of baseball, and so in 1857, the Knickerbockers proposed setting up a committee to create a new set of laws that took into account the different versions and would be accepted by all of the major teams. This set of rules, which John Thorn, the official historian for Major League baseball, has described as like a baseball Magna Carta or Dead Sea Scrolls, sold at auction in 2016 for $3.2 million. They contained many of the rules that are used today, such as the bases being exactly 90 feet apart, both sides having nine players and each game lasting nine innings. The final rule, presumably included at the insistence of the Knickerbockers, was that if any team turned up 15 minutes late, they forfeited the game.

Be it to appease rival baseball clubs or conservative netball viewers, many of these early sporting laws came about to make games more appealing or palatable to the players and public. But rules are established for myriad reasons, not just to create a sport that keeps everybody happy. Another important purpose they serve is to keep everybody safe.

HEALTH AND SAFETY GONE MAD!

For the first few decades of American football, in the second half of the 19th century, teams used tactics that were almost the exact inverse of those used in the earliest days of soccer in the UK. Initially, players would try to manoeuvre the ball around the opposition by throwing it to each other, rather than running directly towards the goal line, ball in hand, as is more common today. The big change occurred thanks to a man called Lorin Deland, who had a brainwave when he attended a match between Harvard and Yale in 1891. Deland was an aspiring actor who also ran a greetings-card company. He had never played any sport to a decent level, but he was interested in military history and saw similarities between football and war. He was also friends with Bernie Trafford, the captain of the Harvard team.

In the run-up to the 1892 season, Harvard tried out a new tactic devised by Deland (with a little help from Napoleon Bonaparte). The idea was for the bulkiest and strongest players to form a 'flying wedge' that ran at full pelt towards the member of the opposing team whom they'd identified as the weakest. They would mow the guy down, thus creating a hole in the opposition's defence. Another player would run with the ball just behind the wedge, and now that a gap had been forged, he could simply trot through it to score.

It was simple but incredibly effective. Within a year, every team in the country was using some version of the flying wedge, and football had turned from a skilful passing game into an absolute bloodbath. In some cases literally. One particularly feared Yale player, Frederic Remington, would dip his shirt into a pool of animal blood before each game to make him appear even more ferocious.[*]

---

[*] If the name sounds familiar, that's because Remington went on to become quite a famous artist, thanks to his paintings of cowboys and Native Americans.

An example of the 'flying wedge' formation, which was banned in American football in the early 1900s. The tactic found its way into rugby later in the 20th century, and has since been explicitly banned in both rugby league and rugby union.

The new tactic was a disaster for the game. Not only was it repetitive and quite boring to watch, but the players were constantly injured, or worse. President Grover Cleveland abolished the annual Army vs Navy game in 1893 when it turned out that 24 of the naval team had spent some time in hospital the previous season due to football injuries. By 1905, American football had become so violent that 19 players died during the course of the season. Unsurprisingly, there were calls for the sport to be banned.

The man who saved football was another US president, Theodore Roosevelt, who was a big fan of the sport but understood that without reform, the public would soon insist it be outlawed. The previous year, he had negotiated the end of the Russo-Japanese War, for which he would become the first politician to win the Nobel Peace Prize. Getting Yale and Harvard to the table to agree to new rules proved arguably more difficult. Harvard's president, Charles Eliot, wanted the game banned altogether, while Yale's Walter Camp had come up with the rules in the first place, and so took the idea of anyone wanting to tinker with them as a personal attack.

Eventually, thanks to Roosevelt's public admonishment of the college heads, imploring them to 'set an example of fair play', they came to the table and a new set of rules was agreed, including many of those that define the game today, such as allowing the forward pass by a quarterback that begins most plays. Crucially, the flying wedge was no longer allowed. As a result, there were 'only' 11 deaths on the football field over the next two seasons. Despite the slow start, the modern game had been born. Fatal accidents in American football are thankfully now vanishingly rare.

However, the sport still carries its risks.* The National Football League (NFL) has embraced technology to improve safety. In 2019, it launched the NFL Helmet Challenge, which so far has awarded more than $1 million to innovators who have managed to come up with new, safer helmets. And since 2022, some players have been equipped with smart mouth-guards that can give data on how dangerous different types

----

* A 2017 study looked at the brains of amateur and professional players, and found that 87% of them, and 99% of those who competed in the NFL, showed signs of chronic traumatic encephalopathy – brain degeneration caused by repeated head impacts. In the general population, it's around 6%.

of tackle are. These days, there are on average 30 health professionals at every NFL match, specifically to look after the players. The rules have also continued to change – in 2013, for instance, stopping a runner by using your head was made illegal. All this has been done by the league to ensure its players are safe. But in some sports, the rules had to be changed to keep the spectators safe.

THROWING CAUTION TO THE WIND

On 13 October 1956, several British newspapers reported that a Spanish athlete called Félix Erausquin had recorded one of the longest javelin throws of all time, throwing his spear 83.40m for a national record. There was no mention that Erausquin was just a few months away from celebrating his 50th birthday, and no explanation of how a previously relatively unknown athlete had achieved this feat. Two days later, when more detailed information filtered into the press, he became an international celebrity.

Erausquin came from the Basque region of northern Spain, an area rich in iron ore deposits and whose history has been shaped by mining. Basque iron was the best in the world; it was known as '*bilbo*' after the city of Bilbao, and was mentioned by Shakespeare;* it is probably where Bilbo Baggins gets his first name from. In their spare time, Basque miners

----

* When Hamlet refers to 'the mutines in the bilboes', he's talking about the shackles worn by prisoners on boats which were made from this high-quality steel.

would compete to see who could throw their equipment the furthest. The *palanka*, a heavy metal rod that was used to make holes for explosives, was a favourite object for this pastime.

The traditional way to throw a *palanka* was to spin round, like a discus thrower, and let it slip through your hands when you were at the appropriate point of the rotation. 'What if,' thought Erausquin, 'I try the same technique with a javelin?' He practised the style in the 1940s, while still a relatively young man, but it proved difficult to control the spear. Moreover, other javelin throwers couldn't hide their amusement at this athlete spinning around and launching his spear in random directions, often almost directly into the ground.

Still, Erausquin persevered, and by 1956, he was ready to take his technique into actual competition. Wetting his hands to help the javelin slip from his grasp at the right moment, he not only beat the Spanish record, he began to threaten the world record of 83.66m – as well as anyone standing within 100m of him. In any direction.

The authorities quickly banned the technique on safety grounds, but not before one athlete without Erausquin's years of practice had unsuccessfully tried the method, almost impaling a pole-vaulter. Another, the Norwegian Egil Danielsen, had managed to send one almighty throw in the right direction, recording an incredible distance of 93.70m, a full 10m further than the world record. The authorities wouldn't allow his record to stand, however, and instigated a rule that javelin throwers could not use a technique like this in the future.

Eventually, Danielsen's distance was surpassed anyway, as conventional javelin throwers got stronger and improved their technique. In 1984, a German athlete called Uwe Hohn managed an incredible throw of 104.8m. But again, this record prompted a rule change by the authorities. The javelin event typically takes place in the field part of a stadium, which is enclosed by a running track. The track always has to be the same length and shape, since both sides are used for 100m sprints. Once a javelin throw gets any longer than that, it starts to threaten the runners, or even the crowd, at the other end of the field. Indeed, as the measurers raced after Hohn's throw, which landed a good 5–10m beyond where they were expecting it to, the American commentator excitedly announced that it had landed 'just inside the stadium', and that after this throw 'the weight of the javelin will most assuredly be increased. The stadia are not big enough to hold the javelin any more.'

The commentator was wrong. The rules were not changed to make the javelin heavier, but they were changed to make it less aerodynamic. By moving the centre of gravity forward by 4cm, the spear would now tend to land nose down, rather than coming in flat. This took an average of 10% off the distance any athlete could throw, with the added bonus that the javelin would now make a dent in the ground when it landed, so it was easier to measure the length of the throw.* Hohn, meanwhile, was stripped of his world record, but it is called

* The women's javelin kept its original design until 1999, when women, too, began to threaten to break the 100m barrier.

the 'eternal record' on the official website of the Olympics, where it will presumably remain until a new Uwe Hohn or Félix Erausquin comes along.

The section of the World Athletics rulebook relating specifically to the javelin is just five pages long. It begins by ruling out Erausquin-style throws, simply by stating that 'non-orthodox styles are not permitted', and ends by saying that 'a space must be reserved beside the throwing point for a wind sock'.* The rest is mostly a list of the approved weights and designs of the spear itself. It's all that can be expected for a sport that simply requires an athlete to throw an item as far as possible. But other sports that appear equally straightforward to the casual observer can have the most intricate of rules.

BY FAIRWAY OR FOUL

As we've seen, the first rules of golf were written up in Scotland in the 18th century. They consisted of just 13 laws and fewer than 350 words. But more laws were added, and by 2019, the bodies in charge of the game decided that the rules had become much too cumbersome and so tried to simplify them. The official book containing these new 'simple' laws is available to buy. It's 538 pages long.

....

* This is to allow the athletes to calibrate their throws according to the strength and direction of the wind. For instance, for optimum results it's best to throw a javelin at a slightly steeper angle in a tailwind, compared to a headwind.

At the sport's most basic level, it's all about trying to propel a ball into a hole with a stick, and you would be forgiven for thinking that's that. But the problem is that golf is played on natural terrain. You need rules for what to do if your ball lands in sand, water, bushes or trees, or, in the worst case, hits somebody. There's even a rule that tells you what to do if your ball lands in a rabbit scraping, and that's something that was very important for some of history's earliest golfers.

There's evidence that people have played golf in the Scottish town of St Andrews since the early 15th century, and in 1552, the archbishop of St Andrews gave all local people the right to play the game on the land that is today known as the Old Course.* The reason golf is typically played over 18 holes today is that this is the number of holes on the Old Course.†

The Old Course is what's known as a 'links', so called because the land is a link between the sand dunes beside the North Sea and the arable land which is a few hundred metres from the coast. Links courses follow the lie of the land, and players must avoid (or utilise) the natural humps, bumps and hollows as they make their way around. The land was useless for farming but could be used to keep animals, and some historians think that this explains why golf clubs are shaped like

* There is also a New Course in St Andrews, though it's all relative: it opened in 1895, a year before the first modern Olympic games.
† It used to be 22 holes, but the locals decided that some of them were too easy, and so combined them to make the game a bit more challenging.

shepherds' crooks. Even more speculatively, some think that golf bunkers – the sandy pits you get on the courses – were originally holes created by sheep that were sheltering from the harsh winds in sand dunes. The golf holes themselves might have been rabbit burrows. Indeed, rabbits have long lived in the links area of St Andrews, and they are known to flatten areas of ground around their warrens, just as the grassy patch (the green) around the holes is flattened today. Perhaps, so the theory goes, rabbits constructed the first greens.

In 1797, thanks to years of financial mismanagement, the town of St Andrews found itself skint. The council decided to raise funds by selling the golf course to a couple of local merchants, father and son Charles and Cathcart Dempster, who leased the land to rabbit farmers. However, due to the long-standing church ordinance the Dempsters weren't allowed to stop people playing golf there, and this caused a few problems.

The golfers played around the rabbits for a few years, but rabbits did what rabbits do, and soon there were thousands of them. Worse still, they were digging up the golf course; one survey found 895 holes or partial holes (in addition to the ones that were actually meant to be there) on the course, which was making the game virtually unplayable. And so the matter went to court. The Dempsters had a contract that was signed and sealed, but the golfers had been playing on the course for hundreds of years. Many were also members of very influential families, so they used all their political might to force the nouveau-riche merchants to stop their rabbit-breeding. Not only that, the court decided that the golfers had the right to exterminate any rabbits they saw.

Furious with the ruling, the Dempsters hired a team of men to protect the rabbits. Anyone who was seen threatening the animals was harassed and shooed away. One golfer, John Fraser, was attacked and almost killed by the Dempsters' men, and so in response the golfers formed a similar 'committee' to protect their games. There was now a mini-war taking place on the golf course. It was rabbit farmers versus golfers, and neither side was backing down.

The Dempsters appealed the case, and eventually took it to the House of Lords, which found in their favour. It looked like the days of playing golf in St Andrews were numbered. But then a man called George Cheape came in to save the day for the golfers. He owned some land nearby and was irritated with the rascally rabbits encroaching on his property, so he offered to buy the golf course off the father-and-son team. Presumably glad to be rid of it, the Dempsters agreed, Cheape removed the rabbits, and the area was preserved for golfing. Today, Rule 16.1, as written by the Royal & Ancient Golf Club, still gives explicit instructions for what to do if your ball ends up in a hole made by a burrowing animal: you can move the ball to an area free of holes, with no penalty shots.

The same action is available if your ball comes to rest next to venomous snakes,* stinging bees, alligators, fire ants or bears. If it is next to a cactus, you do not get free relief, but you can wrap a towel around your body to protect you from the spines. If your ball embeds itself in a piece of fruit that has fallen from a tree on the course, you have to either

---

* It's up to the players to agree that the snake in question is venomous.

take a penalty or try taking a swing at the entire ball–fruit combo. All of this has to be codified because golf is an outdoor game played across large tracts of land, and therefore has to accommodate nature in all its diversity. But sporting rules sometimes go beyond this. Scientific advances, paired with a growing public awareness of our environmental impact, mean measures that actively protect nature and the environment are increasingly being built into the rulebooks.

WAXING AND WINNING

Celtic–Rangers, India–Pakistan, Prost–Senna, Boca Juniors–River Plate, England–Australia, England–Germany, England–Scotland . . . England–anyone really. Sport is full of rivalries, but one of the most intense, yet under-reported, is Norway vs Sweden in cross-country skiing.

The two were part of the same kingdom until 1905, but since then, Sweden has always prided itself on its successful cross-country team. For Norway, a much smaller country by population, any victory over their larger neighbour is a cause for celebration. With national pride at stake (along with medals, glory and cash, of course), both teams have spent decades trying to eke out the tiniest advantage, and in skiing, one of the best ways to do that is to find the best wax.

The first people known to have waxed their skis were the Lapps. In the 17th century, they were covering their equipment with pine pitch and rosin to make it last longer. It was a happy coincidence that by doing so, they were able to slide along the snow much more quickly. Waxes work because they repel water.

As you ski, you heat up the snow, which causes water to form. Without any wax, a wet sheet on the bottom of the ski is created, which is fine, but if you can add a wax, you get tiny beads of water instead. These act like ball bearings on the bottom of your skis, speeding you up a great deal. Over the years, all sorts of substances have been tried: candle wax, floor wax, Teflon (though that needed to be heated so much in order to stick it to the skis that it ended up melting them) and even spermaceti – a waxy substance found in the heads of certain whales.

In 1948, a Swedish company called Swix* came up with a new paraffin-based wax that proved a revelation. It helped the country's skiers to glide over the snow at higher speeds, and the company made different versions for different types of snow, tailoring it to cross-country or downhill skiing. In that year's Winter Olympics, Sweden won gold in all three cross-country events, including the relay, in which they beat Norway by a full 12 minutes. Norway had its worst-ever cross-country skiing result in an Olympics. They were furious. This was a blatant attack on Norway's national sport. Norwegian manufacturers banded together in an attempt to stop the Swedish wax from coming into their country. Shopkeepers wouldn't stock it, and were happy to admit that it was because the brand was Swedish. Even when Swix began to be made in Norway by Norwegian workers, patriotic skiers refused to buy it at first.

Eventually, though, Norwegian skiers became sick of their slow waxes. They caved and began to use Swix, which led to a

* The name is a shortened version of 'Swedish wax'.

thaw in the public's stance. But the industry was still innovating. In the 1970s, a recreational skier from America called Terry Hertel brewed up a new wax that he called 'Hot Sauce'. It proved popular, but it was nothing compared to a chemical called perfluorocarbon, which was made by a company called 3M. Hertel had a friend called Rob Hunter, who worked at the company and told him about this magic substance. 3M was selling it to the cosmetics and paint industries in very small amounts, but Hunter and Hertel realised that theoretically it could do an even better job in the skiing world than Hot Sauce. The only problem was that it cost $1,000 per pound. Hertel solved that problem by mixing small amounts into candle wax. He now had a substance that was both affordable and made skiers unbelievably fast.

Over in Europe, Swix had a similar idea, and their labs came up with a comparable chemical that they called 'Cera F'. Suddenly, nobody could win without using one of these fluorocarbons, and so they flew off the shelf – even in Norway. Every professional ski that made contact with snow (and those of many keen amateurs as well) was covered in one of these chemicals.

Then, at the start of the 21st century, studies began to appear that suggested these substances are terrible for the environment and human health. Not only was there a suggestion that being in regular contact with them could cause problems in the human liver, kidney, thyroid and reproductive system, but they also hardly ever break down and are particularly good at leaching into the water supply; for that reason, they're sometimes called 'forever chemicals'. Recently, there have even been some studies suggesting that the more of these chemicals you have in your body, the more susceptible you are to Covid-19.

The ski industry was put under pressure to remove these products, and in 2020, the International Ski Federation announced a new rule banning them from all competitions. This may be the first time that the laws of a sport have been changed to protect the environment, but it almost certainly won't be the last. It's still not clear how the new rule will be policed, but while Sweden and Norway were presumably busy keeping an eye on each other's wax during the 2022 Winter Olympics, Finland and Germany also became embroiled in the controversy. Finland accused Germany of using the now-illegal fluorine waxes to help them win a surprise gold and silver in the women's cross-country events. It was a claim that the Germans would not let slide. They furiously denounced the accusations as 'a lie' and 'outrageous', and went on to say: 'The German Ski Association adheres to all guidelines and rules. And we assume that this also applies to the other nations.'

That second comment was likely a dig at Finland for being unsportsmanlike enough to accuse them in the first place. In most sports, an unjust allegation of cheating is cause for outrage. Being accused of foul play is, after all, a double insult: not only is someone saying that you refused to act within the rules that everyone has agreed, but also you weren't good enough to win fairly.

Since sports are defined by their rules, once someone stops playing by them, the game becomes something else completely. If you're a cricketer who rubs the ball with sandpaper in order to make it more difficult for your opponents to hit it, then that's 'just not cricket'. The great paradox of sport is that most players want to be seen to be playing within the rules, but at the same time, they push them as far as possible. In some sports, rules are regularly broken until noticed by the umpire or referee, and it's agreed by everyone involved that it's part of the game. But for those who take it too far and act beyond the tacitly agreed parameters of the sporting world, there can be lifelong pariah status and bans from the games that they love so much. To protect athletes against these outcomes, it's important for organisers to recognise their motivations. Often it's pressure, culture or money – but sometimes it's simply an overriding desire to win at all costs.

4

SHOELESS JOE'S REDEMPTION

WHY, DEEP DOWN, WE'RE ALL CHEATERS

> I try not to break the rules but merely
> to test their elasticity.
> **Bill Veeck**
> **(baseball club owner)**

Most people have, at some point in their lives, employed a
touch of deception to improve their chances of winning. It
seems to happen regardless of how small the stakes are,
which is why in sport you see it at the lowest levels, as well
as the highest. Comedian Michael Palin was once disqualified
from a conkers tournament on the Isle of Wight for baking
his conker and then soaking it in vinegar to harden it. One
of his comedy forebears, Harpo Marx, was a great fan of
croquet, a sport which was a hotbed of deceit. Marx played
with the Algonquin Round Table, the famous group of 1920s
and '30s writers and artists, but their games were beset by
skulduggery. On one occasion they all stopped speaking to
Harold Ross (founder of *The New Yorker* magazine) for a week
because he'd shoved the ball with his foot – an illegal move.

The Algonquins' response goes to show that nothing fires
up our righteous anger like a cheat. Through deceit or dis-
obedience, cheaters get recognition they don't deserve at the
expense of honest rivals. It's not fair, and we are hard-wired
to hate unfairness when we see it, and even more so when
we lose out to it. Our primate cousins feel the same way: a
capuchin monkey who is given a cucumber for performing a

task will be delighted with the reward. That is, until she sees a fellow monkey being given even more delicious *grapes* for the same task, at which point she'll hurl the comparatively tasteless cucumber at the researcher.

And yet, the monkey who got the grapes doesn't object to the injustice quite so much. And when we're the ones benefiting from the cheating, neither do we. In fact, while it's unpleasant being the victim or observer of cheating, being the perpetrator can be positively thrilling. In a study called 'The Cheater's High: The Unexpected Affective Benefits of Unethical Behavior', researchers had participants perform tasks such as solving as many anagrams as they could in a time limit. They gave them a chance to add extra answers when the experimenters weren't looking and then scanned their brains. The study showed that the experience of 'getting away with something' triggered positive feelings. Regret came only when someone saw that they had hurt a specific, identifiable victim.

We can blame our biology only so much. Sports psychologists tell us that there's plenty more at play when it comes to explaining why we cheat. A lot of it is due to peer pressure. Professor Mia Consalvo, an expert on cheating in video games, coined the phrase 'gaming capital' to explain the fact that the better a player is, the more popular they are in their community. It turns out that someone who has already banked a lot of this gaming capital will do anything they can to keep it, which is why you find cheats at the very top of every sport. If you repeatedly tell a child that they're good at something, they're more likely to use underhand tactics to keep up that reputation than a child who has not had that positive reinforcement. Similarly, students who cheat in exams tend to be the ones who are already close to the top of their class. And these habits are self-perpetuating, since when you believe that those around you are cheating, you're incentivised to do the same to avoid falling behind. Lance Armstrong would probably have won the Tour de France without his years of drug-taking, but he blamed his transgressions on the fact that he was trying to keep up with his opponents, all of whom he perceived to be cheating too.[*]

TOP OF THE FLOPS

All cheating involves some kind of deception, but one of the most common ways to do so during the heat of a match is simply to trick the referee. In football, this is most commonly done by diving, or 'flopping', as it is known in the US.

Serial floppers can also blame their actions on outside pressure, but rather than it coming from peers, they can be affected by fans and the referees themselves. When, due to the 2020 Covid-19 pandemic, English Premier League games were played behind closed doors (with no fans), not a single player was booked for diving in 148 games. Compared to

....

[*] Armstrong denied doping for many years but had to pay out millions in settlements after finally being found guilty. He is still incredibly wealthy thanks to the fact that he was an early investor in the ride-share app Uber. Satisfying, in a way, to know that he's still taking people for a ride.

previous seasons, you would have expected around 10 people to be cautioned in that time. And if you look at the areas of the pitch where dives take place, then the evidence that they're playing up is clear: players love to dive when they are close to a referee. They're also smart in their choice of when to flop and are more likely to dive in matches that are refereed by officials who are statistically more likely to fall for their theatrics.

One of the biggest scandals in rugby union history was also down to fakery. In 2009, when Harlequins played Leinster in a big quarter-final, their best kicker was substituted. When the replacement was injured, Quins wanted to bring back their star player, but the only way they'd be allowed to do this was if one of the team got a 'blood injury', meaning they would be forced to leave the field to get patched up. So when they sent their physio on to treat the injured player, he carried with him a capsule filled with fake blood hidden in his sock. One of Quins' players, Tom Williams, was tasked with biting down on the capsule to feign a cut lip. Williams missed his mouth the first time and had to scramble in the mud looking for the tablet, but eventually fake blood flowed from his mouth and the replacement took place.

The opposing team were immediately suspicious – not least because Williams winked to his bench as he left the pitch. He ran straight down the tunnel and into a room with the match-day doctor, Wendy Chapman. The Leinster physio followed them, looking for evidence to back up his suspicions, but he was locked out. In a panic, Williams asked Chapman to cut his lip for real, to hide the deceit. Under pressure, Chapman agreed, apparently disregarding the medical profession's maxim: 'First, do no harm.'*

Eventually, the truth came out, and the Harlequins manager was banned for three years, the physio for two and the player for four months. Chapman was suspended from the British Medical Council.†

An incident that's often considered the most shameful in football's history took a similar course. In 1989, Brazil and Chile (partially) played an extremely hotly contested match at Brazil's Maracanã stadium to see who would qualify for the World Cup. Brazil were ahead 1–0, when a fan threw a flare onto the pitch. The Chilean star player, captain and goalkeeper Roberto Rojas immediately fell to the floor clutching his face, which was pouring with blood. He was carried off the pitch, and to the horror of watching fans, the entire Chile team walked off with him. The referee was forced to abandon the match.

Suspicions were soon raised, and the Brazilians began hunting for evidence of what had really happened.‡ They

....

* It is often said that this phrase appears in the Hippocratic Oath, traditionally taken by all doctors. Hippocrates didn't actually use those exact words, but the general gist was there.

† Dr Chapman was later reinstated with a warning, when the council accepted that she had not been part of the conspiracy and had been coerced into helping to hide the plot.

‡ The first person to openly accuse Rojas of foul play happened to be Pelé. A journalist spotted him milling around the locker rooms after the incident and asked him what he thought had happened. Pelé immediately replied: 'Iodine' – in other words, fake blood. He turned out to be right about the cheating, although wrong about the specifics: the blood was real.

found one photographer who'd taken a few shots from directly behind Rojas at the crucial moment, and Brazilian newspaper *O Globo* immediately bought the rights to them. There then ensued a desperate race to get the pictures developed. The woman who ran *O Globo*'s photography lab was asleep in bed, it being late at night by this time, but found herself being woken up and dragged back to the developing room. For the Brazilians, it was worth it: the photos published on the front page the next day showed that the flare had landed close to Rojas but not made contact with him.* He'd thrown himself into the smoke and, as he finally admitted later, pulled out a razor blade he'd hidden in his glove and used it to cut his face. Brazil were awarded a 2–0 victory, and Chile not only failed to make it to that World Cup, they were banned from the following one too. A generation of Chilean footballers missed their chance to compete at that level. Rojas was banned from professional football for life.

As the severity of the punishment reflected, Rojas had gone to a shocking extreme to win – or avoid losing. But perhaps the most shocking fakery in sporting history took place in the 2000 Paralympics in Sydney. A few days after the tournament ended, Spanish gold medal-winning basketball player (and investigative journalist) Carlos Ribagorda admitted that most of his team had no type of disability. The players were supposed to have an IQ of below 70 to qualify for the tournament,

---

* The woman who'd originally thrown the flare briefly became a celebrity, dubbed *Fogueteira do Maracanã* (Firecracker of the Maracanã), and made it onto the cover of *Playboy* magazine.

but medical certificates were forged and no further tests were made. Ribagorda said that at one stage of their first game, when they were 30 points ahead of the Chinese team, their coach had shouted: 'Lads, move down a gear or they'll figure out you're not disabled.'

The team's success was their downfall. A photo of the athletes appeared in the online edition of *Marca*, Spain's most widely read daily paper, and the comments section was filled with people who recognised the players, making remarks like: 'I played basketball against him, he's definitely not disabled.' The truth was out, but not soon enough to stop the Spanish from winning gold. However, while the rest of Spain's Paralympians returned home to a heroes' welcome, the basketball team were sneaked out of the airport in dark glasses, hats and comically fake beards. The scandal had huge repercussions: intellectually disabled events were scrapped for the next two Olympics, wrecking the careers of other athletes, who now could no longer compete.

In this case, the motivation to cheat appears to have been money. Officials would get funding from the government, and the better the teams did, the more money they got. As far as the athletes were concerned, according to Ribagorda many just saw it as a chance for a free holiday in Australia. They cheered when the hooter sounded to end the final, but the enormity hit home at the medal ceremony. As the Spanish national anthem played, 'We just stood there and listened,' said Ribagorda. 'Nobody wanted to talk about it afterwards.' The players were happy enough to cheat when they saw it as a bit of fun, but when the event was over, they began to regret their actions.

For many people, in the heat of the moment it's instinctive to try to gain any advantage. However, paradoxically, once we see the successful result of any underhand tactics we might have employed, we're often reluctant to repeat them. In another study with our friends the capuchins, researchers had the monkeys play a game of shape-matching on computers against humans. When a 'cheat' (a shortcut to the correct answers) was added, 70% of the monkeys chose to use it, versus just over half of the humans. But when they saw positive results from their actions, only 20% of the monkeys continued to cheat, while none of the human subjects did.

This experiment was small, and of course only the humans knew they were part of a scientific study and acted accordingly, but the results suggest we have an innate sense of fairness. And while many of us will happily cheat when given the chance, this sense of unfairness becomes harder to ignore when our actions help us get ahead. That said, and as we've already seen, this instinct doesn't always win out; it's sometimes overpowered by stronger forces. The promise of money can be one, and attaining glory or high status is another, but our culture also has to shoulder some of the blame.

US VS THEM

In the 1980s, economist Fons Trompenaars was working as a management consultant for companies such as Heineken, IBM and General Motors when he came up with his model of national culture differences. According to him, some countries are Universalist, while others are Particularist. People who live in Universalist cultures (such as the UK and Germany) tend to believe that rules are universal and should be followed by everyone, while Particularist cultures (Italy and Spain, for example) largely believe that the rules are particular to your situation. Applied to a sport like football, the model means that players from Universalist countries would think diving is always wrong, while those from Particularist countries would think it's acceptable in certain situations. There's evidence to support the theory. In 2014, the *Wall Street Journal* looked at the number of dives during that year's World Cup. They found that the classically Universalist England was near the bottom of the flops, along with Australia and the Netherlands. Typically Particularist nations such as Brazil, Honduras and Chile, on the other hand, spent the longest 'writhing time' lying on the floor.* In one match, it was only four seconds before Ecuador's Enner Valencia had thrown himself to the ground, clutching his leg.†

The English might call Valencia a cheat, but in South America he might be known as a *malandro*. It's a different mindset, where cunning is prized just as much as skill. The

....

* It's not an exact science, though. Portugal and Argentina are usually described as Particularist, but they were positioned towards the bottom of the *Wall Street Journal* poll.
† During a training session in his home country once, Valencia was confronted by lawyers demanding unpaid child maintenance. To avoid being given papers, he flopped to the ground and feigned injury so that he could be taken from the pitch on a motorised stretcher. Footage shows the lawyers chasing after the buggy before the player jumps into an ambulance and makes his escape.

culture of the *malandro* (feminine: *malandra*) comes from the abolition of slavery, when formerly enslaved people struggled to find regular work and were forced to rely on their wits to survive. Some South American journalists lament the lack of *malandro* players in modern times, replaced by taller, European-style players who grew up in the richer beachfront areas of the big cities.

Of course, it's not right to say that all South American sports players are *malandros*, any more than it's true to say that all northern Europeans are paragons of fair play. And every country has its own subjective interpretation of events. English football fans will never forget the 'Hand of God'* moment, when Diego Maradona punched the ball into the net in the 1986 World Cup quarter-final against England, but will dismiss the Argentinian's claims that Harry Kane dived to win a penalty against Colombia in the World Cup 32 years later, an event that still raises hackles in some parts of South America.

Not only is there too much nuance in this debate to make sweeping claims, but as the sporting world becomes more globalised, different cultures have inevitably influenced and embraced each other's habits. There are fewer *malandros* now where there were once many, and more where there were once none. And as much as they'd like to deny it, English teams are no exception. In 2020, after the England football

---

* This is how Diego Maradona famously referred to his goal, though he later clarified in his autobiography: 'What hand of God? It was the hand of Diego!'

team received another dubious penalty in the European Championships semi-final against Denmark, *Marca* publicly asked English footballers to 'stop giving lectures to the rest of the continent about diving'. Despite cultural differences, it's never the case that 'the others' cheat, while 'we' never would. However, in baseball at least, we have cold, hard data that foreign players in the US are more likely to take performance-enhancing drugs. Ultimately, the reasoning behind that returns to one of the main causes of cheating in general: cold, hard cash.

MONEY, MONEY, MONEY

In 2013, *Sports Illustrated* ran a large survey on drug-taking in baseball. They found that while fewer than 30% of professional players were born outside the US, foreign-born players accounted for almost two-thirds of doping suspensions. The authors concluded that this was the logical result of the huge amounts of money flooding into the game. Their idea is that sportspeople are well able to weigh up the risk of being caught against the reward if they are not. After American, the next four most common nationalities competing in Major League baseball are Dominican*, Venezuelan, Puerto Rican and Cuban – four countries that have much weaker economies

---

* That is, people from the Dominican Republic, rather than people from the island of Dominica. While you're here, the difference is that you pronounce the former 'Dom-MEE-nik-ans' and the latter 'Dom-in-EEK-ans'.

than the US. The money that a top player can make means a lot more to your average Venezuelan than it does to the average American. In fact, the authors found that there was a very strong inverse relationship between the likelihood of a player failing a drug test and the per capita gross domestic product of their country of origin.

The most infamous cheats in the history of baseball were also motivated by money, but the 1919 Chicago White Sox team that included Chick Gandil, Happy Felsch and 'Shoeless Joe' Jackson was all-American. Even Charles 'Swede' Risberg was from California – he got his nickname because his father was born in Sweden.* The White Sox were easily the best team in the country, but were run by the miserly Charles Comiskey, who had a reputation for underpaying his players. As a result the temptation of a quick buck was too great for eight of his team, who agreed to lose on purpose and throw the 1919 World Series. They conspired with gamblers who were planning to bet against the team (the favourites to win the competition) and promised to give the players a total pay-out of $100,000 if they lost.

When the truth came out, the so-called 'Black Sox' scandal rocked the baseball world. The *Chicago Herald and Examiner* considered it a blow to the entire country: 'It might seem unimportant in comparison with disarmament, or world commerce, or the race problem, or prohibition. But at the bottom

* Baseball players are not renowned for their geography skills: one of Risberg's peers, Olaf Henriksen, was also called 'Swede', even though he was Danish.

of every issue lies the national character.' It was a big enough deal to be mentioned in *The Great Gatsby*, and the 1989 Kevin Costner film *Field of Dreams* is based on the legend of 'Shoeless Joe' Jackson, one of the eight players who pleaded guilty. Today, Jackson is largely considered to have been innocent due to the fact that he performed better than any other player during that World Series.*

THE OPPORTUNISTS

Sometimes cheating is much more spur-of-the-moment than the examples we have seen so far. After all, if an easy opportunity presented itself to any of us mid-contest, who could honestly say they'd never take it? Especially if, should the finger be pointed, you can give an innocent shrug and say, 'Who, me?'

In open-water swimming, a typical example is 'ziplining' – grabbing the ankles of someone in front and tugging them backwards and yourself forwards. It's grounds for disqualification if spotted, but such races, with their mass of bodies fighting for the lead while kicking up white water in every direction, are hard to adjudicate from the bank. A similar piece of apparent improvisation came at the 1980 Moscow

---

* Shoeless Joe was virtually illiterate, so much so that his wife would sign memorabilia for him. In fact, there is only one known example of Joe's actual signature on a photograph of him. It sold in 2021 for $1.47 million, which – even allowing for inflation – is a darn sight more than the $5,000 he allegedly received for his part in the scandal.

Olympics, when it was alleged that the Soviets were opening the stadium gates whenever the home javelin throwers were competing so that a gust of wind might give them extra distance. It was a subtle tweak at the margins that they thought might just give them the edge (they won gold).*

But the most ingenious opportunist cheats of all have to be the rowers in the 1936 Berlin Olympics. During the heats, the German team noticed they were able to get away with false starts because the megaphone used by the starter was so big that he couldn't shout 'Go' and simultaneously see around it to keep an eye on them. The British team of Dick Southwood

Rowing coach Al Ulbrickson in 1936, sporting one of the oversized megaphones used in the sport at the time.

---

* Nobody called it the 'Gategate' scandal, but they should have.

and Jack Beresford noticed this cheating in the early rounds, and deployed the same trick themselves in the final. They defeated the German team – with Adolf Hitler watching on. Beresford later described it as 'the sweetest race I ever rowed'.

Opportunist cheats appear in all sorts of races, whether on land or water, foot or horseback. At the 1904 Olympics in St Louis, the first man to cross the finish line in the marathon was Fred Lorz, a bricklayer from New York. Whoops of delight went up from the crowd at having an American winner, until a few of the more beady-eyed spectators pointed out they'd spotted him travelling part of the course by car. It turned out he'd begun to suffer from cramps after nine miles and hitched a ride with his trainer for the subsequent 11, before popping out to jog to the finish. When his deception was unearthed, Lorz claimed it had only been a joke, and he was duly disqualified. You have to admire the chutzpah of someone who uses motorised transport to finish a running race.*

He wasn't the only one bold enough to attempt such a ruse. In 1980, a previously unknown runner called Rosie Ruiz won the Boston marathon, and it attracted a lot of attention. The Boston marathon is the world's largest and oldest annual event of its kind – king among marathons – and the fastest time by a female in its history had just been recorded by a runner no one had ever heard of. She didn't even look out of

---

* Conversely, the 1959 Formula 1 World Championship was won on foot. Australian driver Jack Brabham ran out of petrol on the final lap of the deciding race, so climbed out of his car and pushed it over the finish line.

breath and had barely broken into a sweat. Eyebrows were raised, particularly when she was interviewed afterwards and didn't seem familiar with some of the most basic running vocabulary. When her win was announced, one photographer in particular expressed surprise, given she'd bumped into her on the subway as the race was being run. Although Ruiz always maintained her innocence, she didn't appear in any of the official race photographs until the end of the marathon. It's thought that she intended to skip most of the race and then jump over the barriers to join the pack near the finish line, but when she did so, she accidentally entered right at the front of the race.

Similarly, in 1990, a jockey called Sylvester Carmouche was banned from horse racing for 10 years after hiding in a heavy fog cloud during a race and waiting for the rest of the horses to run around the track before emerging well in front and winning the race. Like Ruiz, Carmouche was caught because he finished so inconceivably far ahead of the rest and at such speed. It was also noted that neither he nor the horse were dirty; no other jockey had noticed him overtaking them; and a videotape of the event showed no sight of his colours at any time. He protested his innocence at first, but later admitted it.*

These brazen cheats were all following in the footsteps of their forebears. Bare-faced rule-breaking has a long history. There were no Olympics scheduled for AD 67, but the Emperor Nero bribed officials to hold them then anyway,

---

* This hastened the end of Carmouche's career, but today his son Kendrick is one of the US's best black American jockeys.

because it coincided with his tour of Greece, meaning he could take part. Nero competed in the four-horse chariot – or at least that was the name of the race, and a description of everyone else's vehicle, but Nero actually drove one with 10 horses. Perhaps due to the increased horsepower, he was thrown from his chariot and didn't finish the race, but the judges declared him the champion anyway, with the logic that he definitely would have won had he not fallen. It turned out he'd been right to bring the games forward, since he died the next year. After his death, with the danger of retribution now removed, the result of the race was declared null and void.

KEEPING IN THE LOOPHOLE

You could argue that rather than castigating all cheats, we should be lauding some of the more creative mavericks who think outside the box in their pursuit of success. These are the innovators, the ones who push what is possible. As we have seen in the cases of javelin and bobsled, some of the rules that define sports today came about as a result of people finding a loophole. And sometimes whether someone is a cheat or a hero can depend on whether or not these loopholes are closed during an event or after the athletes are victorious and nothing more can be done.

The way Olympic badminton competitions are organised was changed after some audacious rule-bending took place in 2012. The women's doubles tournament began with a round robin series of games that determined which teams got through to the knockout stage, and who they'd play against if they did. Sixteen teams entered, with half of them set to make it to the next round. Some of the pairs – namely one Chinese, one Indonesian and two South Korean teams – did so well in their initial matches that they were guaranteed a place in the knockout stage before they'd played their final round robin match. This happened to leave China and Korea playing each other, even though neither had any incentive to win. In fact, China had an incentive to lose, because if they'd beaten Korea, they'd have ended up playing a second Chinese team. If they lost, they'd end up on the opposite side of the draw to their fellow countrywomen, leaving open the possibility of an all-Chinese final – obviously a desirable outcome for China. So they attempted to lose the game. Mid-match, their opponents realised what was happening and also tried to lose, to avoid the second Chinese team. The game turned into a farce, with all four players deliberately hitting the shuttlecock into the net or sending it out of play. In the end, both teams were disqualified for not trying, despite their argument that losing was their best chance of getting gold. Of course, it was the tournament structure that was at fault, and it was duly changed for the next Olympics.

One player who got away with exploiting the rules – for one game, at least – was Eddie Gaedel. In baseball, the rules say that the pitcher must throw the ball into the strike zone – an imaginary rectangle placed between a batter's knees and the midpoint of their torso. With this in mind, in 1951 the St Louis Browns revealed their new player: the 3ft 7in

Gaedel. Not only did his diminutive stature mean that there was not much to aim at between the knees and the midriff, Gaedel would crouch right down to ensure his knees were as close to his head as possible. In the end, the strike zone was just 1.5in high. In his first game, the pitcher missed this area four times, which allowed Gaedel a free walk to first base, at which point he was substituted for another player who did the rest of the running. Realising that Gaedel was not a baseball player in any real sense, just someone who had been signed for his height, the league voided his contract the next day. But for that one game, he was a legitimate player and certainly not a cheat.

Baseball sometimes seems to be the spiritual home of creative cheating. Given the ball has to be pitched into a very specific area, it's relatively easy to predict its path, and so pitchers will try anything to counteract this and make the ball fly unpredictably through the air. In the 1960s, the Chicago White Sox (somewhat in the spirit of their predecessors, the Black Sox) would keep their balls in a humidifier and take them out just before the game, making them wetter, heavier and harder for their opponents to hit. A Seattle Mariners pitcher called Rick Honeycutt was less successful with his ball-tampering: he taped a drawing pin to his thumb and used it to scratch one side of the ball to make it travel unpredictably. He was caught when an umpire saw him making unusual rubbing motions with the ball. On further investigation the ref also found a scratch on the pitcher's forehead where he had absentmindedly itched himself with the pin during the game.

Pitchers had to resort to this secrecy because tampering with a baseball was, and is, explicitly against the rules due to an incident in 1920.* Until then, it was accepted that pitchers would sometimes throw 'spitballs', where they used saliva or hair grease to make the ball fly out of their fingers much more quickly. Unfortunately, a player called Ray Chapman was killed when an unexpected spitball hit him flush on the head. The league explicitly banned the practice, although in an acknowledgement that it had been an integral tactic for some players, and a key to their success, it allowed certain pitchers to continue using it until they retired. Legendary spitballers such as Gaylord Perry, Preacher Roe, John Boozer and Urban Shocker were granted exemptions until their careers ended, and the final legal spitball was pitched in 1934.†

---

* The only thing that can be rubbed on a baseball is a special mud gathered annually from the Delaware River. In fact, all balls are rubbed with this mud, so that they're rough enough for pitchers to get a grip on them. The man who collects it, Jim Bintliff, keeps the exact location secret; if challenged during his collection trips, he claims that he's gathering it to put on his roses.
† The verb 'to spitball', which means to throw out ideas, hoping that something sticks, could be related to baseball, the idea being that a spitball has an imperfect flight, just as spitballed ideas might be imperfect. Alternatively, it may be related to the other meaning of 'spitball' – a rolled-up, moistened piece of paper that might be fired at a schoolteacher by a pupil. To be honest, nobody knows for sure. We're just spitballin' here.

BE WARY OF GREEKS ON CUPS AND VASES

It's one thing to break the technical rules that define a sport, but quite another to break the ones that keep participants safe. In combat sports, cheating almost always involves making the game more dangerous, but even so, it has been happening for as long as those sports have existed.

In a lesser-visited part of the British Museum, tucked away in the furthest corner from the main entrance, is Gallery 20.* The room is stuffed to the brim with Greek pottery; if you don't like Greek pottery, this is not the room for you. But the illustrations on these items can tell us a great deal about life around 500 BC, when they were made. And in particular they can tell us how sports were played. Though the artists aren't here to tell us exactly what they were trying to illustrate, with a little guesswork three of the items scattered around Gallery 20 – a vase, a cup and a drinking bowl called a kylix – can do the job of explaining all the ways to cheat in pankration, one of the oldest sports in the world.

Pankration was the ancients' version of the Ultimate Fighting Championship (UFC) – hand-to-hand combat with almost no constraints. The word translates as 'all force', and the sport was supposedly used by the gods Heracles and Theseus to defeat the Minotaur and the Nemean lion

....

* Fortunately, these days you can explore it from the comfort of your own home, as the British Museum has made all its galleries available on Google Street View.

A pankration competitor being punished for eye-gouging. Though that may be the least of his opponent's worries, as he also seems to be kicking himself below the belt.

respectively. Pankration athletes became legends, and the sport was a common motif for decorating pots. The kylix in Gallery 20 shows one fighter gouging the eyes of his opponent; the vase depicts a vicious, desperate bite; and the cup appears to show one of the combatants attempting to grab the other's genitals. These are the three moves that were illegal in pankration;* anything else was fair game. On each pot, an umpire is standing to the side of the fight, with a branch in his hand ready to give an admonishing thwack to the cheater. On

* The same rules – no biting, eye-gouging or groin strikes – were instigated in the first-ever UFC fight.

the vase he is also holding a palm leaf, a prize which would be bestowed on the victim of the illegal bite. The moral is clear: cheaters never prosper.

TYSON'S FURY

Two thousand five hundred years later, the former world heavyweight boxing champion Mike Tyson performed similar, and similarly illegal, antics in Las Vegas. Famously, he bit a chunk out of his opponent Evander Holyfield's ear while attempting to regain his championship belt. Initially, Tyson wasn't disqualified – it was only when he bit Holyfield's *other* ear that the referee decided to stop the fight and awarded Holyfield not just the belt, but the winner's cheque for $35 million. The event was not commemorated on a vase, but certainly was recreated in photographic form: Tyson later claimed that he made more than $3 million by charging people for photos of him pretending to bite their ears.

In 2014, Tyson told the press: 'It was just one moment in which the competition can make the blood in your veins boil and it overpowers your rationality. Sometimes you become something that you are not.' But he wasn't talking about his own actions – he was sympathising with Uruguayan footballer and textbook *malandro* Luis Suárez, who had been banned for four months for biting his Italian opponent Giorgio Chiellini in a World Cup game. Suárez had form: he had previously been banned for a total of 17 games for biting two other opponents. In fact, the *New Statesman* magazine calculated that you were more than a thousand times more likely to be bitten by Suárez when playing football against him than by a shark when swimming in the ocean.

In 1983, basketball player Tree Rollins was banned for four games for biting an opponent during a brawl, an event that led to the *Boston Herald* running one of the great sporting headlines: 'Tree Bites Man'. But there were (perhaps sensibly) no punning headlines when English rugby union player Danny Grewcock bit the New Zealand hooker's finger during a match against the All Blacks in 2005. He got a four-month ban, even though the review board accepted that the bitee Keven Mealamu's fingers had 'inadvertently entered' Grewcock's mouth before he chomped down. And in 2001, the Sevilla striker Francisco Gallardo was suspended for biting down on the penis of a teammate while celebrating a goal. The Royal Spanish Football Federation thought that while he couldn't be found guilty of cheating, he had failed to act according to 'sporting behaviour and decorum'.

Why is biting considered such an offensive kind of cheating? In football and rugby, players kick or tackle each other with much more force, and in boxing they're literally punching each other in the face throughout. It was a point that Uruguayan president José Mujica made after the most recent Suárez incident, when he said: 'We didn't choose him to be a philosopher, or a mechanic, or to have good manners – he's a great player. I didn't see him bite anyone. But they sure can bash each other with kicks and chops.' According to experts in sports ethics, part of the reason we abhor biting is that we consider it to be disgusting and 'animalistic'. And if, as we've seen, play is used by children as a way of learning how to be good adults, then things like biting (as well as using offensive language and spitting), which we teach kids not to do at a young age, are particularly taboo.

WON'T SOMEONE THINK OF THE CHILDREN?

So are children likely to go around biting each other in the playground just because they've seen Luis Suárez do it? News outlets hold sportspeople to a higher value system due to their supposed influence on our children. It's become such a trope that some people called for England footballer Raheem Sterling to be banned from playing for his country due to a tattoo of a gun on his leg, ignoring the fact that it's in memory of his father, who was shot dead when Sterling was two. The tattoo is meant as a reminder to Sterling that he will never touch firearms in his life.

But the evidence doesn't support the reactionary press (*plus ça change*). Dr Michael Skey, a senior lecturer at the University of Loughborough, wondered to what extent young football fans are influenced by their idols, and so interviewed youth players and their coaches. He found that the kids particularly venerated three players whom he called 'the holy trinity': Lionel Messi, Cristiano Ronaldo and Neymar. In fact, he couldn't find a single young footballer who didn't know who those players were. But while he found plenty of evidence that the children wanted to emulate their heroes' skills on the pitch, even going so far as to include moves they'd seen the players' avatars perform in video games, there were no examples of children imitating their non-football related activities.

We asked Dr Skey if children may be encouraged to cheat when they see their idols do it. Might kids feign injury because they see Neymar rolling around on the floor pretending to be hurt? Skey said that his observations suggest that children are more than able to make their own minds up about right and wrong, rather than slavishly copying their heroes. And while there are sometimes changes in the way that children play the game – kids today are more likely to berate referees, for instance – responsibility for that comes down to the full sporting family: players, managers, officials, journalists and even politicians. It's not simply a question of them watching their heroes behave badly and copying what they see.

The truth is that if you see a child cheating in sport, it's most likely because children are humans. And humans sometimes like to cheat.

5

TWO GLASSES OF WINE FOR BREAKFAST

WHY DOPERS DON'T ALWAYS STICK TO STEROIDS

The Kentucky Derby is coming up. This year,
the horses may be subjected to a surprise drug test.
Isn't everything a surprise to a horse, though?
David Letterman

Whatever its effect on children, few would argue that biting
your opponent is anything other than a piece of egregious
cheating. But injuring the opposition is not the kind of
rule-breaking that triggers most pearl-clutching. That comes
when athletes cheat by acting against themselves – by taking
banned substances.

Ever since records began, athletes have been ingesting
substances to gain an extra edge in competition. In the days
before protein powders, ancient Greek wrestlers would eat 5kg
of lamb a day to build up muscle; in place of steroids, the phys-
ician Galen suggested taking 'the rear hooves of an Abyssinian
ass, ground up, boiled in oil, and flavoured with rose hips';* and
some classical Olympians are known to have taken psyche-
delic mushrooms to help them recover from fatigue or injury.†

....

* Traditional Chinese medicine also uses gelatin from donkeys'
hooves (and skin) to treat coughs and dizziness. There's no evidence
it works for those maladies, and there's no reason to think it had any
more than a placebo effect on the Greek athletes.
† The science behind psychedelics is more promising: there is
some evidence that they may help deal with the high incidence of
depression and anxiety in former athletes.

But modern doping came to the fore in 1952, when the Soviet Union took part in its first Olympics, winning eight gold medals in wrestling and weightlifting, and destroying the American team in the process. The strength of the Soviet athletes was even more surprising, given the country arrived off the back of some of the worst famines in history.

A decade earlier, a Maryland doctor and chemist called John Bosley Ziegler – who somewhat confusingly preferred to be known as 'Montana Jack' – had been badly injured in the Pacific theatre of the Second World War. He was told he would never walk again, but refused to accept this and hit the gyms. As he built up more and more strength, he found that not only could he walk, but he had natural ability as a bodybuilder. While training, he made friends with a strongman called Bob Hoffman, the most coveted trainer in the bodybuilding world. Hoffman's training methods and Ziegler's medical background appeared to be the perfect combination, and the two joined forces to create new ways of sculpting muscle.

In 1954, Ziegler managed to pull a few strings and became the team doctor for the US in the World Weightlifting Championships in Vienna. He watched in awe as the Soviet team smashed more and more records, but noticed odd things about the athletes, who were often unnaturally hairy and sometimes couldn't even urinate without catheters. Intrigued, Ziegler invited one of the Soviet doctors to a local bar, plied him with booze and learned that the strongmen were bulking up using testosterone. The hormone was not illegal at the time, partly because there were very few drug rules, and partly because it occurs naturally in small doses in all humans.

At this point, Ziegler could have petitioned the authorities to ban testosterone injections, given the damage he could see it was doing to the Soviet athletes. Instead, he decided to go in the opposite direction: anything the Commies could do, Americans could do better. He returned to the US, and along with Hoffman set about coming up with his own hormone-based bodybuilding system.

Initial trials with pure testosterone were unsuccessful. The athletes didn't bulk up much and complained of side effects,* so Ziegler looked for a synthetic version – including scouring the Nazi experiment books that the Americans had confiscated during the Second World War. Eventually, he came up with methandrostenolone, which he marketed as Dianabol, one of the world's first artificial anabolic steroids.

Ziegler tried the pills on himself and found that he started to build up even more muscle. As an added bonus, unlike the Soviet athletes he had seen in Vienna, he was still able to urinate. Before long, he was hawking Dianabol tablets – or, as his customers called them, 'Doc Ziegler's mysterious pink pills' – to professional bodybuilders. His gym became famous across the US, as it began to produce the best lifters in the country. Hoffman took the credit, writing an editorial piece entitled 'The Most Important Article I Ever Wrote'. It was full of tips on which exercises to do in order to end

* One early adopter said that after his first dose of Ziegler's hormones, he would get an instant erection on seeing any female.

up like one of Ziegler's clients, but made no mention of the drugs. Ziegler, meanwhile, was getting frustrated, as the bodybuilders began to ignore his recommended dosages. Realising the dramatic impact the pills had on their muscles, they were taking more and more of the drugs, while ignoring side effects such as enlarged prostates and much smaller testicles. 'What is it with these simple-minded shits?' said Ziegler. 'I'm the doctor!'

By the 1960s, steroids had not just seeped into other sports so much as crashed into them like a tidal wave. After the 1968 Mexico City Olympics, Dr Tom Waddell, who had come sixth in the decathlon, said that according to his observations, a third of the entire US track and field team had used steroids. Four years later, another US athlete, Jay Silvester, estimated the proportion was as high as 68%. Just before those games, US weightlifting champion Ken Patera said he was looking forward to competing against the Soviet giant Vasily Alekseyev: 'Last year,' he said, 'the only difference between him and me was that I couldn't afford his pharmacy bill. Now I can. We'll see which are better – his steroids or mine.'

In 1976, the International Olympic Committee (IOC) finally explicitly banned steroids. Athletes had been tested for performance-enhancing drugs since 1968, but in those days there was no way to detect steroids, so the tests looked for 'hard drugs' such as heroin or amphetamines. They also tested for alcohol, which resulted in the first-ever example of an athlete being banned from the Olympics.

TWO BEERS AND A SHOOTER

Hans-Gunnar Liljenwall was a schoolteacher from Stockholm who excelled in the modern pentathlon, a five-discipline sport that rewards skills traditionally used in the armed forces: shooting, riding, fencing, running and swimming. In the pentathlon, one competition is held but two sets of medals are awarded: one for team performance, and another for individual performance. Coming into the 1968 Olympics in Mexico City, Sweden was one of the best countries in the world at the sport, and was set to excel on both counts.

Sven Thofelt, the head of pentathlon's international governing body, was also Swedish. Thofelt had been part of a group of Swedes who successfully petitioned to have alcohol put on the restricted list for the modern pentathlon. Their campaign began after an incident in 1965, in which Austrian athlete Herbert Polzhuber drank 10 beers and an entire bottle of cognac before the pistol-shooting event, fired all his bullets into a mound next to the target and then passed out. The decision was controversial, since almost all the competitors drank some alcohol before the shooting competitions to steady their hands and their nerves. In the month before the 1968 Olympics, the head of the British team said that the upper limit of 0.04% blood alcohol level would at least still allow his team to have a couple of glasses of wine for breakfast on the day of the event. On the day of the pentathlon, that didn't seem to help the Brits, but Sweden took third place in the team event, behind Hungary and the Soviet Union. They also won the individual event, thanks to their star performer,

Björn Ferm. To celebrate, the team left for a well-deserved break in the resort of Acapulco soon after receiving their bronze medals.

However, a few days later, Thofelt was summoned back to the athletes' village, along with Liljenwall, to see the Olympic officials. There was a problem with the teacher's drug test. He had registered a blood alcohol content of 0.07%, which may not seem like much – you'd still be allowed to drive in England (though not in Scotland) with that amount in your system. But it was well over the Olympic threshold. The Swedish team protested, saying they could provide eyewitnesses who would say that the whole team had a beer at 6 a.m. on the day of the contest, but no more, and so Liljenwall couldn't possibly be over the limit. There must be a problem with the testing process, they argued.

But their complaints fell on deaf ears, and attacking the system only made the IOC less sympathetic to their protests. The team had to return their medals, with news outlets enjoying the irony that it had been Sweden that had insisted on the alcohol ban in the first place. The team were an international disgrace, with the *New York Daily News* running the headline 'Alcoholic Swedes Lose Pentathlon Medal'. This feels a bit harsh, considering Liljenwall's blood had less than two beers' worth of alcohol in it.* And it seems especially unfair

* As more evidence of the arbitrary nature of the rules, at the next Olympics 14 competitors tested positive for Valium before the shooting; it was banned by the pentathlon federation but not the Olympics, so no disqualifications were made.

in light of the fact that in the same event, a German athlete started punching his horse in the face when it wouldn't make a jump, for which he was not penalised.[*]

Although the team had to return their bronze medals, Björn Ferm was allowed to keep his gold. Ferm topped the scoring in the horse-riding and swimming parts of the competition, and performed well in the running and shooting, but he struggled through the fencing, despite his tactic of sitting on the floor and reading novels between bouts. In the end he came ninth in that discipline, jointly with a Soviet athlete called Boris Onishchenko, which was still enough to keep him atop the overall pile. Onishchenko, meanwhile, went on to have an interesting doping trajectory of his own. Eight years later, in the same Olympic event, he would become one of the most famous cheats in history. It was also down to doping, but there were no drugs involved this time. His was one of the most egregious examples of what we now call 'technological doping'.

TAKING THE PISTE

Onishchenko came into the 1976 Olympics as a bit of a legend, but at thirty-nine he was getting on and in danger of

....

[*] The animal welfare side of modern pentathlon was still being debated at the time of writing. At the 2020 Olympics, a German coach was seen punching a horse, and so authorities appear set to remove the equestrian part of the sport. An assault-course race is the favourite to replace it.

losing his touch. People were still in awe of him, though; when one hit registered in the fencing even though his épée appeared to be inches above his opponent's head, the Canadian athlete commented that he was 'so fast, you couldn't even see it'.

It was astonishing. Onishchenko was scoring hits without his opponents seeing *or* feeling them, and sometimes without his sword seeming to be anywhere near the other fencer. Fencing is a very quick sport, so most people put Onishchenko's seemingly invisible hits down to a trick of the eyes. An electronic device in each competitor's sword registers a hit when it touches their opponent's body armour, but almost nobody thought to question the machine. However, a twelve-year-old fencing fan called Nicholas Bacon, who had been invited to watch the event as he was awaiting an operation on a brain tumour, sensed something was wrong. As luck would have it, he was sitting behind double Olympic fencing champion Mary Glen-Haig (later to become one of the first female members of the IOC), who heard Bacon's loud protests, strode out onto the piste and demanded that somebody investigate.

On inspection, it was discovered that Onishchenko had wired up his épée so that it would register a hit whenever he pressed a small button on his handle. He was immediately disqualified, and when he got back to the athletes' village the USSR volleyball team threatened to throw him out of a window for bringing shame on the nation. He was expelled from his position in the Red Army, got a personal dressing-down from the Soviet president Leonid Brezhnev and had to pay a

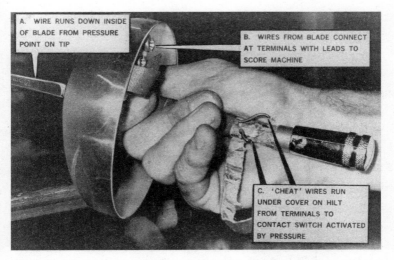

A. WIRE RUNS DOWN INSIDE OF BLADE FROM PRESSURE POINT ON TIP

B. WIRES FROM BLADE CONNECT AT TERMINALS WITH LEADS TO SCORE MACHINE

C. 'CHEAT' WIRES RUN UNDER COVER ON HILT FROM TERMINALS TO CONTACT SWITCH ACTIVATED BY PRESSURE

Boris Onishchenko's plan was foiled when they noticed this apparatus in his épée.

500-rouble fine. He went on to become a taxi driver in Kyiv.

Sporting equipment can provide ample opportunities for this 'technical doping' style of cheating. In most events you bring your own, and only cursory checks are made. There have long been rumours of motors hidden in bicycle frames, for instance, but only one person has ever been found guilty of that – Belgian cyclist Femke Van den Driessche in 2016. In 1957, meanwhile, the world record for the high jump was beaten by Soviet athlete Yuri Stepanov, but it turned out that he'd been wearing extra-bouncy soles in his shoes. Both these examples kept the nefarious technology well hidden, but just as often people have tried to bend the rules in plain sight.

HOWZAT FAIR?

A cricket bat must have very precise dimensions and be made of specific materials. Thirty-three paragraphs in the sport's rulebook are devoted to this, with three additional appendices. Many of these rules exist thanks to two incidents that took place more than 200 years apart.

In 1771, there wasn't even a rule that indicated how large a bat should be, and so in a match between Chertsey and Hambledon, a batter called Thomas 'Daddy' White strode out to the centre with one that was much wider than his stumps, making it impossible for any bowler to hit them.* A week later, the teams met again, but the 'monster bat' (as it would later be dubbed by cricket historians) did not make an appearance: the teams had decided that cricket bats could not be excessively large. An official law soon followed.

Two centuries later, when Australia faced England in 1980, Aussie Dennis Lillee realised that there was no rule saying what a bat should be made of, and so turned up with one made from metal. His friend owned a company that made aluminium bats, so Lillee decided to use one in a big match as a marketing stunt to help him with sales. The opposition captain complained, but so did the captain of Australia, on the grounds that Lillee wasn't scoring as many runs as he would if he used a willow bat. Having listened to all the complaints,

---

* This game is also notable for one ball passing straight through a gap in the wicket, resulting in a law being made that the stumps must be close enough together that a ball cannot slip through.

the umpire made Lillee swap his bat for a wooden one, at which point the Australian hurled his metal one away in a strop. He reflected afterwards that 'I now hold the record for throwing an aluminium bat the furthest in a Test, and I know it will stand forever.' Since then, the rules have stated explicitly that all cricket bats must be made from wood.

In 2021, a study by the University of Cambridge found that the best material for a cricket bat is actually bamboo, since it is stronger and cheaper than willow, and results in a better sweet spot. But for baseball players, a third type of wood, cork, is the material of choice. At least for the creatively minded . . .

THE CORKED-BAT INCIDENT

On 15 July 1994, the Cleveland Indians lined up against the Chicago White Sox (of Black Sox and ball-humidifying fame). It was a crucial match. In the first inning, White Sox manager Gene Lamont accused the Indians' star player, Albert Belle, of using a corked bat – a ruse whereby you cut off the top of a bat, scoop out the middle and replace it with cork to make it lighter. The bat was confiscated, but Belle's team knew that if it was inspected by officials, it would be revealed that it was indeed corked, and Belle would be suspended. So Belle's teammate Jason Grimsley went on a mission to swap the corked bat for a legal one.

While the game was going on, Grimsley removed some ceiling tiles in the stadium clubhouse and climbed into the narrow tunnels above, carrying a torch in his teeth and a replacement bat in one hand. This was especially tough because Grimsley was a massive guy, 6ft 3in in height and weighing 180lb. Crawling on his belly, he dragged his body through the boiling-hot bowels of the stadium, trying to find where Belle's incriminating bat was being kept. At one point he thought he was in the right place, so removed a ceiling tile, only to come face to face with a janitor sitting on a sofa directly beneath him. The janitor looked up, and their eyes met. Grimsley slowly replaced the tile as though nothing unusual had happened and continued; we can only imagine what the janitor thought. After 35 minutes, Grimsley finally found the correct room, lowered himself in, replaced the bat and dusted his footprints off the fridge as he climbed onto it and back into the ceiling.

He escaped without being caught, and the Indians went on to win the game. Unfortunately for Grimsley, though, he hadn't been able to replace the bat with another of Belle's because *all* of Belle's bats were corked, so he replaced it with a teammate's. That one had the teammate's signature on it, which rather gave the game away. Belle was subsequently suspended for seven games.

To add insult to injury from the Indians' perspective, studies have since found that corked bats don't even produce the desired benefit. The theory behind the cheat is that the cork core helps you swing faster – and it does – but any power you gain thanks to the extra speed is lost due to the altered bat's lack of weight.

Comically large bats, hidden bicycle motors and electronic épées make for entertaining media fodder, but technological doping is a serious issue in sports. Just as with other types of cheating, the lines are blurred, since the advantages that athletes can get by having better – but legal – equipment can make all the difference in elite competition. It means that for many competitors, sport is not a level playing field. When the Soviet Union was the only country to inject its weightlifters with testosterone in 1952, the world rightly called foul. But is it within the spirit of sport that an athlete from a certain country has an inherent advantage because their country can afford better technology?

SWIMMING DOWNHILL

During the 2008 Beijing Olympics, a new swimsuit caused a great deal of controversy. The technology had been developed by Speedo, alongside NASA, and everyone who wore it reported that they swam much faster. Australian Libby Lenton said it made her feel like she was swimming downhill. It worked by squashing the muscles down, which made stronger, bulkier athletes much more aerodynamic. It also trapped a layer of air, making swimmers more buoyant. And the results bore this out: 94% of all the swimming races in Beijing were won by someone wearing the suit, and in 2008 and 2009 more than 200 world records were broken. But the suit cost more than $500, which put it out of the reach of some swimmers in developing countries. Even a number of richer countries' athletes found themselves hampered because they had sponsorship deals with other swimsuit companies. Speedo responded to criticism by handing out free suits at the Olympics to anyone who wanted them. Much to their delight, several competitors who had contracts with Speedo's rivals switched over to the new suit. But it was just too good, and the swimsuit was soon banned by the authorities.*

It's a long way from the original women's suits that were popularised in the early 20th century by the first woman to try to swim across the English Channel, Annette Kellerman. Kellerman excelled at swimming as a child in Australia, and when she turned eighteen, she travelled to the UK hoping to capitalise on this financially. She managed to negotiate a deal with the *Daily Mirror*, which paid her a daily rate to train for her Channel swim, knowing the story would sell newspapers. People turned up every day to watch her prepare by swimming from one bay to the next around the south-eastern coast of England. At the time, the sight of a woman in a swimsuit was a spectacle in itself.[†] She wrote of one of her attempts:

> *I was seasick every half hour. But I stuck it out for six and three-quarter hours. You will wonder that I remained in the water so long, suffering from sea-sickness and the chafing of my bathing suit, and cold and weariness. But dad and*

....

* Other Speedo innovations include elite goggles that are blue–grey tinted to promote calmness in the wearer, and women's swim caps that allow for hair to be gathered at the back in a perfect shape to create a 'fin'.

† In some places, women's swimsuits as we know them today were considered so outrageous that they were banned. Kellerman herself claimed she was arrested in Boston in 1907 for sporting one that finished above the knee. The judge in the case eventually agreed to let her wear it, so long as she wore a long skirt over it until the moment she entered the water.

*I were desperately poor – we must have money. And I kept
saying to myself, 'The longer you stick, the more you get!'*

She never actually made it all the way across the Channel,
but Kellerman did build a rich and varied career from the
fame she garnered while trying. As well as performing swimming and diving stunts around the world, she starred as
'The Diving Venus' in a hit Broadway show that ran for four
years; she featured in a number of films, including one in
which she became the first Hollywood actress to appear nude
in a movie; she wrote popular swimming manuals; and she
campaigned for a woman's right to wear a one-piece swimsuit in the water, rather than the customary heavy dress and
pantaloons. We have her to thank for the bathing costumes

An official measuring a woman's 'Kellerman' swimsuit in Atlantic City,
1921, to make sure the distance between knee and suit conformed to beach
standards. The patrol was also on the lookout for ogling men, described in
newspapers as 'bald beach lizards'.

we wear today, which for a brief time were known as 'Annette Kellermans'.*

Another sport in which the technology has exploded over the past 100 years is cycling. In the Tour de France, changing gears with a lever wasn't allowed for the first 34 years; until 1937, when going up a hill, cyclists had to stop, remove their rear wheel, rotate it, then reattach it to access a larger gear. Today's bikes are miracles of engineering by comparison. While hidden motors are obviously beyond the pale, there is plenty that you can do within the rules to improve the performance of a cyclist and their bike. Former director of British Cycling Dave Brailsford used the term 'marginal gains' to refer to minuscule individual improvements in equipment, fitness and tactics, which add up to significant time differences overall.

Great Britain has by far the best recent record in Olympic cycling. A peak was reached in 2016, when husband and wife Jason and Laura Kenny won five gold medals between them, putting their family 19th in a theoretical medal table, ahead of countries such as New Zealand, Canada and Greece. However, Team GB's victories have often seemed to be at odds with the athletes' form; for instance, the nation's cyclists had performed well below par at the World Championships immediately preceding the 2016 Olympics. Cyclists from other countries were befuddled, including Australian Anna Meares,

----

* Kellerman was not in favour of the next major swimwear innovation, the bikini, which arrived on the scene in the 1950s. She described it as 'a very big mistake' for most women.

who said: 'The British are just phenomenal when it comes to the Olympic Games, and we're all just scratching our heads.'

The answer may well be found in British Cycling's finances. For the 2000 and 2004 Olympics, Team GB's cycling budgets were around £5 million and £8 million respectively. The team managed four medals at each of those Games. For the next three Olympics, the budgets went up to £22 million, £26 million and then £30 million for the 2016 Games. With so much money available in the run-up to the Olympics, Team GB's cyclists managed to top the table with a dozen or more medals each time. There's no suggestion that Team GB broke any rules, but they were able to push their equipment right to the limit.

The research and development department of British Cycling is known as the 'Secret Squirrel Club', after the James Bond-like rodent in the Hanna-Barbera cartoon. This reflects the mysterious, behind-the-scenes, pivotal work it does. For the 2016 Olympics, this team of 'boffins' – as the press likes to call them – provided aerodynamic helmets, moulded carbon shoes and skinsuits that reportedly cut three seconds from the British time in the team pursuit discipline. British cyclists even had special chains on their bikes that were cleaned in 'ultrasonic baths',* then covered in a lubricant that was dubbed by its manufacturer as an 'advanced military grade additive'.

....

* Ultrasonic cleaning sees intense, high-frequency sound waves being passed through extremely pure water. They generate tiny implosions in the water as they go, and these implosions act on the surface that needs cleaning, dislodging even the tiniest of contaminating particles.

All of these advances work for one championship only – after that, all the other teams are able to adopt the same innovations – and each one was well within the rules, although that might not have offered much in the way of consolation to athletes from countries without such huge budgets. But then one person's technological doping is another's sporting innovation – and not only do innovations in sporting equipment help individual athletes to glory, they shape the very sports themselves, and even find their way into the non-sporting world.

6

EXPLODING BILLIARD BALLS AND FORMULA 1 TOOTHPASTE

HOW NEW EQUIPMENT CAN CHANGE SPORT – AND THE WORLD

> When I hit the ball in the net, I look daggers
> at my racket, reproaching it for playing so badly
> when I myself have been trying so hard.
> **Craig Brown**

Just as with cycling, every year Formula 1 motor racing sees new inventions, which tend to teeter on the border of legality. Opponents object, and then the innovation is either banned or integrated by everyone. Racing cars need as much downforce as possible; it helps drivers to control steering, and also means they can reach high speeds without (almost) taking off. For this reason, at top speed an F1 car could theoretically be driven on the ceiling of a tunnel, with the downforce (which in that case would be directed upwards) essentially sucking it onto the driving surface and preventing it from falling to the ground. In pursuit of improved downforce, in 1978 the Brabham team put a huge fan on their car, which was ostensibly to cool the engine down but actually blew the car downwards to stick it to the track. All the other teams objected, of course, not simply because the new 'fan car' was faster, but also because the blades would fire out small stones from the track at all the other cars. Eventually, for the sake of the sport, Brabham agreed to stop using the car, even though it was technically within the rules.*

---

* Another piece of technology introduced into Formula 1 was seatbelts

Brabham's new motor-racing innovation for the 1978 season. The sport's governing body, the FIA, was not a big, ahem, fan.

While this particular innovation didn't take off (in either sense of the phrase), many other Formula 1 inventions have not only been embraced by the sport, but have subsequently found their way into our day-to-day lives. For instance, the system which allows electric and hybrid cars to retain some of the energy they would otherwise lose from braking – known as a kinetic energy recovery system (KERS) – was originally invented for (non-electric) Formula 1 cars. The same technology is now even used on remote Scottish islands such as Fair

. . . .

– though initially they weren't accepted. Some thought that they removed the 'romance' from the sport, while others preferred the idea of being thrown clear of a crash, rather than being held in the vehicle. They were made compulsory only in 1972.

Isle and Eigg, where it can be fitted to wind turbines to make them more efficient.

Formula 1's technological expertise has also been employed in less obvious areas of our everyday lives. With the suspension of motor racing due to the Covid-19 pandemic in 2020, the McLaren racing team turned their efforts towards making ventilators for the NHS. They made more than 100,000 individual components in just 10 weeks, helping the production of ventilators in the UK to rise from 50 a week to 200 a day. And this wasn't the first time that healthcare was aided by motor racing.

In the early 1990s, Great Ormond Street Hospital surgeon Marc de Leval carried out more than 100 operations on babies born with congenital heart defects. When a number of the operations were unsuccessful in quick succession, he decided to study what might have been going wrong. He found that while large errors such as a machine breaking down were rare, multiple small errors often added up – with disastrous consequences. In particular, he realised that there were frequent problems with the delicate but complicated procedure of moving a patient from the operating theatre to the intensive care unit.

Dr de Leval and his fellow medics Allan Goldman and Martin Elliott (who were both Formula 1 fans) realised that the surgery handover team had a lot in common with a pit-stop team, who in every race would refuel a car and change its tyres in a matter of seconds.* The hospital got in touch with

----

* Refuelling has since been banned in F1. This was for safety (to avoid gallons of highly flammable liquids being present in a high-pressure situation), cost (fuelling rigs are expensive to lug around)

Ferrari and sent a team of doctors to the British Grand Prix, where they observed the Italian team's practice sessions. They picked up two things that have since been integrated into their handovers. Firstly, each member of the team was given a specific job to do, in a specific order, and in silence. Previously, there had been a lot of talking things over, as staff announced what they were doing and questioned who was doing what. Secondly, they gave one person total authority to oversee the whole process. In Formula 1, it was the team member with a massive lollipop who stood in front of the car, while at Great Ormond Street it might be the surgeon or the anaesthetist, but whoever it was, everyone knew who was the boss – even though, sadly, they didn't get to carry a huge lollipop.*

Pit-stop technology has also been used by air traffic controllers: in the same way that Formula 1 teams use complicated algorithms to work out which of their two cars should come in first, so airports use them to work out the order in which planes should land. And it's even used by pharmaceutical companies: GlaxoSmithKline learned similar lessons to Great Ormond Street Hospital and streamlined the way in which its teams changed over. It means the company can manufacture an extra 6.7 million tubes of toothpaste a year.

While Formula 1 is an obvious sport for technological

....

and to improve the sport, since cars were being overtaken while they topped up, and the organisers wanted the important parts of the race to take place on the track itself.

* Actually, the lollipop isn't used in F1 these days either. Now, each person in the pit presses a button once their job is done, and when all the buttons have been pressed, the driver gets a green light.

advances, it is arguably not the most influential in terms of sporting technology crossing into the mainstream. The lowly bar sport of pool is at least partly responsible for one of the most ubiquitous materials in the history of mankind.

PLASTIC FANS

In the late 19th century, if you wanted to play pool, you needed a table, a couple of cues and three elephants. They provided the ivory needed to make the balls. In fact, you arguably needed 150 elephants, since only the best ivory was good enough, and so just one in fifty tusks could be utilised. If it were still the case today, for conservation reasons the sport would certainly be forced to find new ways to make the balls, but back then it reached the same conclusion because of the ruinous financial costs.

Michael Phelan was the son of an Irish immigrant who had settled in New York and opened a series of pool bars in the city. These were quite seedy joints, often in the basement of saloons, and when his father died, Michael decided that he wanted to make pool a more reputable game. He was a man of simple tastes: when profiled by the *New York Times*, the paper said that he worked from 9 to 5, played chess in his breaks and ate the same lunch each day of oysters and a mug of ale.* He disliked gambling and dissuaded his patrons from

----

* At the time, oysters were a food of the working class. They were cheap thanks to the huge supply: on a typical day, more than 6 million oysters might be hauled out of New York harbour.

doing so. His first attempt at a respectable pool hall failed, since the New York pool scene was populated by men who saw gambling as part of the game.* But when the gold rush hit California, he saw his opportunity and opened a magnificent pool hall in San Francisco, where speculators who had hit it rich could spend their new-found wealth.

Even so, Phelan saw one big issue stopping pool from becoming a sport of the masses, and that was the equipment. The cues and tables were wildly inconsistent between one establishment and the next, and the balls were extremely expensive. So Phelan set about standardising the cues and tables, inventing a new type of bouncier cushion that is typical of today's tables and placing advertisements in newspapers, offering $10,000 to anyone who could come up with an alternative material for billiard balls.

In stepped John Wesley Hyatt, a printer from Albany in New York state. He had access to cellulose, a common ingredient of paper, and collodion, a clear liquid that hardens when it comes into contact with air – printers used it to cover the tips of their fingers, protecting them from paper cuts. Teaming up with his brother Isaiah Smith Hyatt (and probably influenced by similar work being done by a chemist in England called Alexander Parkes), he mixed these ingredients with various oils and solvents and came up with something he called 'celluloid', named

. . . .

* The first North American world snooker champion, Cliff Thorburn, cut his teeth playing pool for money against hustlers in the US. He once played a guy called Cornbread Red for 54 hours and said: 'I knew he had really come to play when he laid out two pairs of socks.'

because it was 'like cellulose'. He used this celluloid to make billiard balls and distributed them to saloons. Cheaper and more uniform, the balls were a hit, but there was one problem: celluloid is extremely flammable, so when the balls struck each other, the friction would sometimes cause a small spark and a loud bang. This could be accepted by most establishments, though one bar owner in Colorado said that every time two balls hit each other with excessive force, the noise meant that 'instantly every man in the room pulled out his gun'.

The Hyatts never claimed their prize from Phelan. They didn't need to. After adding a few more ingredients to make their invention more stable, they did indeed find that they had a material that was perfect for billiard balls. They sold a fair number of those, but celluloid was much more versatile than that, so they used it for dentures, combs, corset clasps, shirt collars and more. The Hyatts' billiard-ball experiments had given the world its first successful plastic.

That was in the 1870s. One hundred and fifty years later, mankind had manufactured the equivalent of a billion elephants' worth of the stuff. Some of that is in the form of sporting equipment, and plastic has led to significant changes in many sports, including one that was originally played by the First Peoples of Canada as early as the 12th century.

LACROSSE PURPOSES

Lacrosse is a bit like hockey, but the stick has a little net on the end so you can carry the ball with you, while your opponents try to knock it out. As a result, there are a lot of sticks flailing around during a game, and it can be quite dangerous. The sticks used by the First Peoples were traditionally made from hickory, and if you got clobbered with one of those, you were at risk of serious injury. With the invention of plastic sticks, the game became not only much safer, but also quicker and more skilful, since the lighter equipment was easier to manoeuvre. No matter how good they were, any team playing with the old hickory sticks would be easily beaten by a team wielding plastic implements, and so these days demand for the original sticks has all but dried up. As a result, the UK lost its last-ever maker of wooden lacrosse sticks in 2014, when Tom Becket, the master craftsman of Hattersleys Sporting Goods, retired.* Becket is a no-nonsense Mancunian whose favourite sport is bowls rather than lacrosse. Even he is happy to admit that the game is much better for having plastic sticks.

Hattersleys' sticks were made from hickory imported from the Americas. The wood was cut, soaked in water and bent into shape by a team of six men, including Tom, and then strung with catgut and leather by a group of highly skilled women. The procedure would take years to perfect, and some people could simply never pick it up. A lot of the skill came from *feel* as opposed to precision: when it was right, you just *knew*. Lacrosse players would come to Tom with old sticks, saying that they wanted a new one that felt the same but perhaps with a thicker end, or a deeper net, or maybe one that

* In the same year, the UK lost its last cricket-ball maker, as well as its last gold-beater – that is, someone who hammers a sheet of gold until it's extremely thin gold leaf.

Native American lacrosse game featuring hundreds of players, depicted by artist George Catlin, who watched numerous matches in the 1830s and declared the sport 'most beautiful'.

was weighted slightly more in the handle. When Tom retired, he was the last person to have this very specific skill, which had been passed down to Hattersleys' workers over the course of a hundred years, since lacrosse first came to British shores.

In 1876, a group from the Haudenosaunee First Nations People* came to the UK and played the first-ever games of lacrosse in the country, against a team of Canadians of European origin. One very interested spectator was Queen Victoria, who watched the likes of Scattered Branches (captain), Pick the Feather, Wild Wind and Outside the Multitude take on the Canadians. She pronounced the game 'very pretty to watch'

---

* The Haudenosaunee are often also known as the Iroquois, though the former is their official name, which means 'people of the longhouse'.

and commented that she thought it would be a good sport to be played in girls' schools. She didn't much like the way that field hockey players would bend their backs when they played the game; it wasn't a very ladylike posture. The lacrosse players she saw played much more upright, and presumably the players toned down the violence a little, given their royal spectator.

The Haudenosaunee lacrosse team were a hit, and they went on a tour of the UK, always travelling by train. According to lacrosse lore, passed down through generations of stick makers, the train was chugging through Manchester on the way to a match and got held up just outside Hattersleys' factory, where the company manufactured cricket bats at the time. As the train waited, a spirit from the Haudenosaunee tribe drifted from the train and into the factory, where it found the owner, Thomas Hattersley, and whispered to him that they should start making lacrosse sticks instead.

That's the story anyway. What is certainly true is that after the Haudenosaunee matches, the royal approval meant that lacrosse did indeed become a popular sport in girls' schools in the UK. But in the US, lacrosse continued to be mostly a men's sport, and as it evolved there, body contact became a major part of the game. Since an ocean and a gender line split the men's and women's sports, they came to be very different, almost as distinct as netball and basketball.*

....

* The women's field is larger than the men's; in fact, until the early 2000s, it didn't have a boundary at all. Women could simply use any playable area (i.e. any space they could reach without having to charge through a bush or climb over a building).

The first girls' school to embrace lacrosse was St Leonards in St Andrews, where it was introduced by its headmistress, Louisa Lumsden, who had seen the game played while on a trip to the Americas.* Her pupils enjoyed it so much that after they graduated, some went on to introduce it into English schools. One, Rosabelle Sinclair, moved to the US, and introduced the country to the British version of the women's game. She resisted the temptation to adjust the rules so that it would be closer to the men's game, stating: 'Lacrosse, as girls play it, is an orderly pastime that has little in common with the men's tribal warfare version except the long-handled racket or crosse that gives the sport its name. It's true that the object in both the men's and women's lacrosse is to send a ball through a goal by means of the racket, but whereas men resort to brute strength, the women depend solely on skill.'

While the men's game followed other sports in improving player safety, by adopting plastic sticks and giving its players protective equipment such as helmets and face masks, the women's game stuck with hickory sticks and didn't see the need for helmets. But that is now changing. Since wooden sticks have become all but extinct, the women's game is becoming faster and more similar to the men's. Body contact is much more common now, as are swipes with a stick – which for the most part just bounce off players due to the lightness of the equipment. Protective eyewear is now mandatory, and it seems very likely that helmets will be required soon as well.

....

* Lumsden was one of the first five women to attend Cambridge University. Later in life, she led the Aberdeen branch of the suffragists.

Sinclair, who in 1992 became the first woman to be inducted into the National Lacrosse Hall of Fame, would not have approved. Lacrosse is one of the clearest examples of how while sport requires the creation of new equipment, when that equipment changes, it can also completely change the way a sport is played.

POLES APART

A similar change, related to new materials, took place in the world of pole-vaulting in the 1960s and '70s. In this case it was the adoption of fibreglass, which allowed athletes to reach greater heights* – though, as ever, not everyone was happy. The 1960 Olympic gold medallist Don Bragg was one of the most outspoken critics of the new technology.† Bragg was a legend in the sport, in the days when the poles were made from aluminium. He was almost killed once when his pole hit a power line as he boarded a train at Philadelphia's 30th Street station. His bag caught fire and his pole melted, but Bragg was miraculously unhurt. He made it to the stadium, said, 'I need to borrow a pole,' and went on to win the competition.

....

* Previously, poles were made from either aluminium or bamboo. Indeed, the first fibreglass poles were known as 'synthetic bamboo'.
† The other big name to come out against fibreglass was Bob Richards, the only man to win two Olympic golds in pole vault. He was also an ordained priest and was Billie Jean King's church minister when she was a child, inspiring her to take up tennis. In his day, he was known as the 'Vaulting Vicar' or the 'Pole-Vaulting Parson'.

Bragg hated the new equipment and what it was doing to his sport. When a young vaulter called George Davies reached a height of 15ft 10in, five inches higher than Bragg's own Olympic record, he said: 'That's catapulting, not vaulting.' This accusation clearly didn't cause the manufacturers of one of the most controversial poles – the Catapole 550+ – to lose too much sleep. And fibreglass does have one advantage that Bragg perhaps didn't consider: it doesn't conduct electricity.

Bragg wasn't the only one bemoaning the new poles. Come the 1972 Olympics, and with the Cold War dragging on, the Eastern Europeans were using older equipment and relying on the precision of their technique, while the freewheeling Americans would launch themselves over the bar utilising the flip of their fibreglass poles. The IOC, under pressure from the Europeans, banned the Catapole just before the Munich Olympics on the grounds that it contained carbon fibre, which was already prohibited. When it was pointed out that not only did the poles not contain carbon fibre,* but that the IOC was mistaken and carbon fibre was not explicitly banned after all, they changed their tune and said they'd ruled against the equipment because it had not been commercially available to all teams and therefore gave the Americans an unfair advantage. When it was *then* pointed out that it was perfectly possible for the other teams to buy the poles, they were simply banned under the dubious maxim of 'Our game, our rules'. All

---

* Carbon fibre and fibreglass are admittedly very similar substances, but the main difference is that the latter (as the name suggests) contains strengthening fibres that are made from glass.

Catapoles were confiscated just hours before the competition, and the American team had to beg or borrow 'legal' poles from their opponents. On the day of the event, American vaulter Steve Smith was so exasperated after not qualifying for the final that he threw the vaulting crossbar and his vaulting pole as if they were javelins, before storming off the field.

The Catapole incident was a turning point in pole-vaulting history. Having won 16 gold medals in a row, to date American athletes have won only two more Olympic pole-vaulting competitions. That's fewer golds since 1972 than the French and the Russians. And the same number as the Poles.

Aside from the very earliest sports, such as running and wrestling,* after your players and your rules, your equipment is the third vital component if you want to play. It can come in the form of complicated aerodynamic items that have been manufactured with pinpoint accuracy by computers, or bespoke pieces that have been developed over hundreds of years thanks to human ingenuity. Many pieces of sporting equipment are enough to define the sport: there's no mistaking the purpose of a pole-vaulting pole, for instance, irrespective of the material it's made from. But there's one piece of equipment that is found in most of the world's most popular sports. Whether you hit it, pitch it, toss it, dunk it, pass it, carry it, throw it, kick it or always keep your eye on it, where would the world of sport be without the ball?

---

* And swimming and jumping, we suppose.

7

THE DUKE OF SUFFOLK'S MISSHAPEN KNOB

WHY THE HISTORY OF SPORT IS A LOAD OF OLD BALLS

> Without the ball, you can't win.
> **Johan Cruyff**
> **(footballer)**

Ball games can be found in all cultures. Whenever *Homo sapiens* have found themselves with free time, they've fashioned a ball and kicked or thrown it around. Europeans used pig bladders. The Inuit used sealskin stuffed with moss. In Fiji, it was a large orange. And some Australian Aboriginal people played a game called Marn Grook with balls made from actual balls – kangaroo scrotums stretched and filled with grass.[*]

Marn Grook means 'game ball', and the balls in question were about the size of an orange. The basic rules were that you gave the ball to your best player, who then kicked it high into the air, at which point everyone tried to catch it (with as little body contact as possible). Whoever ended up with the ball would do the next high kick. Men, women, old and young would all play together, and the winning team was decided on by common consensus at the end of the day's play.

The most popular sport in Australia today is Aussie rules, which was invented in Melbourne in 1858 as a way of keeping

----

[*] While the Kurnai people used unmentionable parts of a kangaroo, others, such as the Woiworung, used tightly twisted balls of possum skin.

A modern version of Marn Grook, with a ball that these days is made from possum skin, as opposed to kangaroo scrotums.

cricketers fit in the close season. The rules were based on Gaelic football, rugby and soccer. However, since Marn Grook was known to the colonial population, and Aussie rules utilises the high-kicking technique a lot more than other football codes, many people think the modern game was also inspired by the Aboriginal sport.

What is certainly true is that the skills learned in Marn Grook allowed Aboriginal players to excel in Aussie rules, despite the considerable handicaps they faced in society. Around the turn of the 20th century, a team from the Cumeroogunga Mission – an Aboriginal reserve on the Murray River, north of Melbourne – asked the colonial government's permission to leave their reservation to play against local settlers. When their request was eventually granted, the team joined the local association and promptly beat all-comers, not only winning the league in their first two seasons, but doing so undefeated. The press wrote gushingly about the Aboriginal team's skills, albeit in the racist language of the day. The *Bendigo Inquirer* said of one game: 'It was a sight to make the proud Britisher feel humble, or at any rate to shake his confidence in the superiority of the race.'

The Cumeroogunga team continued to thrive, and between 1926 and 1931 they won their premiership trophy in five out of six seasons. This was too much for the league to take, and so officials placed a handicap on the team, forcing them to field players only under the age of twenty-five. It was a thinly veiled attempt to stop Cumeroogunga from playing. And it worked. The younger men were unable to cover the expense of travelling to matches, and one of the best amateur teams in early Aussie-rules history was forced to disband.

The colonists were surprised at the Aboriginals' ability to dominate the ball game, perhaps assuming the concept must have been new to them. But just as the concept of sport is universal and timeless, the same can be said of the ball itself. Every culture has its own. The earliest physical examples we have are from ancient Egypt, but they're tiny balls of cloth held together with string which were found in children's tombs, so we can count them as playthings rather than sporting implements.* The next oldest balls we have are around

---

* That's not to say there's anything wrong with inventing something solely for children to play with. You need only to look at the imaginative range of toys on the market today to see that the desire

3,000 years old. They were found in a cemetery complex in Xinjiang, China, alongside the remains of a man wearing the oldest-known pair of trousers. The balls are made of leather stuffed with hair, are uniform in size and have marks where they were hit with sticks, which suggests they must have been used in some kind of game. Given that back then trousers were usually worn when riding horses, it is thought that the game may have been something like polo.

HORSE PLAY AND DONKEY POLO

The golden age for *jiju*, or Chinese polo, came during the reign of the Tang Dynasty (AD 618–907). All sixteen Tang emperors enjoyed the game, and at least half were accomplished players. Competitors would wear embroidered jackets and ride on decorated horses, while a military band accompanied them from the sidelines. Literature, ceramics and art were full of references to the sport. For people living close to the capital, it must have felt as ubiquitous as Premier League football does in Britain today. It was among the earliest team sports – possibly even the first – played purely as a form of entertainment for the people. The thrill of attending one of these polo games is invoked by this poem from AD 821:

. . . .

to entertain our offspring is a powerful driver of human creativity and ingenuity. One striking (pre-Hamleys) example of this comes from when Columbus landed in the Americas, to find that the Mayans had invented the wheel, independently of Europeans. But their wheels were tiny, and never used for transport. The only purpose they served was to pull children's toys along.

Mallets are raised like so many crescent moons in the sky.
The ball, as it falls, looks for all the world like a shooting
*   star.*
The players hit right and left and shoot straight between
*   the goalposts,*
Amidst thundering claps of the horses' hooves on the ground.
The spectators cheer and beat their drums at each goal,
They can never have enough of the spectacular sight.
And yearn to see more.

The verse was written by Emperor Saga of Japan, after a game between his team and a group of ambassadors from southern China. Sadly, the final score is lost to history, although it's likely that the game was choreographed to ensure that the result was acceptable to both parties. This was arguably the first-ever international sporting event, and the earliest example of countries using sport for diplomatic reasons. A touch more speculatively, this could also have been the first time a sporting event stopped for tea: Saga was the first Japanese emperor to try the drink, and he loved it so much that he had tea gardens made in the imperial palace and served it at all important events.

A hundred years before this, the only female emperor in Chinese history was on the throne. Today, Wu Zetian is considered to be one of China's greatest leaders. Under her reign, the country became a superpower, invading Korea and suppressing Japan. She reduced taxes, encouraged the spread of improved farming techniques and created a system whereby the most talented would become civil servants, regardless of their social status. She also improved women's rights, allowing them to wear men's clothes and ride horses, and she made the mourning period for a deceased mother the same as for a deceased father. She encouraged religious diversity and promoted literature, art and poetry. And she loved a bit of polo.

In fact, Empress Wu's ascent to power began as the result of a polo game. In AD 633, Emperor Taizong organised a game between the maids living in his imperial palace. The women were split into two teams, and each was coached by a eunuch. Wu Zetian was the captain of the red team, who were dressed in red velvet, with red flowers in their hair. When they defeated the green team 2–1, her performance was impressive enough for the emperor to bring Wu into the court as one of his concubines.

This women's version of Chinese polo was called *luju*, and it's the first example we have of a female team sport. Earlier depictions of sporting women were always individual: there are ancient Egyptian images of women playing with balls; there were female gladiators in ancient Rome; and there was a special women's version of the Olympics – the Hera games – in which participants always ran with their right breast exposed, possibly to replicate the outfit of the legendary Amazons.

The most obvious difference between *luju* and *jiju* was that in the women's game the athletes rode on donkeys rather than horses, a fact that we know thanks to contemporary poetry and art. In 2020, archaeologists discovered the grave of a high-status woman named Cui Shi, who had been buried alongside donkey bones. It's hard to think of an explanation for this other than that Cui Shi must have been a keen *luju* player. Donkeys were not status symbols, and while poorer people would sometimes use them to carry goods or people, a noblewoman like her never would. Additionally, analysis of the animals' bones showed that they hadn't been used to carry heavy loads but seemed to have done a lot of sprinting and quick turning, so the researchers concluded that they must have been sporting donkeys. Women played polo on donkeys because they were slower and smaller than horses. With the saddle closer to the ground, falls were less serious, meaning that the game was safer and therefore more acceptable for high-ranking ladies.

The danger of the men's game is evidenced by the fact that Cui Shi's husband managed to lose an eye in a game of polo. And the sport could often be fatal. In 832, Emperor Muzong died of a stroke while playing. And in 844, his son, Emperor Wuzong, ordered his troops to surround a polo match being played by rebellious officers and massacre all the players – though it seems harsh to blame those deaths on the ball game itself.

Near the top of any list of dangerous sports is a version of polo that really stretches the meaning of the word 'ball': the Afghan national game of *buzkashi*. Rather than aiming for a goal, competitors go for a goat, as they fight, on horseback, to throw a dead animal (usually a goat, but occasionally a young cow) into a hole known as the 'circle of justice'.* The flailing

---

* In some versions, the goat is eaten by the winning team. Apparently, all the tugging and trampling tenderises the meat and makes it even tastier.

An Afghan *buzkashi* player looks on, as an opponent really gets his goat.

arms and hooves, and the fact that players have to lean down to the floor to reach the carcass, means that injuries are common. And even if a competitor gets hold of it, the other players can use full contact to grab it off them. As the *buzkashi* saying goes: 'Every calf has four legs.'*

The traditional form of the game takes place in the north of Afghanistan and is played as part of a rite of passage, such as a wedding or to commemorate a child reaching adulthood. The *tooi*, which roughly translates as 'celebration', is sponsored

---

* Though not always: in some forms of the game, which is played throughout central Asia, two of the animal's limbs are removed before play. Other events are played with a fake goat.

by a local bigwig, who provides the prizes, and whose status is cemented by the number of players he can attract. Some accounts describe games with thousands on each side, and while most are almost certainly exaggerated, it's fair to say that team rosters might number in the hundreds.

A more codified version of the game is played in the towns and cities. These matches typically have around 10 players at any one time, and rather than being financed by local leaders, they might be run by businessmen or even the government. The similarity between the game of *buzkashi* and the fate of Afghanistan over the last few centuries is not lost on the Afghan people, as the country has been pulled from all sides during the 'Great Game', in which various actors – most notably Britain, the US and Russia – have fought for control of central Asia.* And *buzkashi* has often been used as a means of garnering support. Successive Marxist governments would hold huge *buzkashi* contests, and when the US invaded in 2001, one of the first big events in Kabul that was reported in the Western press was a *buzkashi* match that was promoted as an example of the new freedoms. In actual fact, while the Taliban did officially ban the game across most of the country (as they did almost all forms of entertainment), even they permitted the occasional match, probably in an

....

* The term 'Great Game' is usually used to refer to the 19th-century conflicts, with 'The New Great Game' sometimes used to describe more recent conflicts. In a book about sport, though, it seems fair to use it more generally here as a metaphor – with apologies to historians of the era.

attempt to appease Afghans in the north, where they had limited control.*

Traditional *buzkashi* certainly can be violent, with regular injuries and sometimes death, usually caused by trampling as the players all race towards the goat. Modern, urban *buzkashi* is less dangerous, but when the play moves towards the sidelines, the fans have to flee to avoid finding themselves under a 1,000-pound horse. But it's probably fair to say that the most explicit violence in these games is towards the 'ball', as it is violently wrestled to and fro. In other sports, however, the ball has occasionally fought back.

FOUL BALL

In the mid-19th century, the schoolboys at Rugby were enjoying their new version of football, in which the ball was carried in scrums and kicked over goalposts. They had an almost inexhaustible need for balls, but since the sport had only just been invented, there were no specialist manufacturers. They naturally turned to the tradespeople who had the most leather – shoemakers.

The two shoemakers in the town of Rugby, William Gilbert and Richard Lindon, were run off their feet. Making a rugby ball was an onerous task. Not only did the leather need to be prepared and shaped, but the inside was made from pigs'

---

* Since seizing back control of Afghanistan in 2021, the Taliban have taken a softer line on *buzkashi*, with some local Taliban leaders even participating in matches.

bladders, which had to be inserted into the leather and inflated with a clay pipe. When you take a pig's bladder from the butchered animal it is relatively soft and rubbery, but over time it gets harder. This meant it needed to be blown up while it was quite fresh. It was a thankless task – the bladders would stink and were sometimes diseased (a diseased bladder will usually still hold air, so they were rarely rejected).

The shoemaking businesses were small, family affairs, and so Richard Lindon delegated the job of inflating the bladders to his wife, Rebecca (William Gilbert would usually do that part himself). It cost her her life. She inhaled air from one diseased pig bladder too many and died, leaving behind her husband and their 17(!) children.

To prevent anyone else from suffering the same fate, Lindon looked for an alternative way of making his balls. The new wonder material of the day was rubber – Charles Goodyear had invented vulcanisation some 20 years earlier – so this was the obvious candidate. The problem was that rubber was too tough to blow up. However, inspired by seeing an ear syringe, Lindon came up with the first hand pump. His invention not only transformed many of the ball sports that we play today, but also cycling: Irish inventor John Boyd Dunlop used one when he came up with the first rubber bicycle tyres.

Around 1854, a schoolboy at Rugby was playing with one of Lindon's balls when he launched it high into the air and it came down in a chimney. It seemed it would be lost forever, especially when the chimney was blocked up a few years later. But the ball was preserved by the soot, and when the building was demolished recently, it was found. It's the oldest leather-panelled rubber ball known to exist. But there is another, much older object that Guinness World Records lists as the oldest football in the world.

In the 1970s, an old grey item was found above the oak-panelled ceiling of a room in Stirling Castle, Scotland. It bore more than a passing resemblance to the early balls created by Lindon and Gilbert, but logically it must have found its way into the roof when it was renovated – in the 1540s. Tests have since confirmed that it is, indeed, around 450 years old. Today, the ball can be found in the Stirling Smith Museum and is labelled as 'the world's oldest football'.

There's no doubt it's older than any other football we have – the oldest by centuries, in fact. Mary, Queen of Scots was living in the castle at the time and, moreover, she was sleeping in the chamber where the ball was found, so it's possible that she kicked it up there herself and it got stuck. The object certainly looks like a football: it's the right size, and it's made of an inflated pig's bladder covered in leather. But in 2012, a team at Loughborough University mocked up a version to see how it compared to a modern-day ball. They placed the ball in front of a robotic leg and subjected it to five soft blows. The ball was destroyed by the fifth kick. They had shown that while Mary, Queen of Scots may have played with a ball in her castle, there was no way it could have been kicked with any force at all. Given its fragility, it's more likely it was thrown and passed around like a beach ball.

Footballs and rugby balls were slow to evolve from Lindon's original design. The next big leap forward came in the 1960s, with the invention of synthetic materials giving us balls that behaved like leather ones but were more durable and lighter. It's often said that this innovation helped the health of footballers, who were susceptible to conditions such as dementia due to repeated heading of the old, heavy ball. But the truth is that it may not have helped quite as much as is claimed.

It's certainly true that heading the old ball was extremely dangerous, especially when it got soaked in rainwater and gained considerable weight. We've known this since 1966, when an article entitled 'Danger in Heading the Ball' was published in the Football League's official journal. It was written just months after England had won the World Cup; and indeed, three of the 11 players to start that game for England were later diagnosed with dementia. However, while today's ball is very different to the one used by Martin Peters, Nobby Stiles and Ray Wilson, the game is very different too. While modern balls may tend to be lighter, they also travel faster, and players head them more often. The science is still uncertain, but it's possible that the new balls have made matters worse.

Of course, the ball is not unique to games such as soccer and rugby, and every ball sport has its own story about how its balls evolved. And in some of these sports, one of the strongest drivers of change was the invention of television.

NEW BALLS, PLEASE

In the first half of the 20th century, tennis balls were usually white – a perfectly good colour for players and spectators alike to see. But in the 1960s, a young television producer

called David Attenborough became the controller of BBC2
and began looking for new sports that worked well in colour.
He liked the idea of tennis – especially as it could be filmed
with just a couple of cameras. But the problem was, it was
often difficult for viewers to follow the ball, especially when it
landed next to the white lines.

The International Tennis Federation was delighted that
its sport was finding a new audience, and so decided to do
something about the issue. They undertook a study that saw
viewers watching matches involving all sorts of differently
coloured balls, eventually landing on 'optic yellow', which
is the colour of tennis balls today. Ironically, given that the
first event Attenborough televised was Wimbledon, the All
England Club, which runs the tournament, resisted the
change and insisted on white balls until 1986.

Yellow balls are not Attenborough's only contribution to
the history of sport, and arguably not his most important. He
is also responsible for the popularity of snooker.

In the 1960s, snooker had a low profile. There were fewer
professional players than red balls on a standard table, and
the final of the 1968 World Snooker Championship was held
in a working men's club in Bolton.* The match-up between
John Pulman and Eddie Charlton ran over five days and
offered no money to the winner. It was a far cry from the

....

* Five years later, in 1973, the World Snooker Championship was
held in Manchester. A larger city than Bolton, for sure, but it still had
a stoppage for rain, when a crack in the roof resulted in water flowing
onto the table.

World Championship of 2023, when a victorious Luca Brecel walked away with half a million pounds.

The BBC showed the occasional snooker match in those early days, hoping to bring it to a wider audience, but with limited success. They tried a number of things to make it more exciting. For instance, frames often start slowly, with players keen to avoid disrupting the balls too much because of the risk of making it easier for their opponent to score. To combat the resulting tedium for the viewer, the BBC had a neutral third player smash all the reds around the table at the start, before the camera started rolling. This put the balls into positions that allowed both competitors to start potting straight away. Representing too radical a change to the game, the practice was soon reversed.

The balls themselves were another part of the game ripe for innovation. Snooker balls are identical to billiard balls, whose invention led to the creation of modern plastics, as mentioned in the last chapter. But before colour television came along, they were mostly indistinguishable from each other for those watching on their black-and-white screens at home. To solve this problem, TV producer Michael Henderson decided to put numbers on all the balls so that viewers could tell which was which. Unfortunately, the experiment lasted for only one tournament, as the low-resolution cameras meant the digits were completely unreadable.

These early attempts to lift the viewing figures for snooker were unsuccessful, and it might have remained a niche sport had it not been for Attenborough's search for colour-friendly content. The green table, coloured balls and the fact that nobody moved around very much made it the perfect sport to be filmed with a couple of the new colour cameras. With the help of 'whispering'* Ted Lowe, who ran London's Leicester Square Hall, the home of professional snooker, Attenborough devised a new format called *Pot Black*, which saw eight professionals invited to a televised knockout event. Crucially, the matches were over just one frame – no five-day events here.† Lowe provided the commentary, and the show was a hit for people with the new-fangled colour TVs. People even watched on the old televisions, leading to Lowe's immortal line: 'For those of you watching in black and white, the pink is next to the green.'

Pot Black was the making of snooker, eventually leading to the sport's biggest-ever moment: the 1985 World Championship final, in which Dennis Taylor finally defeated Steve Davis at 12.23 a.m., in front of a television audience of 18.5 million – still a record for BBC2, and the most people to have watched any show after midnight on any channel in British history.

* He earned the nickname from the deep, guttural, hushed voice with which he commentated on snooker, and once explained innocently during a game that 'Fred Davis, the doyen of snooker, now sixty-seven years of age and too old to get his leg over, prefers to use his left hand.'

† A 'frame', by the way, is the term for a single game of snooker, from the moment the cue ball is first struck to when all the balls have been potted or one player concedes. The first person ever to clear the table in one attempt in a competition – potting all 15 reds and six colours without the opponent getting a turn in between – was Sidney Smith in 1936. Unfortunately, he did it on the day of Edward VIII's abdication, so the press's attention was elsewhere.

BERTS BOOKS

GODWIN COURT

INDON

LTSHIRE

1 4BB

: 07949 190977

il: bert@bertsbooks.co.uk

, 07 August 2024   11:35

ansaction ID: 85363

9780571372546 A Load of Old Balls :

	VAT:Z Unit £	9.99	Total: £	9.99
		TOTAL DUE	£	9.99
	PAID: Card		£	9.99

BERTS BOOKS

GOODWIN COURT
LONDON
?TSHIRE
1 4BB
T: 07949 150877
Email: hi@bertsbooks.co.uk
D: 07 August 2024 11:05
Transaction ID: 85303

x 9780571372546 A Load of Old Ballts.
VAT:Z Unit £: 9.99 Total: £ 9.99

TOTAL DUE £ 9.99

PAID: Card £ 9.99

Executives hoped that colour TV might do for other sports what it had done for snooker. In the 1970s, they looked to crown green bowls, and just as with snooker, started by making an ill-advised attempt to tamper with its balls.

BOWLING OVER

You might think that changing any element of crown green bowling for the sake of on-screen appeal would be a pointless venture, since the sport is usually played in the beer gardens of pubs and is hardly appointment viewing for most people. But it wasn't always such a niche activity. Until 1997, crown green bowls was one of the more popular events shown on the specialist UK satellite channel Sky Sports. Only when it became sidelined to make space for more televised Premier League football matches did the decline really set in.

Crown green bowls requires players to roll wooden balls about the size of a grapefruit towards a smaller ball, known as the 'jack'. The balls have a 'bias' – a tendency to curve a certain way – which adds to the skill: when trying to get closer to the jack than your opponent, you can use the bias to curl your shot around a ball that's blocking your route. The green is slightly raised in the middle (at the 'crown'), with the almost imperceptible contour adding another layer of difficulty.

Crown green bowlers were the Premier League footballers of the late 19th century. The game was extremely popular in the pubs of Lancashire, where 'panel games' would take place. Publicans would pay the top players (who belonged to a 'panel' of professionals) to take part, and onlookers would gamble at the edges of the green. Players would get a cut of the gate receipts – and sometimes of the gambling takings, which could be hundreds of pounds. Since almost all other sports at the time were strictly amateur, according to some (perhaps slightly exaggerated) accounts, this made the bowlers of Lancashire the most highly paid sportspeople in the world.*

The amount of money at stake meant games took place in all weathers, including snow, when players would typically keep a hot potato in their pocket to keep their hands warm; and in fog, when the referee would stand over the jack with a lamp, while the bowler yelled, 'It's coming!' as he played his shot. When it rained, you might have to engage in 'cobbing': throwing your bowls over the puddles or skimming them across the water rather than rolling them along the ground.

In 1973, the television executives came knocking, hoping to make bowls the next on-screen sensation. But, of course, a few things would have to change. The players were forced to wear a sort of uniform, comprising peaked caps that sometimes obscured their view of the balls and coloured clothes made of nylon cloth that made them all sweat terribly. They were also given coloured balls, which were universally unpopular: some players said they were too heavy, some said they were too light; some said the bias was too much, others that it was not enough. In fact, the balls had been independently checked by

---

* Male bowlers, that is. Women's bowls was played under strict amateur rules until the 1970s. Cash prizes were not allowed, so in the first Ladies' Open in 1935, the top prize was an oak wardrobe, and eighth prize a rug.

one of the country's top equipment makers and, colour aside, found to be identical to the original black balls. All the complaints turned out to be psychological in nature.

Today, the balls used in crown green bowling are black, slightly misshapen spheres. Their shape is what makes the game, since it creates the bias. The story goes that this innovation came in the 16th century, when Charles Brandon, the Duke of Suffolk, was playing a game and one of his balls accidentally cracked in half. Rather than end the match, he ran indoors and broke a wooden knob off his staircase. The knob was slightly flattened on top, giving him a bias, but he saw that it improved the game. It's a nice story. But in fact, the bias probably came about because when the sport was first played, it was very difficult to make wooden balls that rolled in an exact straight line. Early bowls would bend by different amounts, depending on how they were manufactured, and like lacrosse sticks, players would find a bias that they liked and stick with it.

Today, the balls used in bowling need to be consistent. This is true of almost any popular ball sport, and the rules that govern them can seem excessive. The US Golf Association has an 81-page document listing all the brands and models of ball that conform to its rules; the first sentence in the NFL rulebook concerning the ball says that each one must bear the signature of the commissioner of the league, Roger Goodell; and every soccer ball must have the FIFA quality mark, which shows that it has passed seven tests, in which machines check the ball's weight, circumference, roundness, bounce, water absorption, preservation of pressure, and shape and size retention. Of course, such uniformity hasn't always existed. In the first-ever World Cup final, in Uruguay in 1930, there were no exact ball specifications, which led to a heated controversy.

DIFFERENT-SIZED BALLS

The two teams that competed in the 1930 final – the home favourites Uruguay and their bitter rivals and neigh-bours Argentina – each had their own favourite ball. The Argentinians tended to play with a slightly lighter one, while the Uruguayans had an unusual 11-panelled model imported from England. The referee, a Belgian called John Langenus, recalled that when the teams turned up, both captains approached him with their own ball, demanding to be allowed to play with it.

Even before the ball debate, there was animosity circling the game. The pitch was surrounded by armed police who had heard rumours that the Argentinian fans, arriving in Uruguay by boat, had had 150 guns confiscated at customs.[*] The hard man of the Argentinian defence, Luis Monti, had received death threats, which he claimed came from opposing players, and as a result almost didn't turn up. In the end, Monti tried to ingratiate himself with the crowd by helping the Uruguayan players up whenever they fell over.

....

[*] True or not, these supporters fared better than another boatload of fans that got stuck in fog between Argentina and Uruguay, eventually landing the day after the final.

According to FIFA's account, the game began with Langenus tossing a coin to see who would play with their own ball in the first half. Argentina won the toss and raced into a 2–1 lead, before Uruguay, now playing with their heavier ball, rallied in the second half to win 4–2. How much effect the change of ball had on the result, we can only speculate.

In Buenos Aires, a crowd of 50,000 people stood outside the offices of the national newspaper, where updates were shouted through a loudspeaker. When the final result was announced, the Uruguayan embassy was attacked. A mourning parade took place, and two people were reportedly shot for not saluting as the procession went by. One Argentinian newspaper said that all future international football tournaments should be stopped. Eight of the team never played for Argentina again.

With such intensity of feeling, and so much at stake, it's no surprise that these days most sports have clear rules regarding the uniformity of their balls. And it's not just the ball. Elite sportspeople will insist that they train with the exact equipment that they will encounter in their matches. Though in one notable case, during the first-ever Olympics, the precise opposite happened, with surprising results.

8

THERE AREN'T ENOUGH BOOKS ABOUT THROW-INS

WHY TRAINING IS OVERRATED. AND UNDERRATED

They say that nobody is perfect. Then they tell
you practice makes perfect. I wish
they'd make up their minds.
**Wilt Chamberlain
(basketball player)**

The discus is one of the oldest pieces of sporting equipment we have evidence for. In the *Odyssey*, Homer writes about a sporting event held by the Phaeacians, a chilled-out, sea-loving, athletic people – effectively the Australians of the ancient world – in honour of Odysseus, who had washed up on their beach. The Phaeacian athletes suggested that Odysseus take part, but given he'd just dealt with the Trojan War, been a prisoner of Poseidon, escaped the Cyclops and survived a storm sent by Zeus, he decided that he'd rather take it easy. Only when he was taunted for being a useless weakling because he'd turned it down did Odysseus pick up a discus and throw it – and, of course, 'the spinning disc soared out, light as a bird, beyond all others'.

Given the mentions of discus in classical literature, it was an obvious sport for inclusion when the modern Olympics began in Athens in 1896. Even better as far as the locals were concerned, the Greeks were the only nationality to take the sport seriously, meaning the home nation was almost guaranteed a gold medal. Since Greece had gained its independence from the Ottoman Empire in 1828, the new country was very interested in emphasising its ancient roots, and sports such as discus were a perfect chance to do that.

Discuses had been found in archaeological digs, and there were plenty of vases and cups with drawings of men taking part in the sport, as well as the famous *Discobolus* statue of an athlete about to throw. All of these were static depictions, though, and so nobody knew exactly what the correct technique was, or even what a good discus throw looked like. Did you have to throw it as far as possible, or as accurately as possible, or even as high as possible? In early events, organisers hedged their bets and held multiple contests with different aims. The accepted technique was to stand with both legs planted on the ground and twist your torso while keeping your waist static, then let go. In 1896, the undisputed champion of this style of discus throwing was a muscular medical student called Paraskevopoulos. He looked destined for the first Olympic gold.[*]

The modern Games would be strictly amateur, a rule that would remain until the 1980s. They emerged from the brain of a man called Pierre de Coubertin, who was born in France a generation after the country had been humiliated in the Franco-Prussian War. He felt that France's problems stemmed from the fact that its schools concentrated on poetry and philosophy, unlike those in Germany and Britain, which instilled

---

[*] The other big names in the sport at the time, in more senses than one, were also Greek: they included Deschylopoimenolaon and Papamichaelopoulus.

sports and athleticism into their students.* And so, when de Coubertin and his friends concocted this new four-yearly event, they decided to go with the English public-school model, which viewed professionalism as unbecoming of a gentleman athlete.

De Coubertin's interest in education brought him into contact with Princeton history professor William Sloane. Sloane was also interested in international sport, but rather than it improving a country's chances in war, he thought that bringing together upper-class sportsmen from different countries could foster peace. He was made head of the United States Olympic Committee, and naturally looked to the Princeton athletics team – and particularly its captain Robert Garrett, one of the best shot-putters in the country, as well as an accomplished long-jumper and high-jumper – to form the majority of the US squad for the first Olympic Games. The Americans were given a sheet of paper with a list of all the events and were told to place a mark next to the ones they wished to compete in. Garrett looked down the list and selected his specialities: shot-put, long jump and high jump. Also on the list was discus. The word rang a slight bell thanks to his studies of ancient Greece, but he didn't really know what it entailed. He checked the box anyway – if it was a throwing event, he felt that he was strong enough to put up a decent show.

Back in Europe, George Stuart Robertson, a Classical scholar at Oxford University, was wandering down the Strand,

....

* He also loved the novel *Tom Brown's School Days*, by Thomas Hughes, set in Rugby School. He seems to have considered it more of a memoir than a work of fiction.

in London. Passing the travel agents Thomas Cook, he saw an advert promoting a trip to Athens for the first Olympic Games. Robertson knew about the ancient Olympics, but this was the first he'd heard of the modern version. He was a decorated hammer thrower, but since there was no hammer throw, he also chose the discus. He filled in his entry form and bought a ticket to Athens for £11.

Meanwhile, Garrett had to work out what a discus was. Luckily, his team manager was a history professor, so Garrett and Sloane scoured ancient sources to work out the exact dimensions of the discus. They looked at statues, vases and writings, including *Of Gymnastic Exercise*, by the 2nd-century writer Lucian, who wrote that it was 'a lump of brass, circular and not unlike a small shield, but without a handle or a thong'. From their research, the Americans landed on a metal plate with a diameter of 12 inches, and Garrett approached a friend at the Princeton 'machine shop' and asked him to create the first discus ever seen in America.

Meanwhile, the rest of the team were trying to raise funds for the trip to Greece, which would be both expensive and time-consuming.* Sloane had been saving for a year in order to get himself and his wife to the event. Garrett's mother paid for his ticket. But the remaining athletes needed to pay their own way, and even after a fundraiser they were short. So, in an early act of Olympic spirit, Sloane gave up his tickets so that the entire team could remain intact.

---

* The Netherlands didn't provide a team for the first Olympics because they didn't think it was fair for each athlete to pay their own expenses.

They left America full of confidence. Garrett felt especially happy about his speciality, the shot-put, and was sure that he would make a good showing in the jumping events, but he had decided that he probably wouldn't even bother with the discus. When his brassworking friend made the object according to his specifications, Garrett was aghast at what he saw. The disc weighed more than 10kg – about the same as a medium-sized dog – and had incredibly sharp edges. It was almost impossible to hold, let alone throw, and Garrett almost dropped it on his toes the first time he tried to pick it up.

He took the awkward item to the athletics field and tried to throw it. It went virtually nowhere. From reading ancient sources, he could see that an athlete called Phayllus had thrown a discus almost 30m, but Garrett could muster barely half that. Even if the Phayllus throw was an exaggeration, it was so far ahead of Garrett's best throw that he felt like he must be missing some vital part of the technique. He didn't much fancy embarrassing himself in front of the world, but he had already signed up for the competition and so would have to think of some excuse to pull out of the event once they got to Athens.

The Panathenaic stadium, in the Greek capital, had been built more than 1,750 years earlier and could seat up to 80,000 people. It remains the only stadium in the world made entirely of marble.[*] As the American team took in

---

[*] It was funded by a wealthy politician called Herodes Atticus. In those days, providing the money for public buildings was a way of demonstrating your position as an important member of society, and the more magnificent, the better.

The Panathenaic stadium, sometimes called Kallimarmaro, meaning 'beautiful marble'.

their magnificent surroundings, Garrett saw a discus on the floor. It was much smaller than the one he was used to and was made of wood, with a brass core and iron rim. He bent his knees to pick it up, expecting it to have some hidden weight, but, as he later put it: 'It came up like a feather in my hands.' This was the first time Garrett had held a real discus. It was a quarter of the weight of the one he had practised with in America and looked like it would be much easier to throw. With his confidence restored, Garrett decided that the next day, he would throw a discus for the first time. In an Olympic final.

Tens of thousands of Greek spectators cheered as nine athletes, including local hero Paraskevopoulos, came into the arena. The rules of the event were simple: each athlete would throw three times, and the holders of the top three distances at the end of those turns would be guaranteed the top three places. They would then come back for three final throws, and whoever threw the furthest, in any of their six throws, would be crowned the champion.

Paraskevopoulos was up first. With a physique not dissimilar to the famous *Discobolus* statue, he arched his body in such a way that if he had covered himself in chalk and stood in the British Museum, he could almost have been mistaken for it. Uncoiling his body, with his feet planted on the ground, he launched the discus and it flew for miles. Well, 28.5m, to be precise. It would be a tough distance for anyone to beat.

The non-Greeks, who had never thrown a discus before, tried to copy his technique. Robertson managed a meagre 25m, a distance that remains the worst discus throw recorded in the history of the Olympics, while Garrett was so awkward on his first try that the crowd found it hard to stifle their laughs. However, despite the mockery, he managed to heave his disc 27.5m. He was still a metre behind Paraskevopoulos, but it was enough to elevate him into the top three. The top positions would be contested between the American and two Greeks.

The competition reached the final throw, with Paraskevopoulos still well ahead. Nobody got close to his first throw, and Garrett described his own subsequent efforts as 'miserable duds'. But Paraskevopoulos wasn't going to rest on his laurels, certainly not in front of 80,000 of his fellow Greeks. With huge exertion, he propelled the disc high into the air. The throw was measured at 28.95m – a new world record. The crowd erupted.

Garrett walked up for his final throw. He was guaranteed a place in the top three, so had nothing to lose. He closed his eyes, and in a moment of inspiration, decided he'd try a different throwing technique. Rather than keeping his feet planted on the ground and twisting his torso, he pivoted around his left foot, moving his entire body around in a semi-circular path before letting go of the discus. The stadium was hushed, and Garrett opened his eyes to see the referee measuring his throw. To the astonishment of the crowd, the Greek athletes and Garrett himself, it was announced that his throw measured 29.15m, beating the world record that had been set just minutes before and securing him first place in the first-ever Olympics.* The American, who had never even seen a discus until the day before, was the Olympic champion.† As one newspaper in America bombastically put it: 'Lo! a new record in 3000 years was established for the discus by a barbarian from the new world. Thus the oldest civilisations of Europe must eventually give way before young America.'‡

....

* Paraskevopoulos also took part in the next Olympics, but never managed to win a gold. He went on to become a microbiologist, helping to manage malaria outbreaks and treating refugees during the Greco-Turkish War.

† Incredibly, Garrett's feat was repeated at the London Olympics in 1948 by Micheline Ostermeyer, who – among other things – was an accomplished concert pianist and Victor Hugo's niece. She entered the discus event two months prior to the Games, having never seen one previously, and went on to win gold. She put her strength down to all the bashing of the keys as she played the piano, and celebrated her victory by playing concertos by Beethoven, Brahms and Liszt.

‡ Greece's pride was saved when Spyridon Louis, a former soldier

Robert Garrett lifting a competitive discus for the first time. One bonus fact: his brother John became a US diplomat in Europe during the First World War, and work was his middle name – literally. His name was John Work Garrett.

Garrett went on to win the shot-put and finished second in both the high jump and the broad jump, becoming the top American performer at the Games. Robertson managed a bronze medal in the tennis doubles and wrote a poem that brought an end to the closing ceremony. It finished with the lines:

> *Athens, all hail! Hail, O rejoicing throng!*
> *And from our lips receive the tributary song.*

THE MAGNIFICENT WRECK

Most athletes spend their whole lives making slight improvements before eventually reaching their peak, rather than just showing up and winging it. One example of the more studied approach was James Fuchs, the inventor of the 'sideways glide', a way to throw a shot whereby the athlete begins at the back of the throwing circle, shuffles forward and then propels the ball.

Fuchs (whose name, as his obituary in the *New York Times* pointedly says, was pronounced 'Fewsh') created his innovative style as a result of a knee injury sustained while playing American football. He was unable to throw using the standard

who worked in the family business transporting water from the hills outside Athens into the city, won the marathon in dramatic fashion. The Americans were so captivated by the contest that they decided it was worth replicating as a stand-alone event in the States. A year later, the US held its first marathon in Boston, and today, the Boston marathon remains the world's oldest and most famous modern marathon.

method at the time, which had the athlete stop suddenly when they propelled the shot, putting a lot of pressure on the legs. With his new technique, he won 88 events in a row in the late 1940s, setting four world records along the way.

He also won two Olympic medals, despite not being at full fitness on either occasion. The first time, in London in 1948, he was sick, with a temperature of 104 degrees; the press nicknamed him 'the magnificent wreck'. The second time, in 1952, he managed to take bronze despite having a sprained finger in his throwing hand and an ankle injury. He almost certainly would have won gold otherwise. But this level of sporting prowess didn't come along overnight.

Fuchs never did any weight training; he relied on his natural strength (he was 6ft 2in and weighed just over 15 stone) and fluid technique. He said that 'to me, shot-putting is based on fundamental physics' and that his style got him 'more distance than all the muscles in the world'. But where to hone that technique? Fuchs lived in the centre of New York, and all the stadiums were in the suburbs, so he started training in Central Park. However, when park rangers noticed that his shots were making holes in the grass, he was moved on.[*]

In *The Great Gatsby*, F. Scott Fitzgerald says of New York, 'The city seen from the Queensboro Bridge is always the city

---

[*] He was told that he was breaking Title 18, Chapter 1, Section 18-129 of the New York City Administrative Code, which states it is illegal to cause any vegetation in Central Park to be destroyed without written consent. That apparently included blades of grass squashed by his shot.

seen for the first time, in its first wild promise of all the mystery and the beauty in the world.' But in 1952, the view would have been of a huge man in sports gear launching a metal sphere with a mighty grunt, since an area of waste ground under that bridge was the only place Fuchs could find to train after being turfed out of Central Park. Even there, he came across problems, a passer-by complaining to the police that Fuchs was 'indecently exposed' in his training kit. As luck would have it, when the police arrived, they recognised Fuchs and not only allowed him to continue throwing, but took it in turns to retrieve his shot.

As Fuchs would no doubt attest, the best training equipment and location are important, but if training is to be effective, it needs to be directed. Those important connections in the brain are not going to form if your sessions are unfocused. And in modern sport, specialist coaches are looking at more minutiae than ever in the hope of gaining a tiny advantage.

COACH CLASS

When the laws of soccer were first written down, not much thought went into what happened if the ball was kicked off the pitch. In fact, rather than a throw-in being given to the team who *hadn't* last touched the ball, as happens today, the throw was taken by whichever team managed to collect the stray ball first. Fast-forward to 2020, and when Liverpool FC became Premier League champions – their first championship in 30 years – a sixth of all their goals originated from throw-in situations. They were undoubtedly helped by Thomas Grønnemark, their specialised throw-in coach.

Grønnemark is a man of many talents – he was once a member of the Danish bobsled team – but his main skill is throwing the ball in a sport where most people kick it. He is a former holder of the world record for the longest throw-in, but when training for that record, he noticed that there were no books about that part of the game in his local library. He decided to create his own course on the skill, and has since taught it in six different countries. According to Grønnemark (who admittedly may be more than a little biased), not having a throw-in coach is 'the worst thing you can do in football'. There could be something in it: when Grønnemark arrived at Liverpool, they were the third-worst team at keeping possession from a throw-in, but in the year they topped the league, they were also the best at turning their throw-ins into promising attacks.

And it's not just *on* the pitch that a modern sportsperson's life is carefully monitored in search of those tiny improvements that could mean the difference between victory and defeat. In 2020, a study looking at more than 250 female athletes found that over half of them believed their performance fluctuated depending on their menstrual cycle. The science backs it up: a woman's body creates different amounts of the hormones oestrogen and progesterone at different times of the month, and while the former helps build up muscle, the latter breaks it down. The changes in these hormones can have huge effects on how the body deals with stress. When both hormones are high, the body is much less resilient and more prone to inflammation. The result is that some women are much more likely to be injured at certain times of the month. Anecdotally, it appears to make female footballers particularly susceptible to knee injuries, which are certainly considerably more common in the women's game than the men's. For that reason, many top clubs now employ a menstrual-cycle coach. They take saliva samples from the players and test them, giving accurate hormone levels in just 30 minutes. Depending on the results, the coaches can tailor training to include certain types of exercise, nutrition and rest.

In 2019, the England women's national team, the Lionesses, hired a physical performance manager called Dawn Scott, who had already won two World Cups with the US national team. She was there to oversee the general fitness of the team, and that involved personalised programmes based on each player's monthly cycle. The improvements in fitness and performance were so stark and instant that members of England's communications team, and even the wife of the team's chef, started following her advice. Since data science in the women's game lags so far behind the men's at the moment, this kind of system is still in its infancy, but the good thing about that is that teams who get ahead of the curve can gain big advantages over their opponents.

These minute changes to training may seem like they're solely for elite athletes, but the non-playing staff associated with the England women's football team were right to embrace them; adopting some of these tricks can help all of us in our everyday fitness routines. Even for those of us for whom exercise is little more than a slow jog, or even walk, around the park, doing the same training repeatedly and regularly can make a big difference. Take the comedian Eddie Izzard, for instance: Eddie would definitely not have described herself as a professional athlete when she embarked on an eye-watering 43 marathons in 52 days to raise money for Sport Relief. You might expect her times to have become slower and slower as she became more and more tired, but her speed actually improved – from around 10 hours for each run to around five. This is down to the 'training effect', whereby the body adapts remarkably quickly. For example, Eddie's average heart rate lowered and her lung capacity greatly improved in just a few weeks.

Training makes your muscles stronger, of course, but also your bones, your heart and your lungs. You tend to feel less hungry, and your sleep improves. Mitochondria, the tiny powerhouses in your cells, multiply, so that you have more energy. Your body becomes better at regulating its temperature. All great stuff. But it still hurts. No matter what your level, you eventually reach a moment when your body tells you enough is enough. Which makes it all the more baffling as to why people like Eddie put themselves through it. And when you look at some of the feats of endurance performed by humans over the years, even those 43 marathons look almost like a sprint.

9

THE GLOBE GIRDLER'S WAGER

HOW, AND MORE IMPORTANTLY WHY, ATHLETES PUSH THEMSELVES TO THE LIMIT

> At the end of the day we can endure
> much more than we think we can.
> **Frida Kahlo**

The first person to cycle round the world was a thirty-year-old unmarried man from Berkhamsted called Thomas Stevens. He had a muscular physique and a nut-brown tan, and was often seen sporting a hat with a bullet hole in the rim – plus, appropriately enough, a handlebar moustache. Stevens's trip began and ended on the east coast of the US, and he had to deal with constant rain in England, bandits in Turkey, arrest in Afghanistan, closed borders in Russia, stone-throwing mobs in China and a detour through a part of Iran that the locals called the 'Desert of Despair'. He was sponsored by *Outing* magazine, which described him as a quintessential American hero who was 'built like a compressed giant', with 'the stamp of personal courage and chivalrous enthusiasm upon his handsome features'. He finished his journey in 1887, after spending 30 months in the saddle.*

. . . .

* After his circumnavigation, Stevens immediately set off on a trip to Africa to try to find the journalist Henry Morton Stanley, who in turn had gone to find the missionary David Livingstone. Stevens was unsuccessful in this escapade, and Stanley found himself emerging from the jungle two years later.

Annie Londonderry, who appears to be absolutely thrilled to have
made it all the way around the world.

The cyclist who attempted to smash this record seven years later bore few similarities to Stevens. Annie Cohen Kopchovsky was a twenty-three-year-old Jewish American immigrant and married mother-of-three who had never ridden a bike in her life. She had moved from Latvia to Boston with her family as a child. Her parents died when she was a teenager, and she was left to raise her younger siblings, as well as her own three children, which she did by selling advertising space for newspapers. That is, until she left it all behind and reinvented herself as Annie Londonderry,* with the intention of cycling solo around the globe.

She claimed that it began with a bet. A couple of businessmen, chatting over beers, had wagered that no woman could possibly match Thomas Stevens's feat. Annie got word of this and took them up on the challenge. To make her feat more difficult, as well as completing the trip on her bike, she was required to return with $5,000, which she had to earn en route. If she managed it, the men would have to stump up $10,000. Despite the wager being reported in the media at the time, no record of the men has ever been found, and it's likely she invented them to garner more press attention; having worked in the newspaper industry, she had an eye for a good story.

The papers loved a tale of adventure and female endurance:

....

* To help fund her trip, Annie was sponsored by the Londonderry Lithia Spring Water Company, which paid her $100 to carry its placard on her bike and adopt its name. Londonderry water, from a natural spring in New Hampshire, was thought to have magical properties and was said to cure dyspepsia, heart disease, nervous prostration, 'goneness' (faintness, exhaustion) and 'gravel' (kidney stones).

in the late 1870s, you could barely open one without seeing
stories of 'pedestriennes', the popular name for women who
walked. And walked. And kept on walking. There were six-day
competitions between these famous walkers (any more than
that was impossible, since taking part in sport on a Sunday
was banned), as well as solo challenges, such as completing 3,000 quarter-miles in 3,000 consecutive quarter-hours.
These women would stretch the possibilities of human ability,
subsisting on oysters, beef tea, port wine and only the occasional nap.*

Thanks to this public interest, along with Londonderry's
gift for attracting media attention, 500 people gathered to
see her set off from her starting line in Boston. Whether or
not the bet was real, once she'd announced the rules in the
press, she was obliged to stick to them or else the trip would
have been seen as a failure. She had to stop off at nine different places: Le Havre and Marseilles in France; Colombo
in Sri Lanka; Singapore, Hong Kong and Shanghai; and then
Nagasaki, Kobe and Yokohama in Japan. In each place, she'd
have to get the signature of the US consul as evidence. She
was given 15 months – half the time it took Stevens – to complete the trip. Very few people gave her a chance.

Both contemporary and historical accounts of Londonderry's trip give an impression of high-spirited derring-do,

....

* The pedestriennes made walking races so popular that when 20
boys went missing for more than 48 hours in San Francisco, their
families were relieved to find them in a disused warehouse, taking
part in their own self-organised six-day event.

which she made every effort to enhance. One moment she was escaping highwaymen in Marseilles; the next she was on the back of elephants, hunting tigers in India; and when that wasn't happening, she was receiving a bullet to the arm in the Sino-Japanese War.* Always nurturing her plucky image, she carried a pearl-handled revolver with her wherever she went, and claimed to have received over 200 marriage proposals en route.

She probably exaggerated how much of the time she spent actively cycling. Both Londonderry and Stevens spent large parts of their trips travelling alongside, rather than on, their bikes. *Harper's* magazine estimated at the time that Stevens had walked about a third of his route, since the terrain often made cycling impossible. Annie had to do the same, and it was reported that she also made liberal use of trains and steamers, with the justification that she'd promised to travel 'with' her bicycle, and not necessarily on it.

Eventually, in April 1895, Londonderry arrived back in the US. She still had six months of her time limit remaining, and only had to cross the country from San Francisco to Boston. It seemed as though the record was in the bag. She told local newspapers that she would take her time for the remainder of the trip, delivering lectures as she went to complete the

---

* Londonderry claimed she was briefly imprisoned during this war, and at one point, 'a Japanese soldier dragged a Chinese prisoner up to my cell and killed him before my eyes, drinking his blood while the muscles were yet quivering'. Some of her stories should probably be taken with a pinch of salt.

financial part of her challenge – she still had to make more than $1,000 to meet that stipulation.

All was going well, until she reached Stockton, California. She turned a corner at speed, came face to face with a runaway tram and was thrown off her bike. As she hurtled through the air, she stuck out an arm, which buckled under the weight of her body as she landed, injuring it badly. She became tangled in barbed wire, suffered terrible bruising to her face and had to visit a local doctor, who removed pieces of road from her lips. Nonetheless, Londonderry continued pedalling to the end of that day and into the next, but then had to visit a second doctor, who said that not only should she not be cycling, she also shouldn't give her lecture that evening. Reluctantly, she rested, but less than two weeks later she was back in the saddle.

The fall may have set her back in terms of time, but it worked wonders for her reputation. It was covered in newspapers from coast to coast, and she began to be known as the 'circumcycler' or the 'globe girdler'. Tickets for her lectures now sold quicker than ever, and she managed to get more sponsors, whose badges she attached to her outfit. In Europe, she'd swapped the huge dresses in which she'd embarked on the journey for much more practical bloomers, but when she hit Arizona was told that she was not allowed to wear anything quite so shocking in what was a devoutly religious state. It was only thanks to her growing fame and the support of a local cycling club that she managed to coax a special trouser-wearing licence out of the grudging authorities.

By September, Londonderry was over the Rockies and into the final 500 miles of her trip. The end was in sight.

Then, perhaps as divine retribution for daring to wear cycle-friendly clothing, she was freewheeling down a hill when a herd of pigs seemed to appear from nowhere. She yelled for them to get out of the road, but they weren't for moving and she wasn't for stopping. Again she fell from her bike, onto her already-injured arm, breaking her wrist. Despite being 175 miles from home, she turned down medical assistance and finally arrived at the finishing line wearing a home-made sling. She had made the distance, but the journey wasn't a success since she was still $100 short of the $5,000 that she needed to earn on the trip. She sold her bike to an onlooker to make up the deficit, and the 'bet' was won.

Londonderry's experience reads so much like a fantastical adventure novel that it can be easy to forget how tough the reality must have been. She set out with no money to her name, on a bike twice as heavy as the average woman's city bike today. During the first three months, she lost a stone and a half, slept in whatever barns or haystacks she could find and raided farms for food. When she was accosted by robbers in France, she had only three francs to her name, so they let her keep the money out of sympathy.

Even after she overcame some of the initial obstacles, ditching the original bike for a slicker model and risking scandal by switching to men's clothes, her achievement was no mean feat. Cycling aside, for those of us who manage to get lost walking home from the shops or occasionally board trains going in the wrong direction, the idea of successfully finding our way around the world is a daunting one. To do it in the 1890s, alone, with no money and as a woman, decades

before female suffrage in the US, seems nigh on impossible.[*]
Any woman striving for a life outside of domestic confine-
ment and devoted service to her husband and children was
swimming against the current. Even Queen Victoria herself
declared that 'God created men and women differently. Let
them remain each in their own position.'

That's not to say women like Londonderry lacked support;
the crowds that gathered to see her and the breathless newspaper coverage were evidence of that. By the 1890s, the battle
to allow women their own hopes and ambitions, independent
of men, had gained momentum, with cycling playing no small
part in this. In 1896, the American civil rights activist Susan
B. Anthony wrote: 'Let me tell you what I think of bicycling.
I think it has done more to emancipate women than any one
thing in the world. I rejoice every time I see a woman ride
by on a bike.' But as with any movement that threatens the
status quo, it faced virulent opposition from those corners of
the establishment that wanted to preserve it. Doctors campaigned tirelessly about the supposed dangers of cycling to
women, warning, for instance, that it might lead to the frightening condition known as 'bicycle face'. Caused by too much
cycling and almost exclusively affecting women, symptoms

....

[*] American women wouldn't get the franchise until 1920, although
had Londonderry been a New Zealander, she would have gained it the
year before she set off. But the tiny country of Corsica beat the rest of
the world to it: it granted universal female suffrage in 1755, almost
140 years before any other self-governing nation. Unfortunately,
France conquered the island in 1769, revoked this law and didn't
return the vote to women for another 189 years.

An anti-orgasm bicycle seat, advertised here as 'very cool'. For avoidance of
doubt, that means it kept your genitals cold. The modern meaning of 'cool' as
'fashionable' or 'excellent' wouldn't exist for another 60 years.

included bulging eyes with dark shadows beneath them, a
clenched jaw, a pallid complexion and a constant expression
of weariness. The medical community was divided on whether
it was a temporary or a permanent affliction. There was also
concern that bike saddles would overly arouse female riders
and might sexually corrupt them. 'Hygienic' bicycles were
invented, with a dip built into the saddle so that the genitals didn't touch it, thus averting the danger of accidental
orgasms while riding.

Other commentators were a little less hysterical. In 1896,
the *New York World*, for instance, allowed that women should
cycle, and provided some useful advice for how they could
maintain propriety while doing so. Their list of 41 handy
hints included:

Don't faint on the road.
Don't wear clothes that don't fit.
Don't imagine everybody is looking at you.
Don't go to church in your bicycle costume.
Don't try to have every article of your attire 'match.'
Don't scratch a match on the seat of your bloomers.
Don't ignore the laws of the road because you are a woman.
Don't try to ride in your brother's clothes 'to see how it feels.'
Don't scream if you meet a cow. If she sees you first, she will run.
Don't use bicycle slang. Leave that to the boys.

Annie would have required a hefty dose of psychological resilience to overcome this background hum of what might now be termed 'microaggressions'. And to add insult to injury, once she had achieved what was previously deemed impossible, commentators began to speculate that if a woman could do it, perhaps it wasn't so hard after all. When the *Kansas City Star* reported that a German man, Heinrich Horstmann, was planning a similar feat, they sniffily wrote: 'If Annie Londonderry's story be true, there is no glory in such a trip for a man after a woman has accomplished it.'

These words appear more and more misguided as time goes on, and not only because attitudes towards women have changed. It turns out that the longer an endurance race lasts, the smaller the gap between men and women gets. In fact, while male athletes will typically run a 5km race almost 20% faster than a woman, for a marathon the difference is only 10%, for a 100km race it's 0.5%, and once you get to a race over 300km, women typically run faster times. We're not quite sure why this is the case, but it's probably a combination of factors. Women's muscles fatigue less quickly, for instance, and oestrogen helps their bodies exploit fat stores more efficiently. The fact that their stomachs are smaller may also mean they can cope better with the extreme stress. On top of all this, Fiona Oakes, the 2013 winner of both the North Pole and South Pole marathons, thinks that there's also a difference in attitude. 'During the North Pole race, a lot of the men tended to zoom off very quickly. Particularly in that race, it's imperative that you start at the pace you're going to finish in, because if you don't and you slow down in the race, you're going to get hypothermia.' Studies back her up, showing that women are better than men at pacing themselves during marathons, with men typically slowing down about 20% more than women in the second half of the race.

NE PLUS ULTRA-MARATHON

As mentioned in the last chapter, there are many benefits to exercise, and anyone who's dragged themselves up off the sofa for a quick jog around the park will recognise the 'runner's high', an ecstatic feeling that you either have felt or are sick of hearing other runners talking about.* But why

....

* Despite it being an extremely commonly held belief, runner's high is not caused by endorphins. While endorphin levels in the blood do increase when we exercise, they can't cross the blood–brain barrier, which means they shouldn't affect our mood. However, exercise also

anyone would want to take part in arduous and unfeasibly long-distance races is another matter. Ultramarathons (any race longer than a standard 26.2-mile marathon) are increasingly popular. Their participation has increased 1,700% since the late 1990s, and 600,000 people worldwide have now completed at least one. And yet few ultramarathon runners would argue that it's a pleasurable experience.

Testament to the gruelling nature of an ultramarathon is the fact that some competitors have their toenails permanently removed because they consider it preferable to the constant bruising and damage they'd undergo otherwise. A small price to pay, apparently, for the privilege of running hundreds of miles. And it gets much more extreme than that.

In 2017, an American, Courtney Dauwalter, ran a 100-mile race on so little sleep that for the last 12 miles she went blind. Luckily, she was running alongside a relay of pacemakers, and it was her husband who was with her on the final leg. He shouted out instructions as she went, but it didn't stop Dauwalter from stumbling on a rock and ending up with a huge gash on her head. After the race, it took five hours for her sight to return. For those who don't go blind, there are the hallucinations: champion fell-runner Jasmin Paris started to imagine that animals were appearing out of the rocks in the 2019 Montane Spine Race. She took it in her stride and won

....

increases the levels of endocannabinoids in the blood. This is our body's home-made version of the psychoactive ingredient in cannabis, and scientists now believe it's this that puts us in such a good mood after going for a run.

the 268-mile ultramarathon, beating all her male and female rivals despite needing to stop to express breast milk for her baby at various points along the route.

Humans have been voluntarily putting themselves in similarly punishing situations for millennia. More than 4,000 years ago, a young Sumerian king called Shulgi boasted that he'd run from Nippur to Ur (both in modern-day Iraq) – a distance of 100 miles – in order to officiate at the religious festivals in both cities. He then ran back to Nippur, completing 200 miles on foot in a single day. Given that he was king and probably capable of delegating these ceremonial obligations, he evidently didn't have to do this.

According to legend, the first marathon runner, in 490 BC, died in the act.* Having run 25 miles from Marathon to Athens and triumphantly reported a Greek victory to his masters, he promptly collapsed and expired from exhaustion. Patriotism, it turned out, was enough to get him across the finish line, but not a step further. Centuries later, in 1753, one Woolley Morris ran 10 miles in 54 minutes 30 seconds, but he burst a blood vessel and died within an hour of finishing. Across the border in Wales, an athlete called Guto Nyth Brân (which

....

* He was called Thersippus, Eucles, Philippides, Phidippides or Pheidippides, depending on which ancient source you believe – although 'Pheidippides' was probably a copying error by a scribe who meant to write 'Phidippides', since it wasn't really a name that was known at the time. However, almost 2,400 years later, Robert Browning wrote a poem referring to him as Pheidippides, and the name stuck. It's now what people most commonly call him. Correct them at your leisure.

translates into English as 'Griffith of the Crow's Nest') dominated the long-distance running scene in the 1720s and '30s. His talent had been spotted by a shopkeeper, Siân o'r Siop ('Siân of the Shop'), who acted as his trainer and manager – as well as his lover – and entered him into multiple athletic contests. Sadly, after one particularly competitive race, a fan slapped him too hard on the back during the celebrations, causing him to collapse and die in Siân's arms.

For modern endurance athletes, enthusiastic back-slapping is the least of their worries. Extreme cyclist Jure Robič was known for pushing himself to the edge of a nervous breakdown through overexertion. In the famously gruelling Race Across America (RAAM), his support team knew to expect uncontrollable sobbing, rage and paranoia at various points. He hallucinated bears, wolves and aliens, and ended up fighting inanimate objects, thinking they were attacking him. In spite of these distractions, he won the RAAM in 2004, 2005, 2007, 2008 and 2010.* For weeks after each one he'd need to use two hands just to turn a key in a lock, because the pressure of the handlebars had dulled his nerves so much.

We call these people 'endurance athletes', which is exactly the right term for them. The word 'endurance' is associated with hardship. You might endure pain, war or bad company, but you'd rarely say you'd 'endured' a waterslide or a cheese

---

* Sadly, in September 2010, Robič collided with a car when cycling downhill around a corner and was killed immediately. Hundreds attended his funeral in Slovenia, many of them arriving by bike and wearing T-shirts with his face on them.

toastie. It's hard to understand what motivates some of us to eschew the cheese toastie option in favour of pushing our body to the brink of collapse, but for some athletes, these huge distances are not enough, and they set themselves endurance challenges in some of the least hospitable corners of the world, thus facing external threats alongside their physical and mental struggles.

When Benoît Lecomte swam 3,700 miles across the Atlantic in 1998, he had to be surrounded by a shark-repelling electromagnetic bubble. Even so, a blue shark followed him doggedly for five days. About halfway through his swim, Lecomte became so exhausted and distressed that he had to divert to the Azores (via his support boat) for a break. After a week spent recuperating, he returned to the water where he'd left off and resumed his journey. When he finally reached dry land in Brittany, 73 days after leaving from Massachusetts, he announced, 'Never again.' A few years later, he tried to swim across the Pacific.

One of the least hospitable environments on Earth is Antarctica. Any challenge undertaken there requires significant sacrifices. In the case of Colin O'Brady, the first person to cross the continent solo and unaided,* this included choosing between spare food and spare clothes, since he needed to save weight on his sled. His food supply consisted of hundreds

---

* Norwegian Børge Ousland also claims this accolade, but he occasionally used a kite to harness the wind as he crossed the continent on his skis. O'Brady argues this constitutes 'aid'. The matter is a source of heated, if niche, debate in the polar explorer community.

of 1,200-calorie 'Colin Bars', custom made just for him. He brought one pair of pants.

O'Brady had to be careful about how much and how regularly he ate so that the Colin Bars didn't disrupt his digestion. But one night, he awoke in his tent with a ravenous hunger and gorged on about 2,000 calories' worth. This was not part of the diet plan. He paid for it the next day: waves of indigestion were succeeded by an uncontrollable bowel evacuation, to the detriment of his single item of underwear.

Whether they're going blind with exhaustion, having their toenails permanently removed or trudging through Antarctica with pants full of poo, endurance athletes' privations are an inherent feature of their sport. The suffering seems to be part of the attraction. Their attitude is perhaps best summed up by the words of cyclist Udo Bölts. When his teammate Jan Ullrich won the Tour de France in 1997, Bölts would spur Ullrich on, as he struggled up the steep hills, by repeatedly shouting at him: 'Torture yourself, you bastard!'

MOTIVATION'S WHAT YOU NEED

To understand why some people run, swim, cycle, hike or in any other way exert themselves to an extreme degree, Juliana Buhring is a good person to ask. She's the 21st century's answer to Annie Londonderry: in 2012, aged thirty-two, she became the first woman to earn a Guinness World Record for cycling around the world. Official rules stated it had to be 24,900 miles in one direction, starting and finishing in the same place, and any aspiring record-breaker had to cycle at least 18,000 miles of the route. Londonderry's generous use of ferries wouldn't have passed muster.

Like her 19th-century predecessor, Buhring was a relative cycling novice. She trained for eight months before setting out, but before that hadn't ridden a bike since she was five and was using stabilisers. Where Londonderry courted journalists to drum up support, Buhring relied on savvy use of social media to raise funds. She completed the journey in 152 days, knocking a year off Londonderry's time and covering an average of 125 miles a day. Similar to her fellow endurance athletes, she experienced hallucinations: 'Shadows were chasing me, trees were turning into wild animals, people were jumping out at me.'

Buhring said she was motivated by grief. She was in love with an explorer named Hendri Coetzee, who was killed by a crocodile in 2010 while kayaking in the Democratic Republic of Congo. Devastated by this, Buhring set off, 'hoping not to come back'. But while her ride was extremely tough, she was tougher; life had taught her resilience. She was raised in the brutal, apocalyptic Children of God cult. After enduring the years of abuse that entailed, and having lived in almost 30 different countries, she left the group, aged twenty-three.* She credits her mental strength with these traumatic but formative experiences. Thankfully, she did come back from her ride, victorious, and has won multiple long-distance races since.

There is something intuitive about the idea of finding an outlet for psychological trauma in physical exertion. Many

---

* The cult also counted actors Joaquin Phoenix and Rose McGowan among its members, when they were children.

of us have at some point expressed our anguish by punching a pillow or administering a hard kick to an unsuspecting object, at the expense of our toes. And we've all heard someone declare that they need to go for a run 'to clear their head'. Perhaps Buhring and others like her are acting on this instinct, taken to its extreme. And we know that exercise can genuinely alleviate mental suffering. Studies on US army veterans returning from war zones have found that those with post-traumatic stress disorder can be helped by a strict exercise routine. Those who went running for 30–40 minutes a day, three times a week, were more likely to recover quickly. It's thought that this is because the act of running boosts levels of a protein called BDNF (brain-derived neurotrophic factor) in the brain; this protein acts to stop us having the 'fight or flight' panic reaction to harmless triggers in our environment.

This sense that exerting ourselves might have a curative psychological effect seems to motivate many athletes. In 2022, lawyer Victoria Evans rowed solo across the Atlantic, from Tenerife to Barbados. She took fewer than 41 days, beating the previous women's record by nine days. To avoid her boat drifting off course, she never slept for longer than half an hour at a time. Adversities she faced en route included getting locked out of the cabin that contained all her supplies and having to break back in; having all her electronics drenched as huge waves crashed over the boat; and a flare-up of shingles. She acknowledges that her training and voyage were partly a way of overcoming the depression and eating disorder that plagued her when she was younger. As a child, she was never sporty, but she says that as an adult, completing these extreme challenges has been 'transformational' in helping her overcome lurking psychological demons.

From the small amount of research that's been done on this subject, there does appear to be a strong correlation between the tendency to participate in extreme physical challenges and having a history of mental health problems. A recent paper found that 37% of ultra-endurance athletes had previously been diagnosed with mental illness, almost twice as many as in the general population (20%). The proportion increased with the number of hours of training participants did per week: for those exercising fewer than 10 hours a week, 28% had a previous mental disorder diagnosis, while for those who trained for more than 20 hours a week, that figure was 57%.

That's not to say this type of self-medication always does the trick. While it may be a coping mechanism for some people, that doesn't mean it's an effective one. We don't even know which way the causation works yet. It could be that people suffering from depression, anxiety or other psychological disorders are more likely to take up endurance sports to help cope with their conditions; or it may be that endurance sports are causing some of these disorders. Supporting the latter view, a 2008 study into long-distance swimmers and runners found that the more intense their training regimen was, the more disturbed their moods became. While it's long established that moderate exercise is good for our mood, some research suggests that excessive exercise could have the opposite effect.

But regardless of whether it works, there's no doubt many people are driven to tackle these physical challenges in the hope of gaining some non-physical benefit. This is the case worldwide. In Japan, there are Buddhist monks, known as *gyoja*, who run the equivalent of the circumference of the globe in order to achieve spiritual enlightenment. The *sennichi kaihogyo* tradition involves completing 1,000 marathons in 1,000 days around Mount Hiei, which overlooks the ancient city of Kyoto. The task is spread out over seven years, and things ramp up to such an extent that in year seven, the monks have to cover 84km per day over 100 consecutive days, and then 40km per day over another 100 consecutive days, all in straw sandals.* Towards the end, they also have to spend nine days sitting up straight in a dark room without food or water. Over the past 130 years, fewer than 50 monks have completed the challenge. Traditionally, *gyoja* carry a dagger and rope with them, because if they fail, they're supposed to commit suicide. Although no one has done this in the modern era, the route is littered with the graves of historic *gyojas* who didn't make it.

When asked why monks undertake *sennichi kaihogyo*, one priest at a temple in Kyoto said that the idea is to exhaust the mind and body completely, so that both are entirely drained. The idea of the fast is to bring the body as close as possible to death, in order to gain a true appreciation of life. 'When you are nothing, then something, pop, comes up to fill the space,' the priest explained. That 'something' is enlightenment: a deeper consciousness that can be accessed only when all other distractions are removed, and which yields a sense of oneness with the world. While this may sound a little ambitious for

---

* From the fourth year onwards, the monks are also permitted to wear socks.

As if running 1,000 marathons wasn't tough enough for the monks, they must all be done while wearing this hat, known as a *higasa*. A coin is kept in the hat in case the runner dies and needs to pay the crossing to the underworld.

most of us, there are surely elements of it – the stillness; the all-consuming focus; shedding the anxieties and distractions of our frenetic everyday lives – that appeal to us all.

Not all endurance athletes have quite such elevated ambitions. There are more worldly reasons for attempting barely feasible physical feats. The marathon monks can become celebrities through their ventures, and while that may be of no consequence to them, for some people the glory is part of the attraction. This is most obvious when people exaggerate their claims of physical prowess. In 1966, the Chinese press reported that Chairman Mao had swum nine miles of the Yangtze River in 65 minutes. If true, this would have meant he was swimming twice as fast as China's Sun Yang when he broke the world record with his gold-medal-winning 1,500m swim at the 2012 Olympics. Not only that, but Mao supposedly sustained this speed over a course that was ten times longer.

As Annie Londonderry proved, the media often laps up tales of solitary endeavour. In late-19th-century Britain, Matthew Webb became the first person to swim the English Channel.* He swam from Dover to Calais unaided in 1875, which is a distance of 34km, though because adverse currents dragged him in the wrong direction, he actually ended up swimming 64km. To celebrate his success, his home town in Shropshire held such an extravagant parade that, according to the local papers, a pig stood up on its hind trotters in order to get a better view. He was mobbed by crowds when he landed back at Dover, where the mayor announced: 'In the future history of the world I don't believe that any such feat will be performed by anyone else.' Since Webb's swim, there have been 2,777 such crossings.† To be fair to the mayor, no one else was able to do it for another 36 years, despite multiple attempts.

Webb cultivated the attention, partly because he enjoyed it, and partly because he needed the money. After his swim,

....

* Webb had always prided himself on his ability to stay in the water for long periods of time. As a youth, he challenged a Newfoundland dog, known for its ability to do the same, to a contest. The two of them trod water in the Severn River for an hour and a half, before the dog floundered so much it had to be let back onto the boat, and Webb declared victory.

† That's according to the official website (at the time of writing). But since there are 50–100 successful crossings every year, you can be sure that this number is an underestimate.

he raised £2,000 through donations to fund his future career as a professional swimmer, and the Prince of Wales personally gave him an additional £5,000. Even before his swim, he performed water-based stunts, which always took the form of wagers (spectators would bet against him) to ensure that he made a profit.

As time went on, however, Webb's fame waned as his fans lost interest. By 1883, desperate to make a living, he announced his intention to swim through the whirlpools beneath Niagara Falls. Most commentators deemed it suicidal, and he was refused sponsorship on the grounds of it being too dangerous. He proved them right when he drowned in the rapids, in the pursuit, as his friend and mentor Robert Watson put it, of 'money and imperishable fame'.

Acting in pursuit of glory might not be considered especially noble in the West today, but that hasn't always been the case. Ancient Greek storytelling was dominated by the concept of *kleos** – the fame and glory that came with great deeds. For a male, it was an ideal to strive for, and it motivated the actions of almost every Greek hero, from Odysseus to Achilles to Heracles. Typically, *kleos* was attained through feats of military or athletic prowess, and was considered a way of achieving immortality.

It was *kleos* that motivated the original long-distance runner, Shulgi of Ur – at least if his words are anything to go

---

* The English word 'loud' comes from the same root as *kleos*, both deriving from the Greek word for 'to hear'. The key to *kleos* was having people hear about you.

by.* Left on a 4,000-year-old clay tablet is the 'Self-Praise of Shulgi', in which he explains why he ran so far:

> So that my name should be established for distant days and never fall into oblivion, that it leave not the mouth of men, that my praise be spread throughout the land, that I be eulogised in all the lands, I, the runner, arose in my strength and in order to test my running, from Nippur to Ur my heart prompted me to traverse, as if it were the distance of one mile.

Whether in pursuit of inner satisfaction or external approval, athletes employ a range of tricks to attain the seemingly unreachable goals we have seen so far. Before the era of sports science, properly researched diets, training advice and health and safety, some went to bizarre extremes. Their tricks ranged from masochistic to crafty to unintentionally self-sabotaging, but they were almost always imaginative.

CIRCUMVENT YOUR SPLEEN

In ancient Egypt, long-distance runners sometimes had their spleens surgically removed to help them run faster. This

---

* Shulgi became so famous for his run, seen to demonstrate his virility and stamina, that afterwards his name began to feature in erotic poetry throughout Mesopotamia. The year of Shulgi's run was thereafter referred to as 'The Year When the King Made the Round Trip Between Ur and Nippur in One Day'.

isn't as ridiculous as it sounds: in 1922, researchers at Johns Hopkins University in Maryland removed mouse spleens and found that it made them run quicker. It follows that the same could be true of humans, although any attempt to repeat the trial on human subjects would probably struggle to make it past the ethics board.

Fast-forward a few thousand years, and if you were a Tour de France cyclist in the early 20th century, you might have deployed one of these strategies to survive the ordeal:

Take a cocktail of drugs. In 1924, Tour competitors the Pélissier brothers said that the secret to their success was cocaine rubbed into the eyeballs, chloroform rubbed into the gums and 'horse ointment' to warm the knees (doping wasn't banned for another four decades).

Get a Vaseline massage. In the 1920s, hotels along the route complained that cyclists were using the curtains in their rooms to wipe Vaseline off their bodies, after being massaged with it at the end of the day.

Jeopardise your opponents' chances. Maurice Garin spread broken glass in front of his opponents and put itching powder in their clothes to finish first in 1904.[*] He was disqualified for cheating, along with those who came second, third and fourth. The title went to 19-year-old Henri

---

[*] Garin claimed he got through one 24-hour race on strong red wine, eight cooked eggs, 19 litres of hot chocolate, 2kg of rice, 7 litres of tea, 45 chicken cutlets and plenty of coffee, champagne and oysters.

Cornet, who came fifth, finishing three hours behind Garin. He remains the youngest-ever winner of the Tour de France.

Use a faster mode of transport. In total, 29 people were disciplined for cheating in 1904 – the second Tour de France – mostly for illegal use of cars and trains. One of the competitors remained on his bike but attached himself to a car with a piece of string tied to a bit of cork, which he held between his teeth while the vehicle towed him along. Even the victorious Garin received a warning for hitching a ride in a car for part of the race.

Have a cheeky ciggy. Until the late 20th century, lots of cyclists smoked during the race. As they approached a hill, they'd often light a cigarette and pass it round. They thought it opened up the lungs.

There are other less nefarious or even counterproductive tricks that are employed by endurance athletes to help them on their way. Webb swam the Channel while smothered in porpoise fat for insulation (apparently, this didn't bother the live and reportedly playful porpoises he encountered along the way). But what garnered more coverage were the psychological boosts he received en route. His coach, riding in a support boat most of the time, occasionally jumped in the water and swam alongside to motivate him; and near the end of the swim, a boatload of people passed by singing 'Rule Britannia' to perk him up. Gertrude Ederle, the first woman to complete the Channel swim, had similar support:

she employed a bagpiper to accompany her in a boat and play rousing tunes to encourage her.[*]

This reflects an understanding, which we all instinctively have, that one of the most important ingredients of success in endurance sport is mental attitude. One particularly revealing study on this subject, conducted at Bangor University in 2010, asked ten athletes to perform three tasks, one after the other:

(1) Pedal as hard as they could on a cycling machine for five seconds.

(2) Pedal for as long as they could at a sustained level of power, stopping only when they physically couldn't go on any longer. This happened after about 12 minutes, on average.

(3) Once again, pedal as hard as they could for five seconds.

The researchers measured the power of their subjects' cycling at all three stages, and it was the third stage that was the most striking. When asked to perform the five-second burst, straight after giving up because they *physically couldn't continue* with the longer ride, not only were the participants immediately and miraculously able to cycle again, but they generated over three times more power than they had done in

---

* When she swam across the Channel in 1926, Ederle became the sixth person to do so, and the first woman. She did it in 14 hours, beating the previous record by two hours. The first person to meet her at Dover was a British immigration officer asking to see her passport.

stage two. In fact, the force of their cycling in stage three was only 30% less than it had been in stage one.

The truth was, they weren't physically incapable of continuing after 12 minutes at all. It was their minds that told them to stop, not their bodies. As soon as they knew they'd have to go for only another five seconds, their brains gave them full permission to cycle as hard as they could again.

To an extent, then, pushing our bodies to their limit really is a case of mind over matter. But it does help that our 'matter', or physical make-up, is perfectly suited to the task. We don't outperform the animal world in many physical aspects – we can't run as fast as cheetahs (or, in fact, house cats), jump as high as grasshoppers (proportionally), lift as much weight as gorillas* or flex our bodies and withstand as much pressure (again, proportionally) as hero shrews† – but we are extremely good at covering long distances under the power of our bodies alone. Over distances of, say, 100 miles, we can outrun every other creature.

As mentioned in Chapter 1, our legs, feet and buttocks are exceptionally well designed for running, but there are plenty

....

* The average gorilla is between six and 16 times stronger than the average human (depending on which zoologist you ask). Silverbacks can pull down an entire banana tree to access the fruit at the top, with just one arm.

† The hero shrew's spine is so strong it can withstand the weight of a fully grown man standing on it – the equivalent of a human bearing the weight of 10 elephants on their back. It's also so flexible that in a burrow just a few millimetres wider than its body, it can turn 180 degrees and head in the opposite direction.

of other adaptations that come into play. For instance, our sweat glands and lack of fur mean that we can endure the heat generated by sustained exertion much better than most animals. Hunter-gatherers were (and still are) able to track prey like deer and antelope over long distances, until the prey collapsed from overheating.[*] On top of our perfectly proportioned toes, our feet have other adaptations that are suited for running. Not only do we have foot arches that go from front to back, but we also have an arch running from one side to the other. It's most visible if you look at the top of your foot – you'll see it's raised in the middle. This keeps our feet stiff, in the same way that when you bend a slice of pizza as you eat it, it'll stop being floppy and prevent the toppings from falling off.[†] It means we can push off better while running, without our feet collapsing underneath us.

In answer to the question of how people seem to achieve the impossible in endurance events, it's clearly some combination of physical adaptation and psychological motivation. And it might be that they're mutually complementary: perhaps people who complete extreme endurance challenges

....

[*] The 22-mile Man vs Horse Marathon has been held annually in mid-Wales since 1980. A horse normally takes the prize, but humans have won three times, always on particularly warm days.

[†] This fact, which is clear even to a child eating pizza, was discovered by Carl Friedrich Gauss, the19th-century German mathematical genius. Gauss made discoveries in magnetism, electricity, astronomy, statistics and maths, but still called this theory about how bending something makes it stronger his *Theorema Egregium*, or 'Remarkable Theory'.

are partly motivated by a subconscious awareness of human physical superiority in this respect. We all like to be the best at something, after all.

Certainly, psychological strength is essential for getting people to the finish line. But in good news for anyone who hasn't yet completed an ultramarathon and is seized with the urge after reading this chapter, the greatest competitors don't show signs of being naturally stronger, psychologically, than the rest of us. Research measuring mental toughness and analysing the personalities of endurance athletes shows almost no difference between them and the average couch potato. The only exception is that they tend to view what others might see as barriers as opportunities. This open-mindedness is an attitude that can be cultivated. Armed with that, and the ability to articulate the crucial mantra 'Torture yourself, you bastard!', you'll go far – literally.

10

THE ARCHER WHO WOULDN'T LET GO

ENLIGHTENING DISCOVERIES ABOUT SPORT'S BIG WINNERS

Whoever said, 'It's not whether you win
or lose that counts,' probably lost.
Martina Navratilova
(tennis player)

The history of sport is full of serial winners. Sprinter Usain
Bolt will come to mind immediately for many: he is the only
person to win both sprint events (100m and 200m) at three
consecutive Olympics, and did the same in all the World
Athletics Championships from 2009 to 2015 (except for in
2011, when he was disqualified for a false start in the 100m
final – though he did, predictably, post the fastest time in the
qualifying stage).

Interestingly, Bolt has scoliosis: his spine is curved to the
right and his right leg is half an inch shorter than his left.
His right leg, therefore, strikes the race track with 13% more
force than his left, and his left leg is on the ground 14% longer
than his right. Traditional understanding would say that this
unevenness would slow a racer down, but Bolt has clearly
adapted well to it and naturally come up with the most efficient way of reaching top speeds.

The first American woman to win three gold medals in a
single Olympics, Wilma Rudolph, also had to overcome adversity, in her case both physical and societal. She had polio as
a child, and doctors told her she would never walk again –
though her mother assured her she would. When Wilma was

eleven, her mother's view was vindicated when she went outside and saw her daughter playing basketball with the other
kids. After becoming 'the fastest woman in the world' at the
1960 Olympics, she returned to her home in Tennessee but
refused to attend her own victory parade unless they removed
the segregation that was still legal at the time. Her parade
and banquet became the first integrated events in her home
town of Clarksville.

Rower Ned Hanlan could also point to his childhood as
the impetus that made him unbeatable in his discipline. His
family home was on an island in Lake Ontario, and he had
to row several miles to school and back every day.* He later
became a world champion in rowing for five years in a row,
between 1880 and 1884, and lost only six of more than 300
races in his career. In his first world championship race, he
was winning by such a distance that he kept pretending to
fall out of his boat or lose his oars to get the audience interested. In his second, he won the race, then rowed halfway
back along the course to where his opponent was and beat
him a second time.

Babe Didrikson's childhood was all about sports. All sports.
As a kid, she told people she would be 'the greatest athlete to
ever live', and it's fair to say she got pretty close. In adulthood,

....

* Bizarrely, the position of his home – at the far tip of the island
– wasn't where it had started out. During a storm in 1865, a huge
wave swept his family, house and all, into the lake. They rebuilt it
where they and the remnants washed up, on the opposite end of the
island.

she became one of the best female golfers of all time. She won 41 tournaments, including the 1954 US Open, the year after being diagnosed with – and having surgery for – colon cancer. When the cancer returned and she died in 1956, she was still ranked number one in the world.

Golf wasn't Didrikson's only sport. Not by a long shot. In the 1932 Olympics, she won gold in the hurdles and javelin, and silver in the high jump (which should have been gold, but her last jump was unjustly ruled out). She's still the only person ever to have won medals in a running event, a throwing event and a jumping event. In fact, she was so dominant in athletics that when her team, Employer's Casualty, won the Amateur Athletics Championships in 1932, she was its only competitor. The second-placed team had 22 members. In that competition she broke world records for the javelin, the 80m hurdles, the high jump and the furthest baseball throw.* The last of these came in useful when she decided to take up that sport, where she ended up playing in pre-season exhibition games for the St Louis Cardinals and the Cleveland Indians, becoming the first woman ever to play for a major league baseball team. As well as all this, Didrikson was accomplished at pool, basketball and tennis. When asked by a journalist if there was anything she didn't play, she replied: '. . . with dolls.'

....

* The baseball-throwing event was discontinued soon afterwards, and Didrikson's record for longest baseball throw by a woman, verified by Guinness, stands to this day. This makes her the only Babe to have an existing baseball world record. Sorry, Mr Ruth.

Tiger Woods – the male Babe Didrikson (as far as golf goes, at least) – is perhaps the most successful sportsman of the modern era. The PGA (Professional Golfers' Association) Tour is the most prestigious series of golf tournaments in the world, and in the last 60 years, there have been three instances of a golfer winning five or more PGA Tour events in a row: it was Woods every time. He spent a total of 13 years at the top of the Official World Golf Rankings; that's more than the next four on the list – Greg Norman, Dustin Johnson, Rory McIlroy and Nick Faldo – combined. In 2010, Woods was named as the first sportsman to have earned $1 billion, which is testament to his dominance of the sport. But that may not be the most money a sportsperson has ever won. Adjusting for almost 2,000 years' worth of inflation, Woods's financial remuneration may have been dwarfed by the winnings of one Gaius Appuleius Diocles.

Diocles was the greatest Roman charioteer. He had short stints with the Whites, Greens and Blues, before settling in for a long career with the Reds; imagine a top English soccer player playing for Liverpool, Chelsea, Manchester United and Arsenal. Thanks to his 1,462 victories, he racked up 35,863,120 sesterces in prize money. We know this because the figure is recorded in an inscription to the 'champion of all charioteers' etched on a monument in Rome by his admirers in AD 146. We're not certain if he kept all the money himself, but if he did, it would have been enough to provide grain for the entire population of Rome for a year or to pay all of the soldiers in the Roman army for two and a half months. Converting that to modern-day wealth is not an exact science, but by comparing his winnings to the wages of other workers at the time, it has been calculated that he won the equivalent of $15 billion today. Diocles could have used this money to attempt a career in politics, fund the arts or even to raise his own army – for a couple of months, at least. It was certainly enough to leave his stamp on history, in whatever way he desired. But instead, he retired to the countryside to raise a family, and we know little else about his life.

It's understandable, perhaps, that Diocles craved a life of peace and security, having spent his youth confronting the extreme dangers involved in charioteering. When racing, charioteers were attached to their horses by reins that were tied around their waists, meaning that a crash was very likely to be fatal, as they were dragged beneath wheels and hooves. Very few charioteers lived past thirty. As a result, the athletes who won most races, and survived into middle age, were considered to be extremely lucky, and were even ascribed magical powers. Magistrates might ask for charioteers' advice when it came to the supposed illegal use of magic, and it was thought that the best way to ensure your favourite charioteer would win was to put a hex on his opponents.

You might think we live in more rational times today, when we attribute victories or great sporting feats to an athlete's skill or their years of practice, or even a childhood spent overcoming adversity. But sportspeople and sports fans are still some of the most superstitious people out there, often holding beliefs or providing explanations for success that aren't remotely backed up by evidence.

HOT HANDS AND COLD, HARD DATA

The American Basketball Association (ABA) began with much fanfare in 1967, but by the mid-1970s, it was struggling to attract fans, who preferred the more established NBA. As a result, ABA teams were resorting to increasingly creative measures to attract supporters. In 1975, in a game between the Indiana Pacers and the Utah Stars, fans were treated to an extremely unusual half-time wrestling match.

It was the Pacers' final game of the season at their new Market Square Arena, and they were guaranteed a place in the playoffs.* So there was a party atmosphere at half-time as local sportscaster Chet Coppock walked onto the court in a gaudy outfit borrowed from local wrestler 'Dick the Bruiser'. He was accompanied by two 'slave girls' in skimpy *Flash Gordon*-themed outfits. Despite the effort he'd put in, it was Coppock's wrestling opponent, Victor, who garnered the biggest cheers. Victor was a grizzly bear. The result of the bout will come as no surprise: despite having had his claws removed and being forced to wear a muzzle (as well as being heavily sedated), the bear made very short work of the journalist, pinning him in a matter of seconds. He then easily overpowered several more opponents who volunteered from the crowd. To Victor, the spoils.

....

* The Market Square Arena was a vast improvement from the Fairgrounds Coliseum, where they played the year before. The away dressing room of that stadium had only one shower head, and the press room was a refurbished toilet.

Victor eyes up another victim, while a small child looks on, disapprovingly.

In spite of (or perhaps because of) such gimmicks, the ABA lasted only one more season before it folded, but not without making a contribution to basketball that changed the sport forever: the three-point basket.[*] The three-point line is a semi-circle just over 22ft from the basket. If you score from inside the line, that's worth two points. But the ABA also played by the rule that if you shoot the ball into the net from outside that line, then – you got it – it's worth three.[†]

The NBA adopted the three-point rule in 1979, though it took a while for teams to get used to it. Players and fans alike saw it as nothing more than a gimmick. In its first season, teams attempted a three-pointer on average only 1.5 times a game. Even by 2000, the average was only seven times per match. Today, it is well over 30. And one of the 21st century's most famous three-point hitters was Kobe Bryant,[‡] a player who sometimes went through phases when it felt to all spectators like he couldn't miss. It's a phenomenon that is known in the sport as having 'hot hands'.

[*] The bear-baiting ABA wasn't the first league to adopt the three-point rule. In 1962, a Puerto Rican called Eddie Mellado decided to start a basketball league for six-to-ten-year-olds. Given the large differences in height between some of the players, he came up with the scoring system to motivate the smaller kids.

[†] North Korea has its own basketball rules. You get three points for a dunk, four points for a three-pointer that does not touch the rim and eight points for a basket scored in the final three seconds of a game. Miss a free throw, and it's minus one.

[‡] Bryant's unusual first name comes from a type of steak from Japan: his parents saw it on a menu and thought that it would make a good name.

Bryant grew up in Italy in the 1980s, when the Italian basketball league was the second-most important in the world behind the NBA. One of the teams, Sebastiani Rieti, a second-division club based in a town that claims to be at the exact centre of Italy, had a half-time show that in retrospect was even more impressive than a fighting bear. It was known as the 'Kobe Show', and it consisted of a six-year-old Kobe Bryant dribbling on the court, performing tricks with the ball and trying to shoot baskets from long distance. When the game was ready to restart, the officials would have to carry the child off the court, much to the disappointment of the crowd. Kobe was the son of one of the Rieti players, Joe 'Jellybean' Bryant. Twenty-five years later, the boy would be named the most valuable player in the NBA.

The Bryant family had moved from America to Italy when Kobe was six, and they were seen as both curiosities and celebrities. They never had to pay for a coffee since there would always be a fan of the team who was happy to pick up the tab. At the age of seven, Kobe played his first-ever competitive game. His team quickly went 10–0 up, with Kobe scoring all the points, upon which most of the opposing team started crying. A number of parents yelled for Kobe to be taken off the court, which he was, and so he too started crying. From then on, Kobe would always play in games against older children.*

---

* He still dominated against the older kids, helped along by a tip his father had given him: since right-handed kids tended not to use their left hand, and vice versa, if Kobe learned to use both, he would easily be able to steal the ball from players and shield it as he dribbled.

As an adult, having moved back to the US, Bryant played for the LA Lakers throughout his entire NBA career. In one particular game in 2003, they were playing the Seattle Supersonics. It began unremarkably, and the first quarter ended tied at 25 points each. Then, halfway through the second quarter, Bryant found himself unmarked next to the three-point line, holding the ball. With no pressure, he made the shot. Considering he made around a third of these shots in his career, this wasn't a great surprise, but what was to follow was completely unprecedented. If the chance of Bryant making a three-point shot at that time was about one in three, then making two in a row was one in nine. And that's what he did as the clock ticked down towards the end of the second quarter. Then, after the teams came out for the second half, he made a third in succession, and then a fourth and a fifth – something he'd expect to do only once in 243 tries. The crowd could sense something big was happening, and every time Bryant got the ball beside the three-point line a murmur would build, followed by an almighty cheer as he scored his sixth, and then seventh, basket in a row. The probability of him hitting those was less than one in 2,000; Kobe played only around 1,000 games in his entire career, so he was comfortably beating the odds. Two more baskets followed, to make it nine three-pointers in a row. The chances of him achieving that had been more than 20,000 to one against, and yet it had felt inevitable. The biggest shock of the night was that his tenth attempt bounced off the rim and landed in the hands of his teammate Shaquille O'Neal, who passed it back to Bryant to score at the second attempt anyway.

Bryant would eventually score twelve three-pointers in the game, which stood as the NBA record for 16 years.* Today, that game is often cited as the classic example of a 'hot hand'. Similar concepts exist in other sports, with athletes often speaking of being 'in the zone'. It's an appealing idea – we all know the feeling of increased confidence after a couple of good pool shots or strikes down at the bowling alley – but is it backed up by the data?

Bryant's nine baskets in a row may have beaten odds of 20,000 to one, but there are 1,230 games in a standard season, so if all else was the same, you'd expect this to happen on average once every 16 years or so. The NBA has been going since 1949, so you might think that not only is it not surprising that such an event has occurred at some stage in its history, but we're overdue another one. Except most players don't attempt this kind of shot nine times in a standard game. Put simply, with the data we have, it's impossible to say whether Bryant's exploits are evidence of so-called 'hot hands'.

When a player starts to score a lot of points in a basketball match, three things happen: firstly, their teammates start to give them the ball a lot more often; secondly, their opponents start to mark them more closely; and finally, because they think they have a hot hand, they start taking shots that they would normally turn down. Since these dynamics are constantly changing, it's not as simple as saying that if a player

---

* Bryant learned of the previous record – 11 by Dennis Scott in 1996 – halfway through the game, when a ball-boy informed him.

has a one in three chance of hitting a single basket, the second shot has the same probability of going in.

After crunching the numbers, some statisticians have failed to find evidence for hot hands, while others claim it can occasionally exist, but only to a small degree. What they all agree on is that the public's belief in the phenomenon is disproportionate to the reality. If it does exist, it could simply be that during a game, players find and exploit a small flaw in their opponents, which gives them a slightly better than average chance of making a basket.

Whether or not there's such a thing as hot hands in a statistical sense, there's no doubt that the state of mind dubbed 'the zone' – in which a player feels at one with, and entirely subsumed by, the game – does exist. Almost all successful sportspeople experience it, and it's a feeling that most chase throughout their careers. And it's not specific to sports. Leo Tolstoy described it in *Anna Karenina* in the context of farm labouring, for instance:

> *Levin lost all awareness of time and had no idea whether it was late or early. A change now began to take place in his work, which gave him enormous pleasure. In the midst of his work moments came to him when he forgot what he was doing and began to feel light, and in those moments his swath came out as even and good as Titus's. But as soon as he remembered what he was doing and started trying to do better, he at once felt how hard the work was and the swath came out badly. [. . .] More and more often those moments of unconsciousness came, when it was*

possible for him not to think of what he was doing. The
scythe cut by itself.

In psychology, this state of mind is known as 'flow'. It was first studied in the 1970s by Hungarian psychologist Mihály Csíkszentmihályi,* and the phrase 'in the zone' was coined around the same time by tennis player Arthur Ashe – 100 years after Tolstoy's description. Of course, the scientist, the sportsperson and the author were describing a feeling that is as old as time, and which can be experienced by listening to music or reading a particularly engrossing book, just as it can by playing basketball or tennis.

Bodhidharma, a monk living in China in around the 6th century, described the ultimate expression of this feeling as the state of 'Zen'. He achieved it by sitting facing a wall in silent contemplation for nine years.† Had he lived in the mid-20th century, we feel sure he would have been intrigued by a spate of books promising that readers could reach Zen in such diverse fields as motorcycle maintenance and archery.

MEDITATION'S WHAT YOU NEED

Zen in the Art of Archery was written in 1948 by German philosopher Eugen Herrigel. He was inspired by a visit to Japan, where he learned the art of *kyūdō*, a Japanese version

---

* Pronounced 'chick sent me high, ye'.
† Anyone who has appeared on the quiz show *Only Connect* will know how he feels.

of archery in which the goal is to have good technique rather than necessarily hit targets. Herrigel's teacher, Awa Kenzô, told him that the aim of the game was to reach a state of *shin-zen-bi*, which translates as 'truth–goodness–beauty'. The book's message is simple: to be successful in *kyūdō* you must aim to reach Zen enlightenment; and you can reach Zen enlightenment by practising *kyūdō*.

Readers who were already interested in Eastern mysticism lapped it up. A survey of people studying *kyūdō* in Germany in the 1980s found that 85% were doing it for some kind of 'spiritual training'; 61% said they wanted to become more zen; and 49% specifically cited Herrigel's book as the reason they were trying the sport. However, the connection that Herrigel found between Zen and archery, while iconic, may have been misguided.

His teacher, Awa, was something of an eccentric. Awa was born in 1880 into a family that worked in the sake-making industry. At the age of seventeen, even though he had only a primary-school education, he started a school teaching Chinese characters to Japanese people. In his thirties, he founded an archery school, but it was extremely controversial: Awa taught that the correct technique was to have *no* technique and to fire in whatever way you feel is correct in the moment. Shocked by his maverick ways, other archery teachers would throw rocks at him in the street (presumably, the last person you want throwing rocks at you is someone with the accuracy of a master archer).

If Awa's teaching wasn't eccentric enough, one evening he went to his archery range, drew back his bow and then decided he wouldn't fire; he would just hold the pose forever. It would prove his determination, and the power of mind over matter, if he didn't allow the tension in the bow to change his posture. There he stood, for days, until his body gave up the ghost. He thought to himself, 'I have died,' and just at that moment heard a huge, mysterious noise reverberate around the range. He let go of the arrow, and the sound of the flight and the twang of the arrow hitting the target were clearer and more perfect than ever before. He went back to his school and began to teach a new mantra: that an archer should put an entire lifetime of exertion into every shot. Awa's archery lessons were now a way into a new religion that he called *Daishadokyo*.

While Awa was creating his religion, Herrigel came to Japan to learn more about Japanese spiritualism. He knew about Zen from his philosophy studies, but became fascinated when, during a visit to the country, there was an earthquake. Everyone was running around in panic, but he noticed one man sitting quietly, with his eyes closed, in perfect stillness. This man told him that while in this meditative state, he could not be injured by the earthquake. Herrigel ignored the fact that he himself had not been harmed despite not meditating, and asked the man how he could go about studying Zen. The man told him that the best way was to learn some kind of Japanese art, and given he was already a talented gunsmith, Herrigel settled on archery. Thanks to a contact at the local university, he managed to talk Master Awa into becoming his tutor.

Awa was a charismatic teacher who saw himself as the head of a new mystical religion, and Herrigel was an enthusiastic pupil who was desperate to find evidence of mysticism. But their relationship was made even more complex by the fact that neither spoke each other's language. Herrigel hired a translator, Sozo Komachiya, who had the unenviable task of translating Awa's teachings, which would contain complicated metaphors and multiple contradictions. When Awa contradicted himself, Komachiya would stay silent. If pushed, he would explain that it was such an important point that Master Awa was merely repeating himself. In addition to being selective, Komachiya would sometimes make up translations that he knew Herrigel wanted to hear. As a result, modern scholars of Zen and archery accept that Herrigel's work *Zen in the Art of Archery* contains multiple errors, as well as considerable romanticism.

That's not to say that concentration and some kind of 'getting in the zone' aren't important in archery. The sport is incredibly precise. In the Olympics, to get their arrow into the central gold ring archers have to be able to hit a target the size of a beermat from a distance equivalent to seven buses. The greatest male British archer who ever lived, Horace A. Ford, once wrote a book about the sport and began it with a great piece of advice: 'First of all make up your mind to succeed.'

The greatest-ever female British archer also emphasised the importance of having the right psychological attitude, and it certainly worked for her. Alice Legh won the championship every year between 1881 and 1922 – except for when the First World War got in the way, and for four years when she was beaten into second place by her own mother. Legh wrote that the key to mastering the mental, as opposed to physical, side of archery was to remain unruffled, saying: 'I do not deny that it is most aggravating when your arrows absolutely refuse to obey your will; but above all things, do not show temper, or rage inwardly.'

The current world record holder for the longest accurate archery shot, Matt Stutzman, also believes that having the right mindset is central to success in the sport. Stutzman summed up the reason for his success by saying: 'I've always had the mentality that I want to be the best archer in the world.' That he achieved such an aim despite being born without arms is a fairly strong argument in favour of his approach.

Stutzman says that when he started his career in 2011, he googled 'how to shoot with no arms' and found no results. He wasn't to be deterred, though, and the following year, using his feet to draw back his bow, he hit a target more than 280m away. Thanks to his success, there are now at least two other 'armless archers' taking part in elite events, and these days Google searches yield plenty of advice for those with similar aspirations. Stutzman says being an inspiration to other athletes is 'better than winning'.

This single-minded drive to succeed isn't what motivates all archers, though. While it's a relatively solitary pursuit in the West, perhaps lending itself to an individualist mentality, it takes a completely different form in Bhutan.* Those who downplay the importance of winning will say that 'it's the taking part that counts', and that genuinely seems to be

---

* Until 2012, archery was the *only* Olympic sport that Bhutan competed in.

the case for the national sport of this small, mountainous kingdom.

Bhutanese archery is not like anything you'll see elsewhere. Two teams face off, around 140m from each other, with a small target beside them. Each player takes it in turns to be the archer, and his job is to hit the opposition's target; but before doing that, the opposing side yells insults at him. If he hits the bullseye, the archer's team will do a choreographed dance to celebrate. Indeed, Bhutanese archery gatherings are more like celebrations or festive occasions than competitions. They often last several days and revolve as much around singing, dancing and food and drink as bows and arrows. It's an opportunity for communities to come together and engage in a shared tradition

Bhutanese archers in traditional dress, known as *gho*. The *gho* is worn for all formal events in Bhutan, so its appearance in archery is analogous to snooker players always wearing waistcoats

and culture, and almost every village has its own range for
the purpose. It's also a chance for participants to demonstrate
their verbal skills as they strive to taunt the opposition – or
praise their own team – in the most imaginative or poetic way.

Success in Bhutanese archery tournaments might be measured by how wittily players manage to insult each other, or
how impressively their supporters co-ordinate their dance
routines, as much as by the number of targets hit. As Kinzang
Dorji, president of the Bhutan Archery Federation, once said:
'When we play archery, it's not just archery.' But participation
still requires mental fortitude, not least because competitors
stand just a few feet from the target their opponent is aiming
for.* To add an extra element of risk, it's traditional for everyone involved to have a few drinks before the match. Alcohol is
a key part of the festivities, and in fact, history has shown that
getting a little tipsy is not always a barrier to sporting success.

FASTER, STRONGER . . . AND HIGHER?

Ironically enough, given his name, one of the best cricketers of all time, Garry Sobers, scored his last century while
drunk. He was playing for the West Indies against England
at Lord's in 1973, and had been up all night clubbing and
drinking heavily. He decided not to return to his hotel and
instead went straight from the bars to the ground at 9 a.m.

* These days, at least, there is usually a pretty solid barrier, such as a
wall, beside the target, behind which non-shooters can hide, but that
wasn't always the case.

that morning. He changed quickly and immediately went in to bat. After reaching an extremely impressive 132 runs, he begged to be taken off injured (recorded as a 'stomach complaint') as the hangover kicked in. He was revived with a couple of large port-and-brandies, after which the umpires were told his ailment had cleared up, and he was brought back onto the field of play. He reached 150 not out, securing victory for his country.

Sixty years prior to Sobers' exploits, in May 1913, French-born rookie driver Jules Goux cruised to victory in the Indianapolis 500 motor race by a healthy margin of over 13 minutes. The winning drive included several pit stops, during which Goux not only tanked up on gas, but also refreshed himself with chilled champagne. Some accounts have the Frenchman and his mechanic downing as many as six bottles of bubbly over the course of the race, but Indianapolis Motor Speedway historian Donald Davidson has argued that they had *only* two and a half pints of champagne during their first pit stop and then a few sips during each of the others. Whatever Goux's blood alcohol content was, he later told newspapers that 'Without the good wine, I could not have won.'

Meanwhile, the first person to win a gold medal for men's snowboarding (at the 1998 Nagano Olympics), Ross Rebagliati, was almost disqualified after failing a drugs test when trace amounts of cannabis were found in his system. Within hours of getting the medal, he was in a Japanese police station, where officers killed time by asking him how to roll a joint. He showed them by pulling apart their cigarettes and reconstructing them. Rebagliati's medal was allowed to stand as marijuana wasn't on the banned list – plus there was only a tiny amount in his body, which he claimed had got into his system by him passively smoking at a party. He now runs a marijuana dispensary in a ski resort.

Marijuana comes from one of the oldest plants known to have been deliberately cultivated by humans. For longer than we've been writing things down, we've been using it to get high. Alcohol is probably older still. Humans have been looking for altered states of consciousness for almost as long as we've been humans, be it through ingested substances, religious chanting or even just spinning round and round and getting really dizzy.

Sportspeople are at a greater risk of substance abuse than the general population, and researchers are still trying to work out why. People who take part in team sports seem to be particularly at risk, implying it could be partly due to social pressures, with new players feeling they have to partake to fit in. But there may also be something about the competitiveness of elite athletes that makes them more likely to have serious problems. As one researcher at the University of Alberta who had spoken to addicts who'd once played professional ice hockey put it: 'They wanted to be the best at whatever they did, so if that meant being the best heroin user, that's what they did.'

It may also be that drug-using athletes are victims of their own success. Winning makes them feel good, and when they stop competing, they lose the natural highs that come with sport. As well as the 'runner's high' and the 'cheater's high', which we've already encountered, flow researchers have found that getting 'into the zone' and playing sport to a high level puts athletes into a different state of consciousness, in much the same way as narcotics. People take part in sports for many different reasons: to socialise, inspire or even to become more Zen. Winning isn't everything, but when success brings such a buzz, is it any wonder that players are always chasing the next high?

We've already seen that taking part is enough to improve players' mental health in general, but the sporting world is starting to realise that its athletes have their own particular challenges to face. Many sportspeople find it very difficult to do what Gaius Appuleius Diocles managed and retire to a quiet life in the country. As one of the greatest boxers of all time, Sugar Ray Leonard, put it: 'Nothing could satisfy me outside the ring . . . there is nothing in life that can compare to becoming a world champion, having your hand raised in that moment of glory, with thousands, millions of people cheering you on.'

Worse still, a sporting life isn't all about success. Even at the highest level, the vast majority of sportspeople need to deal with failure on a regular basis. For every winner, there's a loser. And losing can be tough to take. The best way to get over a loss, according to sports psychologists, is to embrace defeats and see them as a stepping stone to future success. After all, what's the name of the NBA player who missed more attempted shots than anyone else in the history of basketball? Kobe Bryant. All that's easy to say, since Bryant's career is defined by his successes, but what of those sportspeople who are known primarily as failures?

11

ERIC THE EEL, EDDIE THE EAGLE AND PAULA THE CRAWLER

HOW FAILURE CAN BREED SUCCESS

Failure is not the falling down,
but the staying down.
Mary Pickford

Sometimes the line between success and failure is paper thin; other times it's unmistakeably clear. In 2009, the Dallas Academy, a school that specialises in educating children with learning difficulties such as dyslexia and attention deficit disorder, lined up in a girls' basketball match against the Covenant School, a Christian pre-college prep school with a formidable reputation for sports in that part of Texas. While it was expected that Covenant would win easily – not least because Dallas Academy had just 20 female students to pick from – their resulting 100–0 victory became something of a national scandal.

The Covenant team were 25–0 ahead after just three minutes of the 32-minute match, so their coach, Micah Grimes, responded by ordering his team to stop pressing so far up the court. This slowed down the scoring a little, but Covenant could still steal the ball from their opponents at will, and by half-time the score was 59–0. At the end of the third quarter, their score was in the 80s, and as it ticked towards three digits, the small crowd began to cheer wildly for every basket, encouraging the Covenant team to reach 100. Everybody got a little bit carried away.

Almost certainly for the first time in Texan schoolgirl

basketball history, the result made national news. In response to the uproar, Covenant said sorry for winning so heavily, commenting that the score 'obviously does not reflect a Christlike and honorable approach to competition'. The head of the school personally apologised to the Dallas Academy, praising the losing team 'for their strength, composure, and fortitude in a game in which they clearly emerged the winner'. Despite that blatantly untrue statement, one parent of the Academy team did tell the press that thankfully 'our girls just moved on, that's the happy part of the story'.

The press didn't move on, though, and it was decided that the villain of the piece was coach Grimes. He was fired two weeks later, after sending an unrepentant email to a local newspaper in which he denied deliberately running up the score and said that aiming for 100 points was not a target (though once his team reached that total, with four minutes remaining, they did finally let up and scored no more). He is surely the only coach in history to be fired after winning a game by 100 points to zero.

The whole incident could have been avoided if the league had a 'mercy' or 'skunk' rule,* whereby if one team gets too far ahead, both sides can mutually agree to end the game. Not everyone agrees with the sentiment behind this type of rule. When the US women's football team beat Thailand 13–0 in the 2019 World Cup and celebrated the last goal as if it was their first, many argued that they should have held back once

---

* The term comes from the fact that the famously smelly skunk was used as an insulting term for a team who had 'stunk the place out'.

they had an unassailable lead. But as their former goalkeeper Hope Solo wrote: 'When you respect your opponent you don't all of a sudden sit back and try not to score.' When the team won their next game against Chile by a more modest 3–0, they celebrated their goals with sarcastic clapping that would be more at home at a golf or snooker tournament than a football World Cup.

While the mercy rule is applied in America's school leagues in an ad hoc and uneven way, there are some sports that have it firmly baked into their laws. In curling, for instance, you can forfeit the game at any point if you think you're too far behind.* That rule applies whether you're playing at your local ice rink or in the final of the Winter Olympics. And in the game of goalball, which has appeared at every Paralympic Games since 1972, if a team ever goes 10 points ahead, then they are automatically declared the winner.

Goalball was invented to help the rehabilitation of soldiers who lost their sight during the Second World War. Played on a volleyball court, with two oversized football goals that cover the entire goal line at each end of the pitch, every player wears a blindfold, so that those with partial sight have no advantage over those who are totally blind. The ball contains

---

* Similarly, in the *Harry Potter* books, when playing quidditch, the captains can agree on when a match should finish. The only other way to end a game is to catch the golden snitch, a tiny golden ball that flies through the stadium. In real-life versions of quidditch, the snitch is replaced by a tennis ball in a sock.

Goalball: a completely unique game whose name is so unimaginative that it could describe most of the team sports in this book.

a bell, and the aim is to throw it into your opponents' goal, while they use the jingling sound to judge where it is going and attempt to make a save. Silence is obviously very important so that the players can hear the ball. It's the only sport where it's written into the official laws that the referee must begin each match by telling everyone in the stadium to turn off their mobile phones.

The sort of runaway victory that led to mercy rules and Micah Grimes's dismissal probably wouldn't come high on most athletes' list of worst-nightmare scenarios, however. Much more common is the opposite concern: the fear of failure.

YOU MUST BE CHOKING

Perhaps the most feared form of failure is the deadly 'choke', whereby a player or team manages to suffer an extraordinary loss from a winning position. Imagine you have been given £100, but there's a catch: you need to use it to place a bet. There are two options: you can bet the £100 on the toss of a coin, and if you guess correctly, you will get an extra £100; or you may gamble the £100 on the roll of a six-sided dice, and if you choose the correct number, you'll end up with a total of £1,000. If you get the coin toss wrong or pick the wrong number on the dice, you will end up with nothing.

If you choose the coin toss, this would suggest you are risk averse – you are more interested in not losing what you have, rather than risking it for a bigger reward. And studies show that the more risk averse you are, the more likely you are to choke under pressure. It has also been shown that up to a point, the smarter or more talented you are, the more likely you are to choke. In one study which illustrated this, people who had a better ability to memorise things tended to do worse when asked to solve mathematics problems under pressure. The researchers found that those who were usually able to solve the problems quickly struggled when they got overloaded, and suggested this was because their brains were unable to immediately locate the previous knowledge and so were forced to look for other strategies. The pressure caused them to lose their advantage.

This knowledge is unlikely to provide any consolation to the Aussie rules team Collingwood FC. Over a course of

21 years from 1960–81, they managed to play well enough throughout the season to reach the grand final on multiple occasions, only to repeatedly capitulate when it came to the crunch. In nine finals, they lost eight and drew one (they lost the resulting replay), leading to them coining their very own term for choking – 'the Colli-wobbles'.

When the team eventually did win a final, 30 years after the Colli-wobbles began, rather than an open-topped bus celebration through Melbourne, they opted for a funeral march in which they could finally lay the Colli-wobbles to rest. A marching bagpipe band preceded the parade – a sea of black crosses, wreaths and fans chanting 'No more Colli-wobbles!' In front of a stadium full of cheering 'mourners', a tiny coffin was laid in a hole dug into the pitch, and a master of ceremonies in a black suit and top hat announced that the curse was finally lifted.[*]

Failure can be crippling. In 2019, South African golfer Ernie Els, a former world number one and winner of four major championships, took six shots to get the ball into the hole from just three feet away during the US Masters tournament in Georgia. He joked afterwards that he might need a brain transplant in order to cure his anxiety – a phenomenon known in golfing circles as 'the yips'. The yips is a condition where a sportsperson is suddenly unable to perform a simple task that under normal circumstances they could do without thinking. It is much feared; even writing a section about the

---

[*] It would be another 20 years before Collingwood won the grand final again. Old habits, it seems, die hard.

yips in a book is enough to bring a keen golfer into a cold sweat. It's also sometimes known as 'the jerks', 'the wiggles' or even 'whisky fingers', but the term 'the yips' was popularised by a golfer called Tommy Armour. He wrote that a golfer with the yips 'blacks out, loses sight of the ball and hasn't the remotest idea of what to do with the putter or, occasionally, that he is holding a putter at all'.*

Depending on your personality, playing in front of a crowd can either be enough to bring on a fearsome case of the yips or inspire you to play the game of your life. Psychological research indicates that this is due to two phenomena: the spotlight effect and social facilitation.

BUT MOST OF ALL, YOU LET YOURSELF DOWN

The spotlight effect refers to the fact that we tend to overestimate how much attention people pay to us. This is illustrated by a study in which students were asked to wear bright yellow Barry Manilow T-shirts to a seminar and then asked to guess how many of their fellow students had noticed their eye-catching attire. In the event, the subjects massively overrated how conspicuous they were to others. The problem with the spotlight effect is that in concentrating on what other

---

* Armour's own struggles with the yips are the stuff of folklore. Inspired by the fact that scores of one, two or three under par are known respectively as a 'birdie', 'eagle' and 'albatross', he also supposedly coined the term 'archaeopteryx' for a score of more than 15 over par.

people will think of us, we can be distracted from the task we're supposed to be carrying out – whether that is focusing on a university seminar or playing in the Masters.

Social facilitation, on the other hand, describes the opposite effect, which sees some people perform better in front of an audience. Research on those who exhibit this behaviour shows that when being watched, the parts of their brains that deal with skilled tasks are more active. The good news is that there's a way to facilitate social facilitation: practice. Whether an audience helps or hinders depends on how practised you are at a task. A crowd, it turns out, heightens your brain's default response: if you've practised hard for the moment, then it will remember this and allow you to excel; if not, then you will perform worse than usual.

Positive or negative, these effects can be triggered by fans, family, friends or even sponsors. In 1992, Reebok spent $30 million promoting a head-to-head rivalry over who would be crowned the 'world's greatest athlete' at the Olympics in Barcelona, which backfired when one of the two failed completely. The campaign began as a way to compete with the highly successful adverts being made by Nike. The premise was simple: Reebok would push the question 'Dan or Dave?' into the public consciousness, and the public would choose their favourite between Dan O'Brien and Dave Johnson, the two American favourites for the 10-event decathlon gold medal. Hardly anyone had previously heard of Dan or Dave (decathletes are rarely very famous), but by the time the campaign was in full swing, they were two of the most recognisable sportsmen in America. Everyone knew the ad, kids played at being 'Dan or Dave' in their back gardens, and Reebok sold tons of 'Dan/Dave' merchandise. It was a hugely successful campaign, and bad news for Nike. That is, until the US Olympic trials.

As the competition to see who would go to Barcelona kicked off, there were 'Dan vs Dave' signs all over the stadium, as well as fans wearing 'Dan vs Dave' hats. Dan later said he was taking part in an 11-event decathlon, 'with the 11th event being "dominating Dave"'. The contest began well for both athletes, with Dan miles ahead of the rest of the competitors and looking likely to threaten the world record. Having completed seven of the ten required events (an Olympic decathlon comprises the 100m, long jump, shot-put, high jump, 400m, 110m hurdles, discus, pole vault, javelin and 1500m), he was an extremely impressive 512 points ahead of the pack – as good as guaranteed a place in the Olympics. The next event was the pole vault, in which competitors jump higher and higher until they fail three times. The highest bar they clear is converted to points and added to their cumulative score.

Perhaps growing over-confident thanks to his sizeable lead, perhaps wanting to assert his dominance over Dave, or perhaps pushed by his coaches or sponsors, Dan skipped the early jumps. Better jumpers often do this, eschewing the warm-up on the lower jumps to conserve energy for the higher ones. Dan made his first attempt with the bar at 4m 20cm. It would be an impressive jump, but one that he could easily make in practice.

He missed the first jump. And then the second. Now Dan's entire competition depended on his third and final attempt.

Dan O'Brien failing to clear the bar in the pole vault, much to the delight of Reebok's competitors.

Even though he was miles ahead in the standings, if he didn't register a score in the pole vault, he was out of the competition. He started his run-up, but things didn't feel right. So he started for a second time, and pulled up again. When he finally made the jump on the third attempt, he got nowhere near the bar. He had scored a zero, so not only would he be unable to beat Dave in Barcelona, he wouldn't be going to the Olympics at all.

One of the Nike execs who was watching the moment when Dan failed said it was the only time in his life that he took pleasure in someone else's pain. Reebok hastily scrapped the ads they'd already made and created new ones showing Dave consoling Dan because he hadn't made it. Another showed Dave telling Dan he was sad that he wouldn't be coming to Barcelona with him, only for Dan to break the 'good news' that he would be going – as a commentator for NBC! Small consolation, we can only assume. The gold medal eventually went to a Czech athlete called Robert Změlík. Dave struggled with a foot injury and managed bronze.

After the pole-vault disaster, Dan began to suffer from crippling nerves in competitions, and so went into therapy. His therapist decided not to mention the pole-vault incident (which everyone knew about) and instead wait for Dan to bring it up. It took him three years to do so – at which point the therapist made Dan watch DVDs of the moment he lost that event, over and over.

It obviously worked. At the next Olympics in Atlanta, Dan won gold. A turning point came in the javelin, when Dave, who hadn't qualified because of injury and was there to support him, noticed that Dan's javelin wasn't flying quite right and recommended a different spear. The subsequent throw was the moment that clinched Dan's win. In the end, it wouldn't be Dan's failure that would define him, but rather a feelgood story of redemption, having gone from over-hyped flop to plucky underdog – and there's nothing spectators enjoy more than a victory against the odds.

EAGLES, EELS AND CRAWLERS

In the men's 100m freestyle swimming at the 2000 Olympics, three athletes were ready to compete in the first qualifying round: Karim Bare of Niger, Tajikistan's Farkhod Oripov and Eric Moussambani of Equatorial Guinea. The trio were poised on their blocks as the starter raised his pistol, but the pause felt like a lifetime, and Oripov and Bare dived into the water prematurely. Both were disqualified for a false start. Now the only thing Moussambani would have to do in order to qualify was complete two lengths of the pool. That would be a more difficult feat than anyone had realised.

Moussambani was there thanks to an Olympic scheme that awarded places to developing nations that wouldn't usually qualify, in order to promote the Games around the world and encourage broader participation in sport. When he arrived at the Sydney Aquatic Centre, it was the first time he had ever seen a 50m pool. He had trained in lakes and rivers, and a pool at a local hotel which was 13m long.

Moussambani's technique was unconventional, to say the least: it involved a lot of thrashing of arms, very little propulsion from the legs, and unlike most swimmers, who only raise their heads out of the water to breathe, he bent his neck so his face was almost always out of the water, looking forward. Coming to the end of the first length, he was making slow but steady progress. He then made a tumble turn, which he had just been taught by his rivals, and set off on the return length – but the push off the wall seemed to take the energy out of his legs. The crowd began to wonder if he would even make it to the end, as on more than one occasion he seemed close to grabbing on to the rope that separated the lanes – a disqualification offence. The final five metres were little more than an excruciating reach for the side of the pool, but in no small part thanks to the roar of the spectators, he made the full distance in just under 1 minute 53 seconds. A full 50 seconds slower than the second-slowest racer in the entire competition, sure, but it was a personal best and a Equatoguinean record.

Moussambani, an IT manager in his day job, became a celebrity overnight. Christened 'Eric the Eel' by the press, he got a role as an ambassador for Speedo, and eventually became coach of Equatorial Guinea's national swimming squad. Meanwhile, supermarket cashier and part-time foot-baller Paula Barila Bolopa, the only female member of the Equatorial Guinea swimming team, became a celebrity before she even started her race. Rumours that a 'female Eric the Eel' was about to compete meant that the stands were full to the brim for her event, with reporters desperate to talk to her, win or lose. She also completed her race in last place, though not quite as dramatically as Moussambani. The papers gave her the nickname 'Paula the Crawler'.

The system that had given Eric and Paula their wildcards came about after a British athlete came a distant last in an earlier Olympics. Now famous as Eddie the Eagle, Michael Edwards held the British record for ski jumping, and at the time of the 1988 Winter Olympics, where he made his name, was ranked 55 in the world. This ranking was in spite of the fact that Britain had no ski-jumping facilities, that Eddie had no sponsorship, and that his long-sightedness meant he had to wear glasses under his ski goggles which regularly misted up and meant he often took off from the ramp without being able to see a thing. He also claimed to be scared of heights. But he made it to the Olympics because there were no other British ski jumpers entering that year, so technically he was the best of them.[*]

Eddie didn't come last in the Games, since another athlete was disqualified, but he finished far enough back from the rest of the field that he became famous for his defeat. He also became a very popular personality along the way, winning over the crowds with his loveable good nature.[†] His subsequent celebrity in countries where winter sports dominate led

....

[*] When he was informed of his Olympic qualification, Eddie was living in a Finnish mental hospital – though this was due to him being unable to afford alternative accommodation while he trained, rather than requiring treatment.

[†] Eddie also gained a reputation for being comically accident-prone (not an attribute you want, perhaps, as a ski jumper). When he arrived at Calgary airport for the 1988 Olympics, his suitcase burst open, spilling his luggage everywhere and forcing him to leap aboard the carousel and chase after his clothes.

him to record two songs in Finnish, despite not being able to speak the language (it seems his dodgy pronunciation added to his charm).

But Eddie's fame sparked a backlash from those who felt it undermined both the competition and those who excelled in it. As a result, a new rule was instituted to exclude cheerful but useless amateurs from richer countries, while recognising the benefit of including athletes from the developing world. The rule states that other than wildcards, a competitor needs to have been placed in the top 30% (or among the top 50 competitors – whichever is fewer) in an international competition to qualify. It's almost always referred to as the 'Eddie the Eagle rule'.

When Olympic president Juan Antonio Samaranch made his valedictory address in 1988, commenting that 'at this Olympic Games some competitors have won gold and some have broken records, and one has even flown like an eagle', Eddie became the only athlete ever to have received an individual mention in an Olympics closing speech.

All these stories go to show that failure needn't be calamitous. You can take advantage of your defeat, like Eric, Eddie and Paula; you can just move on, like the Dallas Academy team; or you can use it to motivate you, like Dan. Past failures should never stop anyone from participating in sport, just as a player's gender, nationality or race shouldn't. But as we all know, seldom is the world so simple.

12

THE GREAT AUSTRALIAN BALL-DODGER

HOW CHANGES IN SOCIETY DETERMINE WHO GETS TO PLAY

In the field of sports, you are more or less accepted
for what you can do, rather than what you are.
Althea Gibson
(tennis player)

Even the most resolute sports-avoider in England or Australia
would admit some familiarity with the Ashes, that century-
and-a-half-long rivalry between the two countries' cricket
teams. But less well known is the 1868 series of matches,
which happened 14 years before the Ashes were born. It's the
story of the first Australian cricketers ever to land on English
soil and challenge the natives to a game.

The Australian team was made up of 13 Aboriginal players
and their captain, Charles Lawrence, a colonist who had previously played for England. All the players adopted anglicised
names for the trip, so the team sheet featured:

Dick-a-Dick (real name Jungunjinanuke)
Johnny Mullagh (Unaarrimin)
Bullocky (Bullchanach)
Sundown (Ballringarrimin)
Johnny Cuzens (Zellanach)
Charley Dumas (Pripumarraman)
Redcap (Brimbunyah)
Twopenny (Murrumgunarriman)

The 1868 Australian cricket team, who were more popular with English fans
than the modern-day Aussie team tends to be.

Jimmy Mosquito Couzens (Grougarrong)*
Tiger (Bonmbarngeet)
Peter (Arrahmunijarrimun)
Jim Crow (Jallachmurrimin)
King Cole (Brippokei)

The team stayed for 150 days and played 47 matches
altogether, against various English teams. Fans flocked to
see them, with 20,000 attending the first match in order to
witness the juxtaposition of cultures. Who wouldn't want to

* Jimmy Couzens was the brother of Johnny Cuzens, despite the
different spelling. The singer Isaiah Firebrace, *X Factor* winner
and Australia's entry for Eurovision 2017, counts them among his
ancestors.

see, for instance, the Aboriginal Johnny Mullagh bowl out
the Earl of Coventry? After five months of action, the results
were exactly even, with each country claiming 14 wins and
the remaining 19 games ending in a draw. Sport had proved
itself, on this occasion, a great leveller.

The star of the tournament in terms of cricketing ability
was generally agreed to be Mullagh,[*] who scored 1,698 runs
in total – 500 more than his nearest rival. Cricket aside, however, there was no doubt that it was Mullagh's teammate,
Dick-a-Dick, who was the real star attraction. Before play,
after play and even during breaks in play, Dick-a-Dick would
charge spectators a shilling to throw cricket balls at him as
hard as they could, while he defended himself with a shield
and a boomerang. His hand–eye co-ordination, reaction time
and the way he contorted his body out of the way of the
approaching ball were admired as much as Mullagh's batting.

The Australian First XI provided myriad bonus entertainment during the tour. Most match days featured, alongside
the cricket, an exhibition of boomerang throwing, as well as
various athletic contests between the visitors and the home
nation. Dick-a-Dick, when he wasn't ball-dodging, particularly
excelled at the standing high jump, the hurdles, cricket-ball
throwing and the backwards 100m race. He was so popular

....

[*] In the Boxing Day Test, one of the biggest cricket matches in the
Aussie calendar, the best player is awarded the Johnny Mullagh
medal. In 2021, the award went to Scott Boland, only the second-ever
player of Aboriginal descent to play Test cricket for the men's national
team. When Mullagh died in 1891, he was buried with a bat and some
cricket stumps.

with the fans that after a match at Lord's, an adoring crowd carried him back to the dressing room on their shoulders. This was despite him having scored only eight runs and failing to get anyone out.[*]

Dick-a-Dick gained the attention of one particular fan so successfully that she fell in love with him – and he with her. According to contemporary reports, he wanted to stay behind in England so he could marry her, but the team's coach refused to let it happen; in the end, despite appearances on the field, the team's white managers still held all the power.

When not playing international cricket, Dick-a-Dick worked on sheep stations. Like his teammates, he was used to playing against white opponents. British and Irish settlers had introduced the game onto their sheep and cattle stations, where many employed Aboriginal labourers. The two groups, indigenous and newcomers, often spent their free time playing matches together. And there was one particular settler named Tom Wills, who helped the Aboriginal XI in their rise to stardom.

....

[*] Dick-a-Dick first made a name for himself in 1864, when three white children aged nine, seven and three went missing in the bush near where he lived. The children's father had organised a 30-strong search party, but after a fruitless week of hunting, rain had washed away any fragments of a trail and there seemed little hope of finding them alive. As a last resort, the father contacted the local trackers – Aborigines who were expert in tracing human and animal tracks by following tiny clues in the landscape. Dick-a-Dick, his future teammate Redcap and one other turned up. They set off in the morning, and by studying every broken twig, misplaced leaf and disturbed patch of earth, by sunset they had found the children. It was unlikely the trio would have survived another night in the bush.

Wills's story was deeply embedded in the colonial history of Australia, and even today it's difficult to reconcile the contradictions within it. Three of his grandparents were Irish and English convicts, transported to Australia at the turn of the 19th century. His father, Horatio, worked as an editor for Australia's first newspaper, before buying 125,000 acres of land, on which he farmed livestock. Most of the people employed on the land were Aborigines, and Tom grew up among them, joining in their games, singing their songs and speaking their language.

During his teenage years, Tom was sent to the UK to be educated at Rugby School, which, living up to its name, inculcated in him a love of sports.* In fact, given his dates, it's not impossible that it was Wills who kicked the oldest-known rugby ball into a chimney in 1854. When he returned to Australia in 1861, he quickly became one of its most celebrated cricketers, as well as co-founding the new sport of Aussie rules football. And yet, after five years of fame and sporting prowess, aged only twenty-six, he retired in order to help his father set up and run a new livestock station in Queensland. It was here that disaster struck.

In October 1861, Tom was away from the station base gathering supplies when it was attacked by members of the Gayiri

---

* True to public-school tradition, Rugby also gave Wills a taste for alcohol, which plagued him for the rest of his life. He died aged forty-four. According to an inquest into his death, he stabbed himself in the heart with a pair of scissors 'while of unsound mind from excessive drinking'.

tribe. There followed the largest massacre ever perpetrated by indigenous Australians against white settlers. Tom returned to find the camp devastated and his father murdered, along with 18 others. It had been a revenge attack, triggered by one of Wills's neighbours killing some of the Gayiri. Even worse than the tragedy to which Wills's people succumbed were the reprisal killings that followed. In the weeks afterwards, police and vigilante civilians killed between 300 and 400 indigenous Australians, almost completely exterminating the Gayiri people. According to a man who claimed to have met him later in life, Wills participated in these revenge killings.

And yet, five years after his father's murder, Wills agreed to coach the first-ever team of Aboriginal Australian cricketers, and did so with great enthusiasm. They were so successful that even before they went to Britain, thousands flocked to see them play against settler teams, and they'd usually have the support of the crowds. By all accounts, Wills had a good, strong bond with his team, and he became known over the subsequent decades as someone who symbolised reconciliation between indigenous people and settlers. During a game in Melbourne, one of his players was asked if Wills had taught them to read and write, and he replied: 'What use Wills? He too much along of us. He speak nothing now but blackfella talk.' The tone here suggests that the relationship between Wills and his players was an affectionate one, in spite of – or perhaps because of – Wills's past. Many of the Aboriginals he worked with would not only have participated in the bloody frontier wars between indigenous and non-indigenous Australians, they would also have lost friends and family in the conflict – just as Wills had. Perhaps there was a sense of shared trauma between them, although of course we'll never know.

Either way, Wills's actions in life, and his subsequent legacy, are as messy, uncomfortable and complicated as the society they reflected. In his story, and that of Dick-a-Dick and the First XI team of 1868, lies the tale of colonial Australia, in all its complexity. It's not an anomaly: every social, cultural and political ripple, in any time and place, can be found echoing in the games people play. Sport never exists in a vacuum, and the way it reflects its context – sometimes challenging social norms and triggering progress, other times reinforcing regressive values or practices – is part of what makes it so compelling.

IN BLACK AND WHITE

The story of mainstream sports in the US is bound up with that of black Americans, with their status in sport often mirroring their status in society. In the late 19th century, as America wrestled with the fallout from the Civil War and abolition of slavery, black players began to join teams. In the early 1880s, when Major League Baseball (MLB) was just becoming established, Moses Fleetwood Walker made his debut as a catcher for the Toledo Blue Stockings.* It was never going to

* Walker is traditionally identified as the first black MLB player, but for one game in 1879, a man called William Edward White played – and extremely well – at first base for the Providence Grays.

be an easy ride, and he was released later that year, almost certainly due to racist objections to his inclusion. Before one game in Virginia, Toledo's manager received a letter warning him not to put Walker in the team, or a lynch mob of 75 men would be there waiting for him. Walker didn't play.

Walker's brother, Weldy, became the second openly[*] black American to play in MLB, joining Toledo a few months later. They were both demoted to the minor leagues by the end of the year, and the doors of MLB were closed to black players. From 1887, African Americans were officially excluded from the minor leagues as well. Weldy sent an open letter to the committee that made that decision, writing:

The law is a disgrace to the present age . . . and casts derision at the laws of Ohio – the voice of the people – that say all men are equal . . .

There should be some broader cause – such as lack of ability, behavior and intelligence – for barring a player, rather than his color. It is for these reasons and because I think ability and intelligence should be recognized first and last – at all times and by everyone – I ask the question again, 'Why was the law permitting colored men to sign repealed?'

He was the son of a white slave-owning father who had had three children with one of his slaves, Hannah. This would have made White legally black, but he never openly identified as such, and was always recorded as white.

[*] 'Openly' is a necessary modifier here, as Cuban players were sometimes allowed to play, and so black players would occasionally take part and just pretend to be Cuban.

His words fell on deaf ears, and it was 63 years before the third openly black player appeared in the MLB.* That, as will be obvious to baseball fans, was Jackie Robinson, who marked a turning point for integration in baseball. It always helps when the person fighting for inclusion also happens to be an outstanding player: in Robinson's first seven seasons, he scored the second-highest number of runs of any player in the league; in his first year, he won the inaugural 'Rookie of the Year' award; and two years later, in 1949, he took the MVP award, which goes to the most outstanding player in the National League. It was in no one's interest to exclude him from the game.†

American football followed a similar trajectory, in terms of segregation and integration. The American Professional Football Association, now the National Football League (NFL), formed in 1920, and for its first 13 years included a handful of black players. Then, in 1933, the NFL secretly banned them; that is, the decision was never made public,

....

* The Walker brothers ended up running a hotel together and editing a newspaper covering black issues. Fleetwood went on to manage movie theatres and patent some inventions, including an exploding artillery shell and a device for alerting projectionists in cinemas that their reel was running out.

† Robinson wore the number 42, and that number has since been retired – not just by his own team, the Brooklyn Dodgers, but by all teams in MLB – out of respect for his achievements. The only time you'll see 42 on a MLB uniform is on 15 April each year, Jackie Robinson Day (the day he made his debut), when every single player wears it.

and no one would ever admit to having made it, but between 1933 and 1946, African Americans were entirely excluded from the game.

Even when the ban was lifted, discrimination remained, particularly when it came to the question of the most important players in American football: the quarterbacks. Between the 1950s and 1970s, despite about a third of NFL players being black, there were hardly any black quarterbacks. The unspoken opinion of the era was that while black players could operate in the more physical roles, the ones that required intellectual capacity and strategic thinking should be reserved mostly for whites. Even in 2022, when a record 29% of quarterbacks in the league were black, that compared with 56% of the entire playing roster.

The first black quarterback in American history was also the first black football coach. Fritz Pollard, by all accounts an outstanding player, was appointed to both positions in the 1920s. As player–coach, he led his side, the Akron Pros, to victory in the first-ever NFL championship in 1920.* The following year, he was their top scorer. Pollard didn't live to see the second black head coach in the NFL: he died three years before Art Shell's appointment in 1989.

Astonishingly, given the racial prejudice at the time, in 1921, the two highest-paid players in pro football were an African American – Pollard – and a Native American, Jim

....

* Despite being one of their star players, Pollard didn't get an invite to the championship trophy presentation. The local black business association held a separate banquet for him instead.

Thorpe.* This would have been impossible to predict a few decades earlier.

STICK IT UP YER JUMPER

In the late 19th century, with the controversial flying wedge tactic recently outlawed, Yale and Princeton were still far and away the strongest teams in the country. Harvard won the odd game here and there. Trailing behind were a few teams from other, less prestigious American universities, such as Lafayette College and Lehigh University. That is, until the Carlisle Indians broke onto the scene.

The team was formed from the Carlisle Indian Industrial School, a boarding school for Native Americans that was founded with the questionable aim of assimilating them into white American society. The justification, epitomised by the frightening mantra 'Kill the Indian, save the man', was that if Native Americans weren't taught the skills necessary to survive and advance in the society that had been imposed on them, they risked disappearing altogether.†

In 1899, a football coach named Glenn 'Pop' Warner joined

....

* They didn't get along. The first time they faced each other as opponents, Thorpe hurled racial slurs at Pollard and said he planned to kill him during the game. Pollard, who was famous for receiving torrents of racial insults with a smile, replied, 'You'll find me down there in your end zone.'

† Students at the Industrial School were made to speak English, cut their hair short if they were male, wear Anglo-American clothes and give up all of their traditional customs.

the school, determined to produce a team that could challenge at the highest echelons of the sport. But to succeed,
they had to be creative; the game was extremely physical
and often very violent, but the players at Carlisle were generally smaller and slighter than those in other American
teams. At the Ivy League universities, the emphasis in
training was on masculinity, physicality and toughness.
Their players easily outstripped the Indians in terms of
strength and aggressiveness, and so, echoing the exploits of
the 1874 Scottish soccer team, the Native Americans had to
focus elsewhere.

Fortunately, as Warner discovered, his team excelled in
creative thinking and strategising, so he capitalised on this.
Together, they developed tactics that centred on speed, agil-
ity, intelligence and, quite often, trickery. During a game
against Harvard in 1902, they hid the ball down the back of
one of their players' jerseys (which they'd commissioned the
local tailor to make specially for the occasion, complete with
the required elastic to hold the ball in place). As soon as the
ball vanished from sight, every other Carlisle player pretended to be holding it, cradling invisible balls against their
stomachs. Harvard pounced on them one after the other,
bringing down multiple opposition players, only to find they
were empty-handed. The 12,000-strong crowd gradually
realised what was happening and laughed uproariously.
Meanwhile, Charles Dillon – the one person who was actually carrying the ball, albeit unconventionally – sprinted
freely up the field, leaped across the goal line and scored a
touchdown.

Harvard actually ended up winning that game by one point, but Warner recalled afterwards that his team treated it almost like a victory, celebrating the joy of that moment all the way home. To have humiliated the Harvard side in such irreverent fashion was coup enough.*

'Muscular Christianity' was all the rage in late-19th-century America; that is, the belief that in a religious sense, the human body is as important as the mind and the spirit, and equally in need of perfecting. Protestants across the country were taught that to be a good Christian man, you had to train your body to reach maximum physicality, so that it was best equipped to serve God. It was partly a response to the concern that the Church was becoming 'feminised'. Women were increasingly permitted roles – albeit strictly limited ones – and tended to be more active at a grassroots level. They outnumbered men in many congregations. Protestants hoped their new thesis of muscular Christianity would bring the men back into the fold, and this thinking underpinned much American sport towards the end of the century.

The Carlisle Indians punctured this preachy, self-important rhetoric by mocking their sporting rivals, while also beating them. They loved, for instance, to impersonate the posh Ivy League accents of their challengers in their own indigenous languages. But at the same time, they proved formidable opposition. In 1911, they won 11 out of their 12 games, including

* A similar trick, which Warner deployed in another game, was having pictures of footballs sewn into the entire team's jerseys so that the opposition would struggle to identify the real ball.

against their old foe, Harvard.* The irony was that their school had been founded as a way of teaching them to imitate their Anglo-American neighbours in order to become their equals. But in football at least, the way they attained this equality was by emphasising their own idiosyncratic style.

Carlisle also produced some of the best athletes the US has ever seen. Most notably, there was the aforementioned Jim Thorpe, who in a 1950 Associated Press poll was voted the greatest athlete of the first half of the century, *and* the greatest football player. Brought up as a member of the Sac and Fox tribe in Oklahoma, his native name of Wa-Tho-Huk meant 'path lit by lightning' and presaged an extremely flashy career. He was the first Native American to win a gold medal at the Olympics – in fact, winning two, for the pentathlon and the decathlon, in 1912. His feat was made all the more impressive by the fact that he achieved it in shoes that didn't fit. On the second day of the Games, his own shoes disappeared, possibly stolen in an attempt to jeopardise his chances. A teammate lent him one shoe (it's unclear why he had only one to lend), which was too small, and Thorpe managed to source another from a rubbish bin, which was too big. He also played professional basketball and baseball,

. . . .

* The Carlisle Indians' most famous win came the following year, when they played the Army Cadets football team, which included future president Dwight D. Eisenhower, playing at halfback. Carlisle subjected the Cadets to their worst defeat of the season. It was viewed afterwards as an extremely symbolic victory, coming 22 years after the massacre at Wounded Knee, where US troops killed more than 250 Lakota people.

and excelled in shot-put, hurdles, high jump, ice skating and even on the dance floor – in 1912, shortly before his Olympic victories, he won first place in the annual intercollegiate ballroom-dancing championship.

Thorpe wasn't the only Carlisle athletics star of the era. Another was Tsökahovi 'Lewis' Tewanima, a Hopi runner who won silver in the 10,000m at the 1912 Olympics, setting an American record that wasn't broken for 52 years. The sporting success of these athletes undoubtedly changed how indigenous peoples were viewed by Anglo-American society. But the difference they made shouldn't be overstated. Even the coverage that celebrated them was often overlaid with racism. After Tewanima's showing at the Olympics, he was photographed at the Carlisle school – where he'd been sent against his and his parents' will in the first place – with the headline above reading: 'Savage Hopi Indians Are Transformed into Model Students'.

While America may claim these men as its own great athletes now, and add their achievements to its medal count, they weren't even US citizens at the time. Native Americans weren't granted citizenship until 1924 (although an exception was made for Thorpe, who got his in 1916), and it wasn't until 1962 that Utah became the last state to give its indigenous population the right to vote. There was still a long, long way to go. Nonetheless, some seeds of progress were planted on the sports fields of the Carlisle Indian Industrial School. While Native Americans adopted Anglo-American sports to greater or lesser extents during the 20th century, one cultural exchange went the other way.

We have seen how one Haudenosaunee team influenced lacrosse* in the UK in the late 19th century, but the sport has been played across North America for almost a millennium. These days, a men's team comprises 10 players, but back in the 1500s you'd rarely have fewer than 100 on each side. According to the sport's governing body, World Lacrosse, some games involved up to 100,000 participants. Matches could last multiple days and took place over many miles of land.

Today, Haudenosaunee teams are recognised as competing for their own individual nations, rather than playing under the US flag. When they play internationally, they travel on Haudenosaunee passports, as opposed to American ones. These are usually accepted, although in 2010 Britain denied them entry to a tournament unless they got US passports, which they refused to do since it challenged their sovereignty. They missed that tournament.

In 2017, the UK found that it could, after all, bend its rules, and permitted the inventors of lacrosse to enter its territory on their own passports, in order to participate in the Women's Lacrosse World Cup. The Iroquois team came 12th out of 15 competing countries. The US won; they and

---

* The word comes from the French for 'the cross', referring to the stick, but the original game, of course, wasn't called this. Names for it included, depending on the language of the players, *baaga'adowe* ('bump hips'), *danahwah'uwsdi* ('little war'), *dehuntshigwa'es* ('men hit a rounded object') and *kabocha-toli* ('stickball'). Today, it's often shortened to 'lax' – a bit of wordplay on the part of its English-speaking inheritors.

Canada dominate lacrosse worldwide, and according to the National Collegiate Athletic Association, it's the US's fastest-growing sport[*] – evidence that this essential element of Native American culture has well and truly crossed the cultural divide.

The fastest-growing sport in the UK in 2022 was women's football. Again, it seemed that the victory of the English Lionesses in Euro 2022 bridged a cultural divide, with an increase in women's teams in the country of more than 30% the following year, and four times more girls aged fourteen and fifteen training to be referees, no doubt inspired by refs such as Stéphanie Frappart, who became the first woman to take charge of a men's World Cup game when Germany played Costa Rica in December 2022. The popularity of women's football in the UK is not totally unprecedented, though: for a brief period after the First World War, the women's game was more popular than the men's.

LADIES FIRST XI

For the first few decades of the 20th century, many football clubs drew their players from factories and other workplaces. When the First World War broke out and women replaced men in these workplaces, they also formed their own football

---

[*] According to the Sport and Fitness Industry Association, however, America's fastest-growing sport is pickleball, a combination of tennis, ping pong and badminton that Bill Gates cites as his favourite sport. It was invented in 1965 and named after the inventor's dog, Pickles.

teams.* Spectators flocked to see them, and the games proved
so popular with fans and players alike that they continued to
play after the war had ended.

One of the best teams was Dick, Kerr Ladies, who worked
at the Dick, Kerr & Company munitions factory in Preston.
Their high point came in 1920, when they played St Helens
Ladies on Boxing Day at Goodison Park in Liverpool, the
home of Everton FC, winning 4–0. 53,000 spectators watched
from the stands, while another 14,000 hopefuls were turned
away due to lack of capacity; for comparison, the average attendance for Everton's men's matches today is about
39,000. That attendance was a record for women's football
in England, and it wasn't beaten until 2019.† It raised the
modern equivalent of £140,000, which went towards helping
unemployed and disabled ex-servicemen.

This success, paradoxically, turned out to be terrible news
for the women's game. Male football players and owners of
men's teams panicked that women were challenging their
monopoly of the sport. This threatened their pride and, more
importantly, their profits. Football's governing body, the FA,
proved very sympathetic to these concerns, and in 1921, it
banned its members from acting as referees or linesmen at

....

* The motive for forming these teams, and charging spectators to
watch their games, was often so that they could raise money to send
to the troops.
† Dick, Kerr Ladies also played the first-ever women's match under
floodlights. They used two anti-aircraft lights for the purpose,
personally sanctioned by the secretary of state for war at the time,
Winston Churchill.

women's games, and barred females from playing on any FA-affiliated football grounds. This amounted to an outright ban, given that the FA controlled every viable stadium in the country. The women had nowhere to play, and their sport had been ruled illegitimate.

Explaining the decision, which was unanimously supported within the organisation, the FA stated: 'Complaints having been made as to football being played by women, Council felt impelled to express the strong opinion that the game of football is quite unsuitable for females and should not be encouraged.'

The ruling lasted until the 1970s, and similar bans were instituted in France (1932), Norway (1931) and West Germany (1955), while Brazil made it illegal for women to play football at all between 1941 and 1981*. The justification in all cases was that the sport was unsuitable for the female body, and – as specified in West Germany's case – 'soul'.† In fact, one of the main reasons behind the relaxation of the ban was that a group of women and (subsequently ostracised) male administrators went ahead and organised some incredibly successful tournaments anyway.

....

* Brazilian footballer Formiga is the only athlete ever to compete in a team sport in seven Olympics. It's an even more incredible feat considering that she was born in 1978, when it was illegal for women to play football in the country.
† The German ban was lifted in 1970, although there was an initial stipulation that women should play only in warm conditions, with shorter matches and a lighter ball. The country has bounced back strikingly since those days, though: between 1989 and 2013, Germany won eight of the first 11 UEFA Women's Euro Championships.

ONCE UPON A TIME IN MEXICO

One of the most successful women's football World Cups, in terms of the host country embracing it, was Mexico 1971. However, it was virtually ignored around the rest of the world, especially in England, where the original Lionesses were treated with apathy both before and during the tournament, and contempt after it.

The event did not have the backing of FIFA or any other national men's football association, and would not have happened at all had there not been two football stadiums in Mexico – the Azteca stadium in Mexico City and the Jalisco stadium in Guadalajara – that because they were privately owned were not forced to ban women's games. The English team, which was not allowed to call itself 'England' and was instead known as 'The British Independents Football Club' (though the press called them 'England'), was run by Harry Batt, a Spanish Civil War veteran who spoke five languages and made his living as a bus driver. Batt had become interested in women's football when his wife June began playing, and the couple were manager and assistant manager respectively of the Chiltern Valley club. When asked to put together an English team for the unofficial World Cup, the couple – surely the only time a husband and wife have co-managed an international football team – jumped at the chance.

The first problem for the Batts was to get 11 players together. They had access to the Chiltern Valley XI, but to give them the best chance of victory, they would need to find players from other teams. The issue was that the Women's Football Association (WFA) refused to recognise the tour, as it tried to walk the tightrope between promoting the women's game and not upsetting the men's game so much that it would lose the small amount of funding that it got from the men's FA and the UK government's Sports Council. Anyone who played in the tournament risked a ban when they returned.

In the end, a team was cobbled together. While they were all among the best prospects in the women's game at the time, it is remarkable just how young the roster was: many of the players were in their late teens; the oldest player on the team was just twenty-four; and two of the forwards, Gillian Sayle and Leah Caleb, were only fourteen and thirteen respectively.

A day before the team were due to fly out to Mexico, they were taken to watch a friendly between Manchester United and Luton Town. The game, which United won 2–0, involved such legends as Bobby Charlton, Denis Law and George Best, and the trip was meant to prepare them for playing at an elite level. It certainly gave them a taste of what lay ahead, though the crowd of under 10,000 was nothing compared to what the team were about to experience on the other side of the Atlantic.

Media attention in the UK was non-existent. The players left British soil with no fanfare whatsoever, and not a single journalist was at the airport. The scene in Mexico City could not have been more different. The team walked down the steps from the plane to a tumult of cheers and flashing bulbs.

The police escorted them to their coach, which took them to the hotel, with crowds lining the streets and verges and even hanging off bridges just to get a glimpse of the English women. The windows of the bus had to be kept open along the way due to the oppressive heat, and suddenly missiles started to rain through them. After a few seconds of shock, it became clear that the fans were throwing small gifts and candies at the players.

If the reception on the journey from the airport was raucous, the crowds in the stadiums themselves were even more vociferous. The players – some of whom were only thirteen and fourteen years old, don't forget – came out for their first two games against Argentina and the hosts Mexico and played in front of more than 100,000 spectators.* It's a crowd that only a handful of today's players, male or female, can boast of having played in front of; the men's World Cup final of 2022, for instance, had a crowd of just 89,000.

The tournament was sponsored by drinks company Martini & Rossi, and in an attempt to appeal to a female audience, the goalposts were painted in pink and white, all the stadium staff wore pink outfits, and pop-up hair and beauty salons appeared outside the stadiums. The mascot was a girl with pigtails carrying a football, called So-cheel. She so resembled England's thirteen-year old striker Leah Caleb that the

* There's no official attendance for this match, but newspaper reports from the time suggest that it was definitely more than 90,000 and the team were told that there were more than 100,000 people there.

Brit was called So-cheel wherever she went. The English team made multiple appearances on Mexican TV, featured constantly in the country's newspapers, signed autographs, stayed in luxury hotels and attended cocktail receptions at the British embassy.

The matches themselves did not go so well for England. They were overpowered by both Latin American teams, going down 4–1 to Argentina and 4–0 to the hosts. At the end of the second game, two of the players were struggling with injury: Carol Wilson had ended up with a broken foot after a tough challenge, while striker Yvonne Farr broke her leg but couldn't be substituted as England had already used up their allocation of replacements. She later recalled: 'I sort of just hopped about and hoped no one passed the ball to me. I asked to come off, but what could we do?'*

Despite these losses, the team came away from the tournament with nothing but positive memories. They were greeted back at their hotel as heroes, were invited to watch the final,† and still required a police escort to get back to the airport.

They arrived back in the UK to no reception whatsoever. It must have felt like they'd had a bizarre fever dream: to have left their homes in silence, then having spent a couple

* One member of the team, Trudy McCaffery, summarised the match against Mexico thus: 'Mexico 4 – Us 1 broken leg, 1 broken foot, 3 strained ligaments, 1 cartilage, 1 badly bruised shoulder & various other bruises, cuts, bumps and knocks.'
† Won by Denmark 3–0, with fifteen-year-old Susanne Augustesen scoring a hat-trick.

of weeks living as rock stars, before arriving back in a country that was completely uninterested in their exploits. There were one or two articles in the British press, but they mostly concentrated on the team's defeats and the players' injuries. One report ended with the quote: 'Don't laugh, one day there may be a female Arsenal!'* The few members of the team who were asked to tell their own story were treated with contempt: when Carol Wilson, for example, was asked to speak at Newcastle United Football Club, she was ridiculed by the interviewer. The entire team was given a three-month ban from any WFA competition, the Chiltern Valley team was broken up, and Harry and June Batt were given life bans from any involvement in women's football. The event did have a positive legacy, though. The WFA organised its first trials for an 'official' England team in 1972, partly to delegitimise the Batts' team. This led to the ban on women playing in FA stadiums being lifted, and in 1972, England contested their first official international, against Scotland.

The 14 women who'd played in Mexico were tracked down by the BBC in 2019 and reunited, almost half a century after the tournament. Remarkably, they were all still in good health, despite the warnings in the past as to the havoc sport might wreak on a woman's body.

---

* Let's charitably call this an incredibly prescient prediction: Arsenal's women's team is the most successful in British history, having won the English league title 15 times, including seven seasons when they remained undefeated throughout.

RUNNING OUT OF EXCUSES

In 1922, a Committee for the Physical Education of Girls was established in the UK to settle the debate that still raged over whether exercise was harmful to women's health. The fundamental concern was that it might damage their childbearing prospects. The committee, comprised largely of medical professionals and teachers, was divided. Advocates of women's sports included one Dr Stanley Dodd, who gamely admitted: 'I have never attended a woman who was not better off, sexually and otherwise, for any muscular sports she may have practised.'

But opponents were equally convinced of their position. A headmistress called Miss Cowdroy observed: 'Hard exercise and games such as hockey and cricket tend to incapacitate a girl for motherhood.'

And a Harley Street doctor called Leonard Williams provided further detail:

Biologists have long recognised the existence of the 'third sex' as a social factor to be reckoned with, and they have long viewed with alarm the increase of these human deviations, owing to our modern ideas about physical education for girls. What precisely happens when we thrust [adolescent] girls into a whirl of exhaustive games like football and hockey is that their energy is unnaturally diverted from the natural channel and spent in sport. The result inevitably is a sterile woman, developing all the male characteristics in her composition or, at best, a woman producing weedy, sickly children.

In short: if women play sport, they risk practically ceasing to be women.*

Running was thought to be particularly dangerous. It was common in the 1960s for doctors to advise European and American women against such exercise, on the grounds that they risked a prolapse of the uterus. Out of apparent concern for their health, the IOC refused to introduce a women's marathon event until 1984.

Some of the committee's scepticism about female runners dated back to 1928. That was the year that women were allowed to participate in track and field events for the first time, including an 800m race. As one journalist at the time recorded: 'Below us on the cinder path were 11 wretched women, 5 of whom dropped out before the finish, while 5 collapsed after reaching the tape.' Reports circulated of the sorry state of the women, who fell prostrate with exhaustion, either without lasting the distance or immediately after they staggered over the finish line. Word spread that the only athlete who hadn't collapsed either during or straight after the race fainted in the dressing room. They had clearly pushed their bodies to a dangerous extreme, and as a result, the IOC

---

* The fear that participation in sports can damage a woman's reproductive organs has been surprisingly persistent. As late as 2010, Gian-Franco Kasper, the president of the International Ski Federation, warned that the female uterus might burst when landing after a ski jump. This supported an earlier statement of his that ski jumping is 'not appropriate for ladies from a medical point of view'. (In case you were wondering, there is no medical evidence to support these claims.)

eliminated women's distance running from future events. Between 1928 and 1960, they were confined to sprints.

Except that this wasn't really what happened. Nine women started the 800m race in 1928, and all nine finished it, as the photos testify. Six of the athletes broke the previously existing world record. There's little evidence of extreme exhaustion in the triumphant expressions of those who broke through the finishing tape first. It's true that after the race, a few of the runners walked to the side of the field and lay down, presumably disappointed they hadn't won and predictably tired after their exertions. But that still happens today in almost every elite-level middle-distance race, involving either men or women.

In spite of bans and attempts to dissuade them, women insisted on participating in long-distance running. The first female marathon world record was set by Dale Greig in the Isle of Wight in 1964. The organisers made a special allowance for her to run it, although to avoid falling foul of Amateur Athletics Association (AAA) rules, they made her start four minutes ahead of everyone else so they could claim she wasn't part of the official event. An ambulance followed her around the course in case she collapsed.

Others found more imaginative ways of getting around the rules. Bobbi Gibb applied to run in the Boston marathon in 1966 but was rejected, with a letter explaining that because of her sex, she was 'not physiologically able'.* So she hid in a

---

* Gibb was an experienced runner. Three years earlier, she'd driven across the US with only her pet dog for company. Wherever she

forsythia bush near the start line until the race began, and then emerged, disguised in a hoodie to conceal her long hair and wearing her brother's Bermuda shorts. As her fellow runners spotted the subterfuge, they shouted their support. When she explained that she was afraid to take off the hoodie in case she was kicked off the course, they called to her: 'We won't let them throw you out. It's a free road!'

Gibb finished ahead of two-thirds of her male competitors. But her time didn't officially count, because she hadn't been allowed to enter. Refusing to make the same mistake, a runner called Kathrine Switzer entered the following year under only her initials, thereby not revealing her sex. It became apparent on the day, though, as she proudly turned up wearing lipstick and eyeliner. A few miles into the race, furious race official Jock Semple seized her and tried to drag her off the course, shouting, 'Get out of my race!'* But he hadn't banked on Switzer's boyfriend running alongside her – and being a nationally ranked hammer thrower known as Big Tom Miller. Big Tom threw Semple to the ground, and Switzer went on to

....

parked the car, she'd run, sometimes up to 40 miles a day. Once, she accidentally crossed the border into Mexico on a 25-mile beach run and was detained by US Border Patrol on her way back. She had to call a friend, Ewing Mitchell, who happened to be a celebrity actor known for playing a sheriff in the TV series *Sky King*, to vouch for her so they'd let her go.

* Semple once gave an interview, saying: 'There's enough competition for women. Why do they want to tackle the toughest thing in the world? It's just women and their stubbornness that just want to do something they're not supposed to do, that's all there is to it.'

The Switzer–Semple set-to. You won't see anyone wearing '261' in today's Boston marathon, as the number was retired in 2017, in Switzer's honour.

finish the race. She later said it was partly fear that kept her running, because she was terrified they'd seriously injured Semple.

Switzer was officially disqualified from the race and banned from the Amateur Athletic Union (AAU). But the media storm around her and Gibb's races, and her subsequent campaigning, helped change the rules, so that by the early 1970s anyone could run a marathon in the US, regardless of sex. And fortunately, Semple survived the incident intact and gradually had a change of heart, eventually becoming a stalwart supporter of female runners. Friends of his insisted that he'd really been less offended by women running, on that infamous occasion, than by the fact that anyone had dared to break the rules of his beloved Boston marathon.

Semple was always a fiery character, having spent a tough childhood in the slums of Glasgow, before emigrating to the US in the 1920s. But he was also 'a complex mix of irascible, funny, hot-tempered and lovable'. That was according to one of his great friends in later life – one Kathrine Switzer. After that rocky start to their relationship, the two of them became very close.* She visited him in hospital just before he died, and as she sat at his bedside, he told her, 'I made you famous, lass.' And, she agreed, he was absolutely right. For most of these sporting pioneers, it is the barriers placed in their way that make them famous or worthy of note. The people who end up forging a path for minorities and excluded groups, and fighting for their right to be included, usually don't start out with such noble ambitions. They simply want to play.

GIRL BANNED

That was certainly true of Ewa Kłobukowska, who ran the final leg of the 1964 women's Olympic sprint relay, over-turning a hefty deficit to push the American favourites into second place. The Polish time of 43.6 seconds was the fastest any team had ever run the distance; in fact, the second-placed Americans also beat the previous world record with their

* Semple published an autobiography in 1981, and Switzer turned up at the book launch to surprise him. As he stood at the podium to give his speech, she sprinted onto the stage wearing the same tracksuit she'd worn for the marathon 14 years earlier and shouting – to his great amusement – 'Get out of my race!'

time of 43.9 seconds. As she celebrated with her team, which included her childhood friend Irena Kirszenstein (the two were always known as K&K and were only seventeen years old when they won gold), she teased the officials, pretending to hand the baton to them, repeatedly, before pulling it away at the last second.

Kłobukowska was a sporty but shy teenager who also excelled academically and hoped to become an economist, as well as pursue sporting glory. A few months before the Olympics, she had fractured a bone in her foot, and it looked like she would miss out completely, but she got on the exercise bike, her foot healed, and not only did she take the top prize at the Olympics, it also looked like she had a stellar career ahead of her.

As we have seen in the context of drug-taking, there was much distrust between the Communist states and the West in the 1960s, and one suspicion was that the other side were allowing men to take part in the guise of women in order to win medals and prove their country's superiority. As a result, at an athletics competition in Budapest in 1967, Kłobukowska found herself, along with all the other women, naked in front of three gynaecologists to prove that they were female. Having gone through such a humiliating ordeal with no problems, it was a complete shock when, later that year, she received the results from a cheek-swab test, which said that she had 'one chromosome too many to be declared female for the purpose of athletic competition'. According to the authorities, this woman who had lived her whole life as a woman, with no suggestion that she was anything but, was not female enough to take part in international competition.

The Western press jumped on this as evidence that the Soviets were indeed allowing men to compete as women. Tasteless headlines such as 'Kłobukowska Misses Test for Misses' in the *Washington Post* and 'Who Goes There? Ex-Miss or Missing X?' in *Newsweek* played their part in hounding Kłobukowska out of the sport.* It turned out that she had mosaicism, a genetic condition where some cells in your body have a different make-up to others. In her case, some of them contained the XY sex chromosomes, while others contained XX. The Polish Olympic Committee still considers her case to be a great miscarriage of justice and points out that no other tests were carried out: they didn't measure her hormone levels, for instance, to see if she had more testosterone than her opponents. She was awarded the highest gong available in Poland, the Golden Cross of Merit, and the International Olympic Committee has never removed her gold medal from the record books. World Athletics has expunged her world records, though, which means the American team from 1964 is the only one in history to have run a world record time in an Olympic final and not won gold.

You need only to look at the back pages (and sometimes the front ones) of newspapers today to see that the question of gender in women's sport has not gone away. It's

---

* They were less vocal about Austrian skier Erik Schinegger, who failed a gender test in the same year, after winning the women's downhill at the 1966 World Championships. Schinegger, who competed under the name Erika before his own intersex condition was discovered, publicly handed his gold medal to runner-up Marielle Goitschel in 1988, but she then presented it back to him.

uncontroversial to say that the debate is not black and white, not least because, as Kłobukowska's case shows, biological sex is not always black and white. As is so often the case, international organised sports are currently behind the curve and scrambling to create the rules that will keep everyone happy. In many cases, nobody is.

The trend, in democratic societies at least, is towards inclusion in sport. This is partly because it generally has the support of the masses. It's noticeable, delving into first-hand accounts of the Aboriginal First XI, the Carlisle Indians or the 1971 Mexican women's football World Cup, how positively ordinary people responded to them. With some exceptions, of course, the overwhelming popular response was celebratory and focused on the games themselves, not the backgrounds of the people playing them. The bigotry and repression came from above, driven by vested interests, and with the support of some of the media.

The truth is that in sport, most people love an underdog or an outsider. Ancient Roman gladiators, the lowest of the low in social terms – usually enslaved people – enjoyed enormous popular support.* Perhaps we like them because they make for an infinitely better story. Or maybe the outsiders are easier to identify with – most people are closer to being underdogs in society than overlords. Either way, however

....

* Gladiator schools used to be daubed with amorous graffiti, left by female admirers. Women wore jewellery in the shape of swords and spears to express their fandom – the equivalent of today's football jerseys.

much the people operating the levers of power attempt to suppress this instinct, they'll be fighting a losing battle for as long as the masses have a say in it. Sport is all about the fans.

13

WE'RE GONNA DEEP-FRY YER PIZZAS

WHY THERE'S NO SPORT WITHOUT THE FANS

> I wish people would love everybody else the way
> they love me. It would be a better world.
> **Muhammad Ali**

Més que un club – 'More than a club' – is the motto of Barcelona football team, but it could apply to any professional sports team in the world. The phrase is an acknowledgement that Barcelona games aren't just about 11 of the club's players running around on the pitch, any more than the 2003 Wimbledon final between Venus and Serena Williams was about two sisters hitting a ball back and forth. The reason such games matter is that millions of people believe that they matter. If it weren't for these people – the fans – players and staff wouldn't get paid, stadiums wouldn't be filled, matches wouldn't be broadcast, there would be no market for giant foam fingers[*] and no one would be foolish enough to publish books about sport.

....

[*] It's unclear who invented the giant foam finger that is so ubiquitous at American sports events. In 1971, an Iowan high-school student called Steve Chmelar made a huge hand, with the trademark oversized pointing index finger, out of mesh and papier mâché. He brought it to a basketball game and it was featured in the local paper. As of 2012, he still had the original. In 1978, a teacher in Texas called Geral Fauss made plywood hands in exactly the same shape to sell at football games. Fauss's company has now sold millions of them, and Fauss says he never saw Chmelar's version. Chmelar, however, believes his was the inspiration.

Some supporters impact their favourite sports even more directly. In 1889, a football fan and engineer called John Alexander Brodie went to see his team, Everton, play Accrington Stanley. When Everton sent the ball past the Stanley goalkeeper, to score what should have been the winner, there was nothing behind the posts to catch the ball, and the referee couldn't be sure it was a fair goal. It was disallowed, Everton had to be satisfied with a draw, and Brodie went home determined to fix this problem and avoid any future injustices. Within a year, he was granted a patent for the first goal-net design,* and within two years, goal nets were made compulsory for all FA matches. Fittingly, the first team to put the ball in the back of Brodie's newly designed net was Everton. Brodie later went on to build the world's longest road tunnel at the time, which ran from Liverpool to Birkenhead under the River Mersey, and was also responsible for selecting the site and planning the layout of New Delhi. Yet he claimed the project he was most proud of was the football net.

On occasion fans have helped the officials in real time. In 19th-century baseball games, umpires sometimes consulted the crowd if they weren't sure about a decision. And if a player hit the ball out of the ground, the game had to stop for five minutes while everyone in the crowd went looking for it. Similarly, due to Shrewsbury Town Football Club's ground, Gay Meadow, being right beside the River Severn, for many years a man

---

* Brodie's initial design was a net with bells attached to it that would ring when the ball touched it.

The Shrewsbury Town coracle. Similar boats have been used on the River Severn for centuries. In fact, when the world's first cast-iron bridge was built nearby in 1781, many locals refused to use it, preferring to paddle across the river in their coracles.

called Fred Davies would bring a coracle – a small, round, one-man boat – to the game and run off to collect any stray balls that were kicked into the water mid-match, much to the amusement of the crowd.* His father did the job before him, and he would get a fee from the club for every ball he saved before it disappeared over a nearby weir, at which point it would be lost forever. Until 2018, anyone watching a golf tournament on television who saw an infringement of the rules could phone up and inform the officials. The player might then

---

* Davies did try using a motorboat for a while, but he found that the cost of fuel made his small ball-retrieving business unviable, so he returned to the coracle.

be hit with penalty shots; worse still, if the player had already filled in their scorecard, they would get an extra penalty for claiming the wrong score and might even be disqualified, all thanks to an eagle-eyed busybody sitting on their sofa.

Nowadays, viewers might be less likely to influence the outcome of a game, but they can still impact some of the finer details, such as dress code. The outfits worn in beach volleyball have been a source of much debate over the years, in terms of how spectators might respond to them. Beach volleyball matches often attract huge television audiences; during the 2016 Olympics, it was the most popular sport broadcast, with viewers across the world watching a total of 2.6 billion hours' worth of play. The games tend to have a more fun, 'party' atmosphere than traditional sports. The sand, sun and swimsuits lend matches a holiday-esque, laid-back attitude, which means beach volleyball has sometimes been viewed more as a spectacle than a competitive contest. In 1997, former player Gabrielle Reece went as far as saying: 'Though no one can deny the athleticism, beach volleyball has nothing to do with sports; it has to do with entertainment. Our challenge now is to market it, to get it to the next level.'

Part of that marketing meant emphasising the fact that the sport involved attractive women wearing small bikinis.*

* Because beach volleyball players, both male and female, don't wear many clothes, sponsors have to find innovative ways of advertising on them. They literally do that – advertise *on* their bodies, offering players temporary tattoos of their logos. The top-ranked men's player in 2007, for instance, played with a picture of an ice pack on his left arm and a pair of socks on his right.

Prior to the 2012 Olympic Games, the International Volleyball Federation's dress code for women's beach volleyball stated that bikinis were allowed 'a maximum side width of seven centimetres' and had to be cut at an upward angle towards the hip – i.e. in the style of briefs, not shorts. This is in contrast to men, who could play in shorts and tank tops. Women were also allowed to play in one-piece suits, but because this was inconvenient, making trapped sand more difficult to remove, most found that impractical.

Many female players didn't mind the aesthetics being part of the appeal. One of Reece's contemporaries, 2004 Olympic bronze medallist Holly McPeak, argued: 'If people want to come check us out because they're scoping our bodies, I don't have a problem with that, because I guarantee they'll go home talking about our athleticism.'

Attitudes are changing, as have the rules. Largely out of respect for cultures in which bikinis are unacceptable, since 2012 female players have been allowed to wear shorts and a sleeved or sleeveless top. As it turns out, however, the vast majority have stuck to smaller bikinis, though these days it's for practical reasons rather than their public appeal: players find that they allow a better range of motion and stop them from overheating.

Of course, one of the oldest-known sports often crosses the line between 'sport' and 'entertainment' much more overtly. While still exhibiting skill and physicality, professional wrestling contests are non-competitive, and wrestlers do all that they can to entertain audiences. This usually involves adopting specific personas. In China, where it's a relatively new phenomenon, some of the most well-known professional wrestlers include Curry Kid (wears a paper plate of rice on his head), Bamboo Crusher (who is made up to look like a panda) and Steve the English as a Second Language Teacher (who brings exam textbooks into the ring).

Pro wrestling goes through phases of enjoying enormous popularity. In 1958, it was cited by the *TV Times* as the most popular sport on British TV. During its heyday, the 1960s–'80s, it was always screened at 4 p.m. on Saturdays, and shopkeepers used to complain that all their custom dried up as soon as the programme started. ITV would show it each year before the FA Cup final – the biggest game in the national football calendar – and the wrestling would garner more viewers than the big match.

Babe Ruth worked as a pro wrestling referee both during and after his baseball career.* He loved the spotlight, and the job suited his big, charismatic personality. He was famous off the pitch for living entirely on hot dogs, beer and cigars;

....

* Another celebrity unexpectedly involved in pro wrestling is actor David Arquette. He became obsessed with it after making a film about the sport in 2000, to the extent that it put a strain on his relationship with his then wife Courteney Cox. As the actress recalled: 'It was a lot to handle to see David at this point. He was going to wrestling matches and he was loud, and it was kind of insane. I remember feeling embarrassed.' The oddest thing about this is that it mirrors almost perfectly a *Friends* plotline from a couple of years previously, when Monica (played by Cox) has to end a relationship because her boyfriend has become so obsessed with becoming the Ultimate Fighting champion.

one day, between games, he consumed between 12 and 18 (accounts vary) hot dogs in one sitting and had to be rushed to hospital with acute indigestion. And he loved being an entertainer, particularly for children. Even when he was in hospital with cancer, he spent his time signing autographs on pieces of paper and dropping them from the window to the waiting kids below.

I'M PICKIN' UP BETTER VIBRATIONS

It's not just players who know they're there to entertain the crowd; the people behind the scenes in all mainstream sports are constantly working to engage the masses as well. Sound engineers play a big role in this. When you watch sports on TV, the sounds you hear are often faked because it's not practical to record them in the moment. A sound mixer will be there, watching what's happening and adding the noises you expect at the right moments. In the 2012 Olympics, for instance, the sound recordist took a boat out before the rowing competitions and recorded the noise of his oars slapping the water. He then played these sounds at the right moments during the races. In reality, the sound of the helicopter and chase boat filming the race would have obscured the sound of oars hitting water.

In other instances, real sounds can be used, but they're emphasised to maximise their impact. In gymnastics, microphones are strapped to the bars and balance beams, transmitting the sound of the vibrations – a bouncing, springing noise – as the gymnasts perform on them. In reality, even if you were standing right next to the bar, these sounds would be almost inaudible, but any TV viewer can be privy to them via these mics. And the engineer who masterminded the sound of the 2008 Wimbledon final between Rafa Nadal and Roger Federer, for which the team was nominated for a BAFTA, emphasised the importance of skilful fades. He explained that it's crucial to create a sense of 'hush' during tense points, and so the volume of the crowd is turned down for those moments. But he has to be ready to fade the sound back up within a split second, in time for the cheers and applause that come at the end of a thrilling point. This ensures that maximum excitement is transmitted into people's homes.

Some of the most dramatic sounds in tennis come between games, when the players are sitting or standing next to the umpire's chair. John McEnroe made this most apparent in the 1980s, with his frequent outbursts at umpires. After that, microphones were added to the umpire's chair to make sure any interesting shouting matches between players and umpires were picked up for the benefit of the TV and radio audiences.

In any sport, the narrative around it, with its varied characters, plotlines and human drama, is a huge pull factor. The organisers are well aware of this. It's partly about making sure the viewer can see the perfect drop shot being played or feel the tension as a gymnast wobbles on a balance beam. But it wouldn't be nearly so compelling if broadcasts didn't also emphasise the personalities that get revealed along the way or the tangled back story (and there always is one), of which a particular match is only a part. That's why when rank outsiders Leicester City, at odds of 5,000–1, won the English Premier League in 2016, the entire country seemed to erupt in celebration. At the moment when their victory was secured, Twitter activity in the UK suddenly surged by 86%, and for once, it was almost entirely celebratory. Leicester fans accounted for only a small proportion of that. As one tweeter put it: 'You don't have to be a fan of Leicester to be crying tears of joy today.'*

SEX SELLS

One of the most salient examples of bigger audiences being lured in by a broader narrative was tennis's famous 'Battle of the Sexes' in September 1973. Pitting former men's world number 1 Bobby Riggs against the then women's world number 1, Billie Jean King, this was a contest everyone could engage with, regardless of whether they usually followed the sport. As a result, it was the most-watched tennis match of all time, with over 90 million people worldwide tuning in and a record 30,492 in attendance.† The showmanship on both

....

* Even Leicester's rivals managed begrudging respect for their achievement. The website Nottingham Forest News ran an article entitled 'Should Forest Fans Be Happy for Leicester?' with the conclusion that they could at least celebrate the contribution of the Leicester captain Wes Morgan, who had previously played for Forest.
† The latter record was subsequently broken, with the current record of 51,954 going to another game with a strong narrative: the 'Match for Africa' charity doubles game between Roger Federer/Bill Gates and Rafa Nadal/Trevor Noah.

sides was enough to satisfy them all. Riggs had hammed up his misogynist approach in the lead-up, with statements like 'She's a woman, and they don't have the emotional stability [to beat a man],' and 'Women belong in the bedroom and kitchen, in that order.' His friends claimed it was mostly an act, to drum up publicity. If so, it worked.

On the day, King was carried onto the court on a gold, feather-framed litter that was held aloft by four burly men dressed in togas. Riggs was wheeled in on a rickshaw by six female models dubbed 'Bobby's Bosom Buddies'. He presented King with a giant Sugar Daddy-branded lollipop,* representing the fact she was 'a sucker'. In return, she went to the trouble of transporting a live piglet to the court, which she handed over to him as an embodiment of his chauvinism. The game itself was an easy victory for King (6–4, 6–3, 6–3). In a lesser-known twist to their tale, the two became good friends afterwards (although King admitted she also found him 'insufferable'). She was with him the night before he died and remembers him saying to her: 'Billie Jean, we really did change things that day, didn't we?'

Of course, there was a long way to go. King reflected in 2018, for instance, that there wasn't a single female reporter at the 'Battle of the Sexes' match. As at almost all her other press conferences, the members of the media she faced were exclusively male. One of them said on air as she walked onto

---

* Riggs was sponsored for the occasion by the Sugar Daddy confectionery brand. They paid him $50,000 to wear their logo-emblazoned jacket. He took it off after three games.

the court: 'Sometimes you get the feeling that if she ever let down her hair to her shoulders and took off her glasses, you'd have someone vying for a Hollywood screen test.'

And it wasn't just the battle against sexism that King fought during her career. In 1981, she was outed by her female lover, Marilyn Barnett.* Rather than deny it, as instructed by her publicist, she held a press conference admitting to the affair – and lost all her sponsorships overnight as a result.

But the 'Battle of the Sexes', because of the attention it attracted, certainly helped convince a sceptical world that women's tennis could be just as good to watch as men's. For King, it wasn't about the one-on-one sporting contest itself; it was about how the public viewed it. As she said: 'I was not playing the game to prove that women could beat men, I was playing to prove that women had the same entertainment value.'

The mass engagement with the King vs Riggs contest is testament to the fact that sport is at its most compelling when it's set in a wider context and engages with issues that are of universal appeal. Sometimes, these issues can swamp the sport itself. In 1990, a football match between Croatian team Dinamo Zagreb and Serbia's Red Star Belgrade proved to be a spectacular example of this. Both Serbia and Croatia were part of Yugoslavia at the time, which was on the cusp of splitting into five (and later six, and then seven) separate nations. Croatia had just held its first legitimate elections since the Second World War, which had been won by a pro-independence candidate. Suffice to say, it was a tense time for the region.

....

* Barnett, living up to her name, was a hair stylist.

POLITICAL FOOTBALL

Hardcore supporters of Red Star call themselves 'Delije', meaning 'heroes', while Dinamo fans are the 'Bad Blue Boys' (BBB).* Between them, on 13 May 1990, they initiated the biggest football riot in Yugoslavia's history. It began with stones being thrown by the BBB and ended with Zagreb's Maksimir stadium being torn up and death threats made. There were over 60 injuries as a result of stabbings, shootings, beatings and tear gas. Even some of the players – who were unable to get in more than a few minutes of play before the pitch was stormed – got involved in the fighting.

Many commentators agree that at this point, both Delije and BBB were operating as nationalist paramilitary organisations as much as football fans. Red Star and Dinamo were the two best teams in Yugoslavia, so the sporting rivalry was intense, but this was not just about football. The leader of the Delije, a man known as Arkan, went on to become a warlord in charge of a paramilitary group. He was indicted by the International Criminal Court for crimes against humanity in 1999 and assassinated in 2000.

On that day in 1990, the riot began with nationalist songs being sung and patriotic flags waved. It's often cited as a trigger for the Yugoslavian wars that broke up the country a year later, although it was really much more of a symptom than a

* The name was inspired by the 1983 film *Bad Boys*, starring Sean Penn, which follows the life of young gang members in a juvenile correctional institution.

cause of political tensions. Nevertheless, there's now a plaque outside the stadium that reads: 'To Dinamo fans for whom the war started on May 13, 1990, and ended with them laying down their lives on the altar of the Croatian homeland.'*

There are, of course, endless examples of football and politics becoming inextricably intertwined. Sometimes, that was the intention in the first place. In the 1920s, Austrian football was dominated by Hakoah Vienna, a sports club that had been founded in 1909 by a dentist and a librettist with the explicit aim of helping the cause of Zionism (the founding of a Jewish homeland). At the time, Jews were banned from joining other Austrian sports clubs, so Hakoah was the only option for aspiring sports stars. Hakoah Vienna's football team were soon much more than a political tool, becoming what some have called the 'greatest Jewish sports team of the 20th century'. In 1923, they thrashed West Ham, one of the best English teams, 5–0.† After the game, one of the English

* The same is true, incidentally, of the so-called 'Football War' of 1969 between El Salvador and Honduras. The Salvadorian military did launch an incursion into neighbouring territory after a riot during a match between the countries' national teams, but again, political tensions had been simmering for some time. The conflict is sometimes called the 100-hour war because a ceasefire was quickly agreed.
† The player who scored the final goal of this match, Tibby Wegner, managed to escape to England during the Nazi occupation. He went on to invent the sweatband, and entered into business with tennis player Fred Perry to sell it. It became the first item in the Fred Perry clothing line – still a multi-million-dollar sports and leisure brand today. Wegner also designed the still-iconic Fred Perry laurel-wreath logo. In an ironic twist of fate, the brand has repeatedly

players stormed into their dressing room to announce: 'You are the best team I have ever seen, and believe me, I've seen hundreds of games of football.'

Hakoah was part of the 'muscular Judaism' movement that began alongside muscular Christianity in the late 19th century. It sought to promote Zionism and defeat anti-Semitism by building mental and physical strength among the Jewish people. It was effective in a sporting sense, at least, where its impact is still felt today: the proportion of Olympic medals awarded to Jewish athletes since 1896 is fourteen times greater than Jews as a proportion of the global population.

Hakoah was a sports club that went beyond football, training up some of the best Austrian swimmers, gymnasts and athletes of the era. Uniquely among mixed-gender sports clubs worldwide at the time, its swimming club was founded by three women. When the women's swimming team competed away from home, they'd be accompanied by Hakoah's male wrestling team, who would step in to help in the event of anti-Semitic attacks. The club put forward Austria's only two medal-winners at the European Aquatic Championships in 1927, Hedy Bienenfeld and Fritzi Löwy. Austria didn't get another medal in this tournament until 2002.

The religious or cultural element that underpins many sports teams isn't always so positive. Fans of Glasgow's

....

been embraced over the years by far-right groups, from 1970s racist skinheads to today's fascist Proud Boys organisation. In 2020, the company withdrew its black and yellow shirts after the Proud Boys adopted them as their own call sign.

ever-warring football teams, Celtic and Rangers (collectively known as the Old Firm), have taken a lot of criticism over the years for bringing sectarianism into the stadium.* Celtic fans are traditionally Catholics who trace their heritage to 19th-century Irish expats, while Rangers fans are traditionally Protestants who support a united Britain. These roots are felt so keenly that it's more common to see Irish flags flying at the Celtic end, and Union Jacks flying at the Rangers end, than it is to see Scottish flags anywhere.

In this context, it seems unsurprising that in 2012 the Scottish Parliament passed a law stating that people singing football chants could be charged with sectarian incitement. It targeted football fans exclusively and could be applied when they were within grounds, entering or leaving a match, or travelling to one.† The lyrics of certain songs appear to justify the law. Some Rangers fans would sing of being 'up to our knees in Fenian blood' (from 'Billy Boys'), while Celtic followers might chant lyrics like 'North men, south men, comrades all, soon there'll be no Protestants at all'.

It has always been a minority of fans, on both sides, who have sung lyrics this extreme. And even though they might

....

* Celtic and Rangers fans have acted as warring tribes for as long as the clubs have existed. Back in 1909, the Scottish Cup final between the two teams was abandoned after a riot in which fans started fires on the pitch by burning the goalposts. When the fire brigade turned up, the fans grabbed their hoses and set fire to those too.
† The Act contained the provision that 'a person may be regarded as having been on a journey to or from a regulated football match whether or not the person attended or intended to attend the match'.

be very offensive, it's not quite so clear that these chants definitely amount to sectarianism. Social anthropologist Joseph Webster has shown that the songs don't necessarily incite violence and aren't generally used to antagonise the opposing team at all. They're actually sung to benefit the side that the singers are supporting, and their impact is generally confined to this. This makes sense, given that they're often sung in pubs or on transport where only one side's fans are present and there is no opposition to antagonise. As a result of Webster's arguments (among others), in 2018, six years after it was passed into law, the Offensive Behaviour at Football and Threatening Communications Act became the only bill ever to be repealed by the Scottish Parliament.*

In other cases of political or cultural groups using football as a means to express themselves, the sport itself becomes almost irrelevant. The Italian ultras† are a famous example of organised, extreme football fans, but as author Tobias Jones, who lived with them and studied them in depth, writes: 'One of the ways to spot the ultras is that many aren't paying

....

* Celtic and Rangers are far from unique in the world of football in terms of the intensity of their rivalry. In 2018, a cup final match between the Argentinian teams Boca Juniors and River Plate, who between them boast the support of 67% of the country's football fans, had to be held in Madrid. It was considered too dangerous and potentially explosive for it to be held anywhere in their home country.
† The name 'ultra' comes from 'ultra-royalists' who used extreme methods to try to restore the monarchy after the French Revolution. They were so pro-monarchy that they even thought King Louis XVIII was not pro-monarchy enough.

attention to the game .... Being an ultra isn't about watching the football, but watching each other.'

Ultras are often said to be ruled by a sense of *campanilismo* – pride in where they're from, or literally 'attachment to the bell tower'. Romantic though that may sound, they have a reputation for being involved in violence, bank robberies, drug dealing, fascism and even the occasional murder. A club's ultras will often be at war with each other, and stadiums are sometimes split into different sections for the various rival groups, despite them supporting the same team.

There's no doubt the ultras bring energy to games, leading the chants, waving banners and taking centre stage among the supporters. But they rarely generate a positive atmosphere and are often associated with far-right extremism. In the late 1990s, the most powerful ultras supporting Italian team Varese called themselves Blood and Honour, inspired by an English neo-Nazi organisation of the same name – which is taken from the Hitler Youth motto *Blut und Ehre*.

Jones did find some left-wing ultras during his time in Italy – specifically, those supporting the lower-league team Cosenza. The Cosenza ultras are an anti-fascist organisation whose projects have included finding beds for immigrants and the homeless, opening their own food bank and building a playground for disabled children. One of their most powerful members is Padre Fedele, a Franciscan friar whose two professed obsessions are football and helping the poor. That said, the group is still fanatical, courts trouble with the police, is prone to fighting and often shows limited interest in the football itself: prominent members will face away from the match during play to focus on 'conducting' the crowd instead. But football is by no means alone in having fans who sometimes lose sight of the sport itself.

DISCO INFERNO

In 1979, a promotional event at a baseball game sparked one of the most controversial moments not just in the history of baseball, but also in that of disco music. Disco was hugely popular at the time, with musicians like the Bee Gees and Donna Summer dominating the charts. In 1978, disco tracks had been at number 1 in the *Billboard* charts for 37 weeks of the year. Rock fans were perturbed, fearing this signalled – and was causing – the decline of their own preferred genre. Their self-appointed spokesperson was a DJ in Chicago called Steve Dahl.[*] He'd started an anti-disco organisation called Insane Coho Lips and spent much of his time on air ranting about disco and snapping such records in half or dragging the needle across them.

So far, so unrelated to sports. But Dahl came up with an idea to promote his campaign: he came to an agreement with the Chicago White Sox[†] baseball team, who were due to play the Detroit Tigers on 12 July, that if people turned up with a disco record and donated it for destruction, they'd get in for 98

[*] Dahl may have been a touch biased, as he'd recently been fired from a radio station that had decided to switch its focus from rock to disco music.
[†] It's truly remarkable, when researching the history of controversy in baseball, just how often the White Sox come up.

cents. Dahl's plan was to throw all the records into a dumpster and explode them. Attendance at games had been poor that season, and so White Sox owner Bill Veeck was keen on anything that might boost numbers. He made sure the event was heavily promoted across Illinois, for weeks in advance. On the night, the 50,000 seats all sold out, and another 20,000 people were left outside the stadium, brandishing their records. It was clear that most had come for the explosion, not the baseball.

Two games were due to be played that evening, and in between them Dahl took centre stage and set off his explosives. Shattered vinyl rained down over the field and a crater was gouged into the ground. After that, things got out of hand. Thousands of people stormed onto the field chanting 'Disco sucks!', stoking up a large bonfire, stealing the bases

Disco Demolition Night at Comiskey Park, Chicago. Which rapidly escalated into 'Comiskey Park Demolition Night'.

from the pitch and destroying the batting cage. Police in full riot gear had to be deployed, and 39 people were arrested. Unsurprisingly, the second game was called off.

The so-called Disco Demolition Night was all the more unsettling because, as ushers at the park noted afterwards, it wasn't just disco records that were offered up. Some people seemed to have turned up with any records they could find by black artists, whether they were disco, funk, soul or R&B. Rock and roll was a genre dominated by straight, white males; disco was much more welcoming of, and likely to be created by, black Americans, Latin Americans, women and homosexuals. Many have since argued that this crowd of almost exclusively white people burning thousands of records by largely black and minority artists was an expression of the underlying racist, homophobic and sexist sentiments in society at the time.

Dahl still defends his actions vigorously, and insists the riot had nothing to do with any kind of bigotry. It was, he maintains, simply a bunch of kids trying to undermine a type of music they hated. If that's the case, it was very success-ful. Radio stations and record labels suddenly abandoned their support of disco and reverted to rock; the Best Disco Recording category at the Grammy Awards was cancelled; and almost overnight, the popularity of disco music went into steep decline. But whether the decline of disco was due to the event or whether the event was a symptom of the decline, and whether Disco Demolition Night was about music or cultural forces more damaging than that, one thing is certain: it had nothing to do with baseball.

FIGHTING CHANTS

Whether crowds in sports stadiums are 100% focused on the game or partly swept up in other events, they unquestionably, unfailingly know how to make noise. In Australia, people who shout support for their team and jeer at the opponent are known as 'barrackers'.* Australian cricket even has its own legendary historical barracker, Stephen Harold Gascoigne, more commonly known as Yabba. Born in Sydney in 1878, Yabba got his nickname early on in life for his habit of talking a lot, and loudly. His job as a rabbit-seller allowed him to practise his art as he drove around in a pony cart† yelling 'Rabbo, wild rabbo' in 'a voice that could be heard a mile away', according to the *Sydney Morning Herald*. In the first decades of the 20th century, he made further use of his skill by attending cricket and rugby matches and shouting advice and insults at the players. He was known for his witty put-downs, which included:

'Those are the only balls you've touched all day!' (to a batsman readjusting his groin protector)

'Put a penny in him, George, he's stopped registering' (to an umpire who also happened to be a gas inspector, when a batsman failed to score any runs)

* The word appeared in the 1880s, probably derived from an Aboriginal word, *borak* (meaning 'no'). Aussies used to have a similar phrase, 'to poke borak', meaning 'to poke fun/ridicule', although it's now fallen into disuse.
† Yabba once somehow managed to run himself over while driving this cart.

'Bowl him down a piano and see if he can play that' (to a
bowler, when the batsman was failing to strike any of his
balls)

'Leave our flies alone, they're the only friends you've got' (to
an English cricketer waving flies away from his face)

'I wish you were a statue and I were a pigeon'

Nonetheless, the players were fond of him, and when
English batsman Jack Hobbs played his last match in Sydney,
he went over to shake Yabba's hand afterwards. A statue of
Yabba now sits, silently barracking, at the Sydney Cricket
Ground.

Another famous heckler is Robin Ficker, who vocally supported the Washington Bullets basketball team in the 1990s.
He'd always sit behind the opposition's coaching bench with
a megaphone to distract them. When the Bullets played the
Chicago Bulls, for instance, he read aloud raunchy passages
from their coach's sex-filled autobiography. And when he
mocked the bad dress sense of Utah Jazz coach Frank Layden,
it sent Layden into such a rage that he had to be physically
restrained by security. Ficker was even flown out to an NBA
Finals game by the Bullets' coach so that he could distract
the opposition there – though the plan backfired when he was
ejected from the game within the first quarter.[*]

. . . .

[*] Ficker used to be a practising attorney but was recently disbarred,
following multiple violations over the years that culminated in
him being found guilty of lying to a judge in 2019. In 2022, he
unsuccessfully ran to be governor of Maryland.

Other supporters make a name for themselves not by heckling the opposition, but by showing their love of their own team in the most eye-catching ways possible. Most Newcastle United followers are familiar with the sight of 23-stone Keith 'Beefy' Roberts standing front and centre at every football match, always shirtless, regardless of the weather (frequently inclement at St James' Park), and with an NUFC tattoo stretched across his belly. He's such a well-known feature that in 2011, the club's merchandise outlet released a T-shirt featuring a photo of his bare torso, so that anyone could get the 'Beefy' look.* Sheffield Wednesday have the similarly perpetually topless Paul Gregory, better known as 'Tango' (because he was thought to resemble the orange man in the 1990s 'You've been Tangoed' adverts). Tango had to take a year off his barracking after being banned from their stadium for verbally abusing a steward.† Over in America, NFL fan Emmett John Pearson expressed his

---

* 'Beefy' now sits as an independent councillor on South Tyneside Council. He led his campaign with a promise to crack down on antisocial behaviour (although in 2019, police were called to intervene in a physical altercation involving him and some other councillors and campaigners).

† Arsenal also had to ban one of their fans from attending games – and in this case, it was an even more internationally recognised name than Tango. Osama bin Laden biographers claim that he became an avid Arsenal fan when he visited London in the early 1990s on a recruitment drive. Some people have testified to seeing him at matches, and there were reports that he bought an Ian Wright jersey for his son. After 9/11, Arsenal clarified that he would not be welcome at the ground.

support not with tattoos, but with facial hair. In 1975, he swore not to cut his beard until his team, the Minnesota Vikings, won the Super Bowl. He died in 2013 with a 38-year-old beard.

England's cricket team has an organised group of supporters, the Barmy Army, who follow it everywhere. They started out as a group of around 30 independent backpackers who had gone to Australia for the 1994–5 Ashes tour. They became famous for their vocal, confusingly cheerful and extremely enthusiastic support in the face of England's abject defeat and were dubbed 'Barmy Army' by the Australian media. Now, they're a fully fledged company, selling tickets and merchandise, organising travel packages, giving advice to cricket fans abroad, raising money for charity and releasing their own pop songs. Lord's is the only cricket ground in England that doesn't specifically allocate seats for them.

The songs, more than anything, are the Barmy Army's trademark. They insult their own team as much as the opposition, with verses such as:

> *It isn't easy when your team*
> *Makes a nightmare out of a dream*
> *It isn't easy, patiently*
> *Watching them snatch defeat*
> *From the jaws of victory*
>
> *The Barmy Army marches on*
> *Every hope of victory gone*
> *The Barmy Army stands the test*

Happy that when it comes to losing
We're the best!*

Singing does have the power to distract the opposition. Players have admitted to being put off by the Barmy Army in the past. Australian bowler Mitchell Johnson said he couldn't help getting their lyrics – 'He bowls to the left, he bowls to the right, that Mitchell Johnson, his bowling is shite' – stuck in his head while playing, which wasn't good for morale. In 2016, his fellow Australian Ricky Ponting could still recite in full one of their songs, which insulted the team he'd captained more than a decade earlier.

The first football chants were called 'football whispers' – presumably ironically. Newspapers started referring to them from the 1880s onwards, and they became so well known and popular that they'd be sung at non-footballing events, such as tugs-of-war, rowing regattas and even dinner parties. They often resembled, and were inspired by, war cries. Southampton FC's famous 19th-century chant of 'Yi-yi-yi' was cited as an example of this. These days, the lyrics of football chants are (occasionally at least) a little more imaginative. At one match between teams from Naples and Verona, Verona fans sang, 'We hope Vesuvius goes off,' while Napoli fans responded with

----

* This song ('Barmy Army') was written specifically for the group by lyricist Richard Stilgoe, who also wrote lyrics to Andrew Lloyd Webber's *Cats*, *Starlight Express* and *Phantom of the Opera*. Stilgoe, incidentally, donated all his royalties from *Starlight Express* to an Indian village, which at the height of the show's success amounted to £500 every day.

'Juliet is a whore'. And when Scotland faced Italy in a World Cup qualifying match in 2007, the Scottish fans chanted threateningly: 'We're gonna deep-fry yer pizzas.'

Sometimes, teams come up with innovative ways to silence rowdy opposition fans. In 1970, baseball team the Pittsburgh Pirates played against the St Louis Blues. St Louis was famous for having very loud fans, so the Pittsburgh manager gave his entire team earmuffs to block out the noise. The plan worked, inasmuch as they couldn't hear the insults hurled at them. However, they also couldn't hear the manager's calls, or each other, and after they conceded the first run after a few minutes, most of the players ditched the earmuffs. Pittsburgh lost 6–0.

The sport that boasts the loudest fans, at least according to Guinness World Records, is American football. The previously mentioned roar of 142.2dB, recorded at Arrowhead Stadium in Kansas City, Missouri, when the home team were beating the New England Patriots and attempting to distract the opposing quarterback, was not only as loud as a jet engine, it was theoretically enough to cause pain and hearing damage in fans. In soccer, fans of Turkey's Galatasaray broke the record for the loudest cheer in 2011, hitting 131dB (arguably, it's more impressive in soccer, because you don't have screens and voices over loudspeakers instructing people to cheer as loudly as they can, as you do in American sports). Galatasaray fans proudly refer to their stadium as 'Hell'.*

....

* Despite their great fanbase, the Turkish team have occasionally been on the receiving end: when they visited Chelsea, the home fans taunted them with 'You're shish, and you know you are.'

Noise can be a disadvantage to the players of some sports. On average, golfers actually perform worse when a crowd is cheering them on, as opposed to watching in silence; as do many snooker players. But clearly it's hard for lovers of either game to restrain themselves in the heat of the moment as both sports occasionally eject boisterous fans. In the 1930s, once the final putt of a golf tournament was holed, it was common for fans to fight each other to grab the ball out of the hole. Even in the solitude of their own homes, people can get rowdy. In 2020, police were called to a house of an ice hockey fan in Florida after he continuously yelled 'Shoot! Shoot!' at his television. And in 2013, when Manchester United footballer Nani was sent off in a Champions League clash, one viewer watching the game on TV was so outraged he called 999 to report it as a crime.

I'M A CELEBRITY, GET ME SOME TICKETS

The popularity of sport means that those who court publicity will often make a point of associating themselves with a certain team, but the relationship can work both ways. Delia Smith loves Norwich City football team so much that she became a majority shareholder. During one game, she seized a microphone at half-time, descended onto the pitch and began shouting at the crowd, 'This is a message for possibly the best supporters in the world. We need a 12th man here. Where are you? Where are you? Let's be having you! Come on!' (The rallying cry failed: her team lost 3–2.) And from 1976, Elton John's chairmanship of, and investment in, his beloved team, Watford, triggered a period of great success for the club, culminating in them reaching the FA Cup final in 1984. Elton was seen sobbing in the stands when they lost that game to Everton.

Politicians, of course, have to be careful about claiming attachment to teams, for fear of seeming to pander to their voters. If this chapter has shown anything, it's surely the passion with which some people are devoted to a team or sport. That's why they are quick to spot, judge and ridicule those who are faking it. Few English football-lovers will have forgotten the moment when Prime Minister David Cameron claimed to support West Ham, having mentioned on multiple previous occasions that Aston Villa were his team. In fairness to him, at least both teams play in the same colours.

Perhaps it's strange that politicians want to claim to be among the unruly human masses that constitute 'fans'. Fan behaviour, as we've seen, can be offensive, violent or stupid. At the very least, it's often unseemly. The German media, for instance, has reported in the past on the *'Pinkelproblem'* – the issue of supporters urinating everywhere except where they're supposed to when they attend games en masse. The 1948 Winter Olympics ice hockey final between Canada and Switzerland was marred by Swiss spectators who, when they realised they were going to lose, pelted the officials and Canadian players with snowballs for the remainder of play.

But no professional sportspeople would sacrifice their fans, nor could they exist without them, as they provide the demand that keeps sport alive. They're arguably the most important part of it; after all, they far outnumber the players they come to see. Teams and players alike understand this and will go to great, and sometimes unusual, lengths to make sure their followers feel involved.

In 2014, the Korean Hanwha Eagles baseball team, known for being the worst professional side in the country, installed robot fans in the hope of boosting their chances. The humanoid figures were placed in seats facing the playing field, and could be controlled remotely from home by supporters who couldn't make it to the venue. They bore photos of their puppet masters' faces on screens on the front of their heads and were able to perform Mexican waves and chants. The Japanese announced that they would utilise similarly hi-tech solutions if they won the bid for the 2022 football World Cup (which ended up taking place in Qatar). They said they'd recreate matches live in various locations using holographic technology, so that multiple stadiums of onlookers could enjoy them simultaneously.

Neither of these fixes, while they undoubtedly serve a purpose, can replace the effect of having real people physically there in a stadium, watching a match. This effect became quantifiable at the height of the Covid pandemic, when fans weren't allowed to attend matches. Researchers at the University of Leeds investigated the impact this had on football results, and found that the absence of a crowd reduced home advantage by almost half.

The existence of fans generates an exciting atmosphere, gives players a confidence boost and, crucially, provides the money that allows the sport to continue. But there's also a positive effect on the supporters themselves. Researchers at Murray State University recently found that people who identify as sports fans have lower levels of loneliness, higher degrees of self-esteem and are happier with their lives than those who don't. This is regardless of whether people support winning or losing teams.

These results are unsurprising, once you consider what fandom can offer. There's the sense of belonging to a community, which has been proven to be fundamental to human well-being. When your team wins, there's the euphoria that accompanies this; and when they lose, it's a chance to support and commiserate with each other, strengthening personal bonds. Also, as participants in the study confirmed, people use sport as a way to relieve stress or distract themselves from more serious problems. And there are so many dimensions to sport, and so many angles from which to reflect on and analyse it, as we hope this book has shown, that following just one is enough to keep any active mind occupied and fulfilled for a lifetime. For those who still haven't found their sport, worry not. There are always plenty more out there for you to try.

14

THE PREMIER LEAGUE
OF PLOUGHING

HOW HUMANS CREATE
NEW SPORTS IN THE
MOST UNUSUAL OF PLACES

Deerstalking would be a very fine
sport if only the deer had guns.
W. S. Gilbert

If taking part in sport is an inherent human trait, as we've
suggested, then it's hardly surprising that groups of like-
minded individuals manage to turn even the most esoteric
of situations into some kind of competition. The result is that
for every sport that's familiar to the global masses, there are
hundreds whose existence is unknown to your average football fan or tennis aficionado. At all times in human history,
and in every corner of the world, people have been coming up
with new games to play. This has generated an extraordinary
diversity – and that's just among the ones that are discover-
able; most are probably lost to history or unknown outside
the small communities that play them. The lesser-known
sports that we *can* find out about deserve to be celebrated, or
winced at, in all their peculiar, imaginative and sometimes
grotesque detail.

History records many bizarre and inhumane games taking place in previous centuries, when health and safety,
animal welfare and, often, basic human rights were less
prevalent. Goose-pulling, for instance, was a popular diversion all over Europe and North America from the 1600s
onwards. It involved hanging a live goose upside down from
a tree or pole, while competitors galloped beneath it on

Goose-pulling. This painting was made by Frederic Remington of 'coating himself in blood before an American football game' fame (see p. 58).

horseback trying to pull its head off. The goose's head and neck were smeared with grease to make the task harder, and the person who succeeded was rewarded by getting to keep the goose. In the case of the 17th-century New York version, they'd also have to buy everyone present a drink at the local tavern afterwards.

Even at the time, some people objected to the barbarity of goose-pulling. In 1664, in New York, the Protestant Dutch Church led protests against it, as well as against 'kissing games',* and petitioned to ban both. As a compromise, the

---

* Kissing games were controversial for centuries to follow. Their rules varied from one place to another, with the common feature being that they provided an excuse for people of the opposite sex to kiss each other at some stage (*plus ça change*). From the 1880s on, there was

local courts banned goose-pulling but allowed kissing games to continue. But despite local objections, goose-pulling continued to be broadly popular in parts of Spain, Belgium and the Netherlands (it was the Dutch who brought it to America). It still happens today in some places, though dead or plastic geese are used now.*

The Basque town of Lekeitio, which has a strong seafaring tradition, has adapted the game for the water. Once a year, a dead goose is strung across the harbour, and competitors leap from boats and cling to the goose, trying to behead it. Meanwhile, people pull at either end of the rope, tightening and slackening it to try and dislodge the player; if they're successful, the competitor plunges into the water below.

The Dutch used to play a very similar game to the Basque version, with almost the exact same rules, but they grabbed a different animal. *Palingtrekken*, or eel-pulling, was terrible for the eels involved, but good for the morale of working-class communities, who gathered in huge numbers to play. When an Amsterdam ordinance in 1870 banned it on the grounds of animal abuse, the masses were displeased, and the sport

a spate of them in British Sunday schools and temperance societies, which horrified the Church. *The Christian Million* newspaper said of them: 'teachers and senior scholars indulge for hours together and [they] form the great attraction of many gatherings'. Their journalists attended a dance where a full hour was devoted to 'kissing and kissing'.
* In Spain, live geese were still used until the end of the 1980s. The practice was reintroduced in the 1970s after being banned for a few decades by General Franco, although the ban had more to do with suppressing Basque culture than with animal welfare.

went underground (figuratively, of course). In 1886, when police tried to shut down an illegal game of *Palingtrekken* in Amsterdam's Jordaan neighbourhood, it triggered a riot so vicious that 26 people were killed.

SHOOTING A BIRDIE

The Brits' taste in blood sports around this time was a little different. Although some goose-pulling was recorded, they were much more interested in a sport called sparrow-shooting. The name was not deceptive. From the early 18th century, sparrow-shooting clubs began to proliferate around the country, with the aim of shooting as many as possible. The birds were blamed for destroying grain crops, so it was in farmers' interests to make sparrow-hunting a popular recreation.[*] Tournaments were arranged by pubs, which would award clocks, watches, stuffed birds and beer to the person who brought back the highest number. First, though, the sparrows had to be caught so that they could be released for the shoot, and this is where the 'batfowlers' came in.

Batfowlers went out at night, when sparrows were nesting, armed with large nets. They spread them over ivy-clad

---

[*] Fortunately, this British mode of culling wasn't as effective as Chairman Mao's order in the 1950s that every single sparrow in China be killed to save the grain. It had the opposite effect to the one intended: sparrows were driven almost to extinction in the country, meaning there was nothing left to eat the insects, which in turn destroyed all the crops. It was one of the major causes of the Great Chinese Famine, which killed an estimated 36 million people.

walls or trees, then shone lights at them so that the sparrows would awake, fly towards the light and land in the nets.
Batfowlers usually operated in gangs and gained a reputation for being tough and intimidating. One man living in
the Cotswolds in 1910 described his local bird-catchers, the
Badsey Batfowlers, as:

> . . . a ragged company, singing ribald choruses to the
> accompaniment of mouth-organs, tin whistles, Jews' harps
> and comb and paper, shouting out rude remarks to the old
> grannies who came to their doors to see what all the row was
> about . . . any labourer plodding his weary way homeward
> was chivvied and chaffed until he was out of earshot.

Sparrow-shooting, as with many blood sports, served both
economic and recreational purposes. Sports often develop in
this way, out of more practical activities. And in an age before
globalisation, when many more societies were based entirely
around farming, these activities were frequently agricultural.
One striking example of this is the extreme popularity in the
19th century of ploughing contests in Britain and Ireland.
Ploughs had suddenly become much more sophisticated,
thanks to the agricultural revolution, and farmers were looking to show them off. They organised competitions from the
1810s onwards, where labourers would be judged on the neat-
ness of their ploughing, furrow shape, straightness and speed.
It was also a good way for farmers to keep hold of their workers: the prospect of winning competition prizes and taking
part in the associated revelry might keep them in the fields
and away from the temptation of the growing cities' factories.

By the mid-19th century, these competitions were so popular that almost every agricultural locality held one each year, and up to 8,000 people would attend.* Champion ploughers were traded like Premier League football players are today, with landowners pitting their ploughmen against those of their rivals and negotiating deals and swaps. The competitors could be awarded a full year's wages if they won.

The sport of ploughing has survived into the 21st century. There's now a World Ploughing Championship, which in 2023 was held in Latvia. British champion Mick Chappell was chosen to represent England, and when asked how he prepared for a tournament, Chappell said he made sure to drink five pints of beer the night before.† But it's in Ireland where ploughing contests are most widely appreciated: the Irish National Ploughing Championships attracted 300,000 visitors in 2022.

KNOW THE ROPES

Another sport which is taken particularly seriously in one part of the world is tug of war, which, as we have seen, is big in Taiwan – though there they play the official Tug of War

---

* The first county-wide ploughing contest, held in Kent in 1867, was the brainchild of the MP William Hart-Dyke. Comedian Miranda Hart and gardening presenter Tom Hart-Dyke are descended from him.
† Chappell has only one leg, having lost the other to a sugar-beet harvester when he was seventeen. It happened while he was out working in the fields, so he climbed into his tractor and drove back to the farm for help – leaving his severed leg behind in the machinery.

International Federation (TWIF) version. It is also played in various other guises across the world. In fact, there's a tomb in Egypt, built around 4,500 years ago, that depicts Egyptians playing a sort of tug of war, but without the rope. Each team is made up of four competitors who line up behind each other, each holding the waist of the person in front, and the opposing teams face off. The front players on each team grab each other's arms and lean backwards, effectively pulling on each other, with everyone behind them in the line pulling too. It certainly looks like a ropeless version of the game we know today, but as with early depictions of running races and wrestling bouts, there are no accompanying hieroglyphics to confirm the rules. Perhaps, rather than toppling each other over, the aim was to remain balanced in an equilibrium.

The Vikings also had a version of tug of war, but they used animal skins instead of rope. Athletes are described as pulling at either end of a walrus or ox hide, with a pit of fire burning between them. The loser would, of course, end up in the fire. However, descriptions of the sport come from the sagas, stories which are part history, part mythology. We'll probably never know whether such competitions actually happened, but we do know that at roughly the same time, the Chinese were practising their own version. During the Tang Dynasty, the emperor used to organise mass tug-of-war games, sometimes with over 1,000 participants. The rope was up to 170m long, and unlike the modern version, it had multiple other ropes tied to it that split off in different directions, allowing more than two teams to play.

Tug of war in South Korea, where it's called *juldarigi*, has UNESCO cultural heritage status. It's played with enormous, thick ropes, as much as a metre in diameter, that weigh up to 40 tons. Usually, the western side of a village will compete against the eastern side, or the men against the women (unmarried men count as women). It's another sport conducted with an agricultural aim in mind: it's been played for centuries as a ritual to bring about a good harvest. It also tends to have a ribald element: the opposing teams traditionally trade crude, sexually suggestive insults as they play, and sometimes each team has a player whose role is to stand on the rope jeering at the opposition.

For a game mostly associated with primary-school sports days in the UK, tug of war can be very dangerous. In 1997, a huge event in Taiwan went so badly wrong that it ripped off two of the contestants' arms.* The problem was that with 1,600 people taking part, 80,000kg of force was placed on the rope. Predictably, it snapped. When this happens, that enormous amount of stored energy suddenly has to be transferred somewhere. In this case, it rebounded straight into the arms of the tuggers at the front and was powerful enough to tear them off. Accidents like this aren't as rare as you'd hope. In a 1978 attempt to break a Guinness World Record, 2,300 students in Pennsylvania pulled on a 2,000ft-long rope. When that one broke, it left five of them

----

* The arms were reattached afterwards using nerve-grafting technology, and both players regained the use of their hands. Though they probably stopped using them to play tug of war.

with missing fingertips, and one without a thumb. In other events, participants have even occasionally been killed. The TWIF is clear that if their guidelines are strictly adhered to, these accidents should never happen.* It's all about strength-testing the rope and making sure it's the correct material (not being nylon is a good start) so that it doesn't break under the pressure.

Tug of war falls into a specific category: games that most of us have played casually at some point, never suspecting that there are official, highly competitive versions out there.

PILLOW FIGHTS

Every year, the small coastal town of Ito holds the All-Japan Pillow Fighting Championships, in which hundreds of people compete. Different regions hold their own contests to decide who qualifies for the national tournament. Each match involves two teams of five people, who begin by lying under duvets, pretending to be asleep. At the whistle, they leap up and hurl pillows at each other. The aim is to prevent the pillows from striking your nominated 'king', and one defender per team is permitted to carry a blanket to fend off attacks.

America is following suit and recently set up the world's only professional pillow-fighting league, with matches available to

---

* TWIF rules include the stipulation that no doping is allowed; your shoes must be no more than 20% longer than your feet; and sitting down is strictly banned.

watch on pay-per-view channels.* Here, players compete in a fighting ring, hitting each other with pillows rather than throwing them. There are three rounds, each confined to 90 seconds, since the exertion is too extreme for players to go on for much longer than that. Many of the players are mixed martial arts (MMA) fighters looking to diversify, as well as aiming for the $5,000 prize. Although it's a new sport, with the first championship held in February 2022, participants clearly have high hopes for it. Brazilian MMA fighter Yuri Villefort said: 'I've been in martial arts my entire life, and I can tell you that this is going to be bigger than all of them.'

SEE-SAW

The ancient Romans turned see-sawing into a spectator sport, thanks to a contraption called a *petaurum*. There are scant references to how they used it, but we know it required a very long board – much longer than today's see-saws – that was supported in the middle. A person would sit at either end, catapulting their opponent high in the air and being flung up in turn. Players passed through burning hoops as they went up and down.

Those who took part in this game were called *petauristae*, which came to mean 'acrobats'. There's an account of

---

* Toronto set up its own semi-professional pillow-fighting league in the early 2000s, but it closed down in 2011. Only women were allowed to take part, and the rules stipulated that you couldn't put bricks in your pillowcase. The league was founded by someone called Stacey Case.

one performing a trick, missing his landing and falling to his death in front of the emperor Nero's box, spattering the emperor with blood.*

SACK RACE

Mo Farah, the most successful long-distance runner in British history, broke the world record in 2020 for the furthest anyone's ever run in an hour: 21.33km. But that wasn't his first world record. In 2014, he achieved the fastest time ever recorded in a 100m sack race. He had to do it in less than 40 seconds, and on his first two attempts, he came in at 42. Fortunately, the third time around he managed 39.91 seconds.† Farah was not a sack-race expert, though, so his record didn't last long; in 2017, it was smashed by father-of-two Stephen Wildish, who did it in 26.2 seconds.‡

. . . .

* Nero would have loved this, famously bloodthirsty as he was. One game he liked to play involved him dressing in furs and being locked in a cage, before being released, at which point he'd gallop around like a wild animal and bite the genitals of men who'd been strung up for the purpose.

† Similarly, former world champion hurdler Sally Pearson broke her first world record in an egg-and-spoon race. She managed to run 100m in 16.59 seconds, without dropping the egg. Naturally, she commented that she was 'happy to give it a crack'.

‡ Wildish's other achievements include mowing a 150m-long cock-and-balls into the field behind his house, which could be clearly seen on satellite images. When asked about his training regime for beating Farah's world record, he joked that he got 'some funny looks when on the treadmill in the sack'.

And it's not a new sport. Cambridge University claims (dubiously) to have the world's oldest athletics club, thanks to its first annual University Games, which were held in 1857. The event included running races of 100 yards, 440 yards, 880 yards and a mile, along with high jump, long jump, shot-put, hurdles – and the sack race.

STAIR-CLIMBING

If you've ever raced someone up a flight of stairs or simply tested yourself to see how quickly you can get to the top, you'll understand how the sport of competitive stair-climbing originated. Today, multiple events take place around the world, although most are in the US and Asia, given this is where most of the tallest buildings are. For extra streamlining, runners often shave their legs and heads in preparation for these contests, and competitors tend to get hacking coughs as they ascend, since the air is usually dry and air-conditioned. Participants call themselves 'step-brothers' and 'step-sisters'.

Suzy Walsham, who has won the women's race to the top of the Empire State Building ten times, has answered an age-old question: after conducting various test runs, she has found it is faster to walk, taking two stairs at a time, rather than running and taking them one by one.

SLIPSTREAMING

Many cyclists have, at some point in their lives (and we don't recommend this), positioned themselves behind a lorry to catch a bit of its slipstream, hoping to be carried along behind it effortlessly. The idea is that the lorry diverts air around its sides, reducing the air pressure in its wake. The cyclist supposedly encounters less drag, and even feels some forward suction.

For most amateurs, this never works quite as effectively as you'd imagine (and certainly doesn't make up for the danger of being invisible to the truck driver), but some have really mastered the art. Denise Mueller-Korenek holds the world record for the fastest person on a bicycle, hitting 184mph in 2018. She was towed by a vehicle driven by racing driver Shea Holbrook until she reached 100mph. Then Holbrook released her, driving in front of her for the next 3.5 miles, as Mueller-Korenek pedalled to stay in the slipstream. Had she veered just a few centimetres off course, she would have been struck by a hurricane-level wall of wind and hurled off the bike. As it was, she sheepishly admitted afterwards that they'd accidentally gone almost 10mph faster than the 175mph safety limit they'd set themselves.

Back in 1899, the cycling speed record was held by a man named Charles Minthorn 'Mile-a-Minute' Murphy. He became, as his nickname suggests, the first person to ride a bike for a mile in under a minute. He persuaded an engineer to build two miles of railway track specifically for him to cycle along, and after 12 years of planning and various failed attempts, he finally managed to complete a mile behind a train in 58 seconds, before the train braked too hard and Murphy's bike crashed into the back of it, flinging him through the air. He was caught by two bystanders and came out of it remarkably unscathed, commenting that 'Grown men hugged and kissed each other. One man fainted and another went into hysterics, while I remained speechless on my back.'

KEEPING A BALLOON IN THE AIR

No longer just a game played at under-twelves' birthday parties, there is now a Balloon World Cup, in which competitors try to keep a balloon from touching the floor.* Contests are one-on-one, and the aim is to hit the balloon to a spot where your opponent won't reach it in time. In a nod to its

The Balloon World Cup, whose first iteration in 2021 was watched by around 8 million people on the online streaming service Twitch.

* One of the authors of this book briefly co-held the world record for keeping a balloon in the air (two people). In the proud tradition of Sir Garfield Sobers, she did so with a glass of wine in hand throughout.

birthday-party-in-the-living-room origins, soft furnishings and various other obstacles are installed to add a layer of difficulty.*

The Balloon World Cup is particularly popular in Latin America, but whichever country you visit, you'll find enthusiasm for some obscure, creative or underappreciated sport. Sometimes this will be a nationally beloved pastime and something that is almost unknown in the rest of the world.

JEUX AVEC LES FRONTIÈRES

Almost everyone in Bhutan has seen or played a game of *khuru* at some point. Simply put, it's giant darts. The game is broadly the same as normal darts, except that it's played outside, the target is at least 20m away, and the darts are much heavier and about five times the size of the ones you find in British pubs. The target, however, is not much bigger than a British dartboard, meaning hits – which are worth one point – are very rare, and a single point is often enough to win you the whole game. The sport was traditionally played exclusively by men, but these days the women's tournament attracts bigger crowds. Aum Dechey, a mother-of-two who

---

* The Balloon World Cup is organised by esports caster Ibai Llanos and Gerard Piqué, better known as one of the best Spanish football players of the 2000s. Piqué played for Barcelona, Manchester United and the Spanish national team. He has two children with singer-songwriter Shakira, and she attended the 2021 Balloon World Cup. The couple had split by the time the 2022 one came around, but there is no suggestion the competition was to blame.

takes part every year, is such a devotee that she says given a choice between food and *khuru*, she'd always choose *khuru*.

Meanwhile, one of the most popular games in Kazakhstan is a horse race called *Kyz kuu*, literally meaning 'catch the girl'. A man and woman compete on horseback, wearing traditional dress. The woman gallops past the man, at which point he gives chase and tries to grab her. If he fails to catch up with her by the finish line, she gets to chase him back to the start, whipping him all the way.

But neither of these sports can rival kabbadi in India, in terms of the scale and enthusiasm of its following. With evidence that it dates back 4,000 years, today it's the most-watched sport in the country after cricket. On their turn, a player has to enter their opponents' territory and tag as many of the opposition as possible before returning safely to their own half of the court, with the stand-out feature being that they have to do so all in one breath. To prove they aren't inhaling, they have to chant the word 'kabbadi' loudly while conducting their raid.

In China, a sport that's less exhausting, but no less exhilarating to those involved, is cricket fighting. It's been a widespread practice for at least 1,000 years.* As with human combat sports, the crickets (almost always male) are placed in a ring to face off against each other. And just like human boxers, they are weighed beforehand – to the nearest

---

* Crickets started out as coveted, non-combative pets in China, highly valued for the 'songs' they generate when they rub their wings together. Emperors used to keep them as pets by their bedsides.

hundredth of a gram – so they can be weight-matched with their opponent.

Unlike human fighters, the crickets are given herbal baths, incentivised with maggots before fights and trained by coaches who poke them with mouse whiskers. They are also permitted conjugal visits by female crickets. It's a huge industry, with the biggest games broadcast on national TV.

Similarly, spider wrestling is so common in the Philippines that it had to be banned in some parts of the country in the 1990s because it distracted children from their schoolwork: kids were skipping lessons in order to hunt spiders for fights. The spiders (almost always female in this case) win if they kill their victim or manage to wrap her up in a cocoon. Techniques for improving spiders' combat abilities include feeding them chilli peppers, starving them for a day before a fight and (just like human stair-climbers) shaving their legs.

Invertebrates also get swept up in some of the more unusual sports in Europe. Finland has both a mosquito-killing championship, where you have to swat as many as possible in five minutes, and an ant-nest-sitting competition, to see who can last the longest while sitting on – you guessed it – an ant nest. Famously, the Finns also organise wife-carrying races, a boot-throwing contest and a heavy-metal knitting championship.*

....

* Competitors are asked to knit on stage while a heavy-metal
band performs behind them. Points are awarded for style, with the
inaugural winner, Finland's Giga Body Metal, combining knitting and
heavy metal with sumo and Japanese kabuki theatre.

The Finns certainly seem to excel in bizarre, niche sports, but the rest of Europe is not far behind. Some similarly off-beat events are deeply rooted in each country's culture and history, such as *fierljeppen* (literally 'furthest jumper') in the Netherlands.* Due to their country's flat, wet geography, the Dutch have always needed to navigate large amounts of water in order to get around. Historically, farmers used to get from one patch of their land to another by pole-vaulting over the canals that divided it.

Today, the technique is practised out of fun rather than necessity. *Fierljeppen* contests are slightly different to main-stream pole-vaulting, in that the pole is rooted to the spot – placed upright in a river. The athlete has to sprint towards the water, leap onto the pole and use their momentum to pro-pel it forward while also climbing up it as high as they can, enough so that it will deposit them on the other bank.

Norway, meanwhile, has the ominously named *dødsing*, or 'death-diving', where rather than hurl themselves across the water, competitors throw themselves into it. The catch is that they do so from a great height – over 30m for the top com-petitors – and have to maintain a belly-flop pose until the last moment. Falling through the air with arms and legs out-stretched and stomach set to hit the water first, they curl into

----

* Another Dutch contribution to the 'quirky sports' category are the Headwind Cycling Championships. The event takes place on a storm barrier facing the North Sea, and organisers ensure it happens during a storm. The aim is to race into the wind for 8.5km. In 2019, the competition had to be abandoned halfway through on safety grounds because it was too windy.

the foetal position at the last second and are awarded points depending on how late they manage to leave it.

Another European pastime that's definitely not for the faint of heart is Estonian *kiiking*. The Estonians took every child's fantasy – to be able to go over the top on a swing, performing a full 360-degree loop – and made it a reality. The arms of their competitive swings are solid metal, and the swinger is fixed to the seat by their feet.* It's a contest to see who can propel themselves over the top and all the way round with the longest swing-arm. The current world record is 7.38m.

While it may not be able to boast the adrenaline-pumping heights of *fierljeppen*, *dødsing* or *kiiking*, Britain is certainly no stranger to bizarre, very localised sports, past and present. Among the most well known are cheese-rolling, where participants hurl themselves down a steep slope in Gloucestershire in hot pursuit of a round of Double Gloucester cheese,† and bog-snorkelling, a swimming race through 110m of wet peat in mid-Wales. But in almost every locality, there's a similarly unconventional sporting event to be found.

Witcham, in Cambridgeshire, boasts an annual pea-shooting tournament. It was conceived in the 1970s by a

---

* There's evidence that Estonian kids have been performing the trick on makeshift wooden versions since the turn of the 20th century.
† The cheese is always the true winner. It escapes every year – unsurprisingly, given it reaches speeds of 70mph – and so the winning person is the one who gets to the bottom of the hill first. St John Ambulance always has a presence there, and they have their work cut out: they say they always end up treating 30 to 40 people for their injuries.

headmaster who kept confiscating shooters from his pupils and decided the children's skills could be put to better use. Participants have to hit a target from 12ft, and contestants, who now come from miles around,[*] have to bring their own shooters, which must not exceed 12in in length, and to which the more serious players add laser or telescopic sights. Competitors have to use the official tournament peas, so there's no chance of anyone cheating with pre-smoothed, extra-streamlined ones. The sign for the White Horse pub in Witcham now features four-time men's world champion Ian Ashmeade, atop a noble steed, brandishing his shooter.

Lincolnshire, meanwhile, has the Haxey Hood game. This, too – like most unusual British sports – comes with an accompanying imaginative back story. These tales are easy enough to verify when they date back to 1970s schoolboys, but less so when they claim provenance from the 1300s. According to Haxey Hood legend, a 14th-century noblewoman called Lady de Mowbray had her hood blown off once when she was out riding. Thirteen labourers chased after it and returned the hood to her, and from this (alleged) incident, the great game grew. Thousands turn up each year to participate, as a 'hood' (these days, a leather tube) is tossed into a melee and four chaotic, unofficial teams compete to kick and roll it to their favourite of four nearby pubs. The contest ends when the hood reaches the doorstep of one of them, at which point that

----

[*] The championships are dominated by English participants, though an American, Dan Sargent, has taken the title twice, in 1996 and 1998.

establishment is declared the winner, and the hood is cere-
moniously drenched in beer. Ample drinking, of course, then
commences.

Every shire has a contest along the lines of Haxey Hood or
pea-shooting, but perhaps the spiritual home of quirky British
sporting events is the small town of Chipping Campden, in
the Cotswolds. It was here that the Olimpicks were established. Not the ancient Olympics or the modern Olympics
– but the Cotswold Olimpicks. They were the brainchild of a
lawyer named Robert Dover, who founded them at the beginning of the 17th century in order to provide ordinary people
with 'harmless, honest sports' and an occasion that embodied
'jollity'. King James VI and I explicitly sanctioned them, and
even lent Dover some of his clothes so he could dress up as the
monarch as part of the pageantry.

The contest included sledgehammer tossing, fighting with
sticks, leaping, dancing, gymnastics, ball-throwing and a
sort of wrestling that morphed over the years into the great
British sport of 'shin-kicking'. A structure dubbed 'Dover's
castle' was erected for the event – a set of mobile, wooden
mock battlements positioned on top of a hill, from which pen-
nants were flown and cannons fired blanks.

The Cotswold Olimpicks became an annual sporting
extravaganza and were so successful that in 1636, a collection of poems, *Annalia Dubrensia*, was published to celebrate
them. We assume, though can't be sure, that there was a
hint of irony in this contribution from one fan called William
Denny, who made the comparison with the ancients:

COTSWOLD GAMES.

The Cotswold Games, launched in the 17th century by Robert Dover. Dover can be seen on his horse in the foreground, keeping an eye on events.

Oh most famous Greece!
That for brave pastimes wert earth's masterpeece
Had not our English Dover thus outdone
Thy four* games with his Cotswoldian one.

The Cotswold Olimpicks have continued on and off (taking an enforced break, for instance, during the British interregnum, and again in the 1850s, when the land they occupied was sold off) up until the present day. It's no surprise that King James VI and I supported them. He was a great patron of sports and even wrote, in 1617, his own *Book of Sports*.[†] This laid out an approach to physical recreation that his people should follow. He published it first in Lancashire, where, the Lancastrian author of *this* sports book is proud to say, he considered it most necessary. A year later, he extended the print run to cover the entire country. The declaration banned local religious leaders from preventing people playing games on Sundays 'to refresh their spirits', as the clergy had been doing. As the King argued:

For when shall the common people have leave to exercise, if not upon the Sundays & holy days, seeing they must apply

* The four ancient games he refers to as being inferior to the Cotswold ones are the ancient Olympics, the Pythean Games, the Nemean Games and the Isthmian Games.
† While *this* James's 'Book of Sports' was ostensibly a solo project, he was married to Anne of Denmark – or Anna, as she always signed herself. Anna involved herself in many of her husband's political affairs and was a keen dancer and horse-rider, so perhaps theirs was a joint effort, too.

their labour, & win their living in all working days? . . .
[I rule that] our good people be not disturbed, letted, or
discouraged from any lawful recreation, such as dancing,
either men or women, archery for men, leaping, vaulting,
or any other such harmless recreation, nor from having
of May-Games, Whitson Ales, and Morris-dances, and the
setting up of May-poles & other sports therewith used.

For the ease, comfort & recreation of our well deserving
people, we do ratify and publish this.

The *other* author of this book, who lives in and is writing
from Oliver Cromwell's birthplace, is less proud to admit that
when Cromwell's Puritans – not known for their love of fri-
volity and recreation – took power, they ordered the *Book of
Sports* to be publicly burnt. Fortunately, its tenets, along with
the Cotswold Olimpicks and similar banned activities, were
restored, along with the monarchy, 11 years later, and have
endured ever since. In Stuart England, as in almost every
other time and place, people always found a way to play.

EPILOGUE

HOW SPORT AND LIFE ARE INESCAPABLY INTERTWINED

We do not cease to play because
we grow old. We grow old
because we cease to play.
G. B. Shaw

If there is one thing that unites us, be it the bog-snorkellers
of Wales, the belly-floppers of Norway or the pillow fighters
of Japan, it's that we all just want to get together and have
some fun. And at the end of the day, that's why sport is part
of every culture and society throughout all of history. It's a
natural human impulse to want to play. The human body
is made for it. Our bodies are healthier for taking part in
it, and since we're social animals, our brains are rewarded
not just by taking part in it, but by watching others doing
it. Our ingenuity has created not just the rules that define
sports, but also the intricate and ingenious items needed
to play them. We are captivated by stories of superhuman
exertions and dramatic victories, and yet we love nothing
more than a gallant loser. But just as the story of humankind is not always a happy one, so that is reflected in sport:
some people have it in their nature to cheat, inequality can
result in grossly unfair contests, and sometimes they reflect
society's greatest ills, with whole swathes of the population
excluded from playing.

The sporting community, from the players to the officials
to the organisers to the fans, comes together every day for

events that not only create drama in the moment, but stories and memories that are passed through the generations – from father to daughter, mother to son – and even recounted thousands of years later, when we can still imagine ourselves cheering on a proven winner or commiserating with a plucky loser. When Liverpool FC manager Bill Shankly said, 'Some people believe football is a matter of life and death. I am very disappointed with that attitude. I can assure you it is much, much more important than that,' he could have been speaking about almost any sport, even cheese-rolling, and for at least some of the people involved, it would be no exaggeration. As the character Dani Rojas says in the multi-award-winning TV series *Ted Lasso*, 'Football is Life'. We would go one step further and say not only that 'Sport is Life', but also that 'Life is Sport'. At a time when the world often seems to lurch from one crisis to another and many of us are consumed with our personal problems, sport is always there in the background, giving groups of people a shared goal and allowing individuals to live only in the moment.

Finally, and with all this in mind, we ask the reader to consider the seminal cricket match in 1882 when the Australian national team beat England on English soil for the first time. Famously, the newspapers called it the 'death of English cricket' and announced that 'the body will be cremated and the ashes taken to Australia'. This was the beginning of the myth of 'The Ashes', which were later embodied in the form of a burnt set of bails in an urn, which is given to the captain of the victorious team every two years. But the history books focus less on a man called

George Spendlove, who was watching in the crowd with his friend that day.

Spendlove had enjoyed most of the match when he began to feel unwell. He stood up from his chair, collapsed, and his friend called out for a doctor. The first to respond to the call was none other than W. G. Grace, the English team's best player, who also happened to have a medical degree. Grace had Spendlove carried into the pavilion, where he treated him, thus delaying the game by 10 minutes, since Grace was supposed to be batting next.

The cricketer was unable to save the fan, and Spendlove died, after which Grace promptly went out to bat. But viewed from Spendlove's perspective, there are worse ways to go, surely. As a cricket fan, he spent his last moments at the famous Oval cricket ground, with W. G. Grace – probably the greatest figure in the history of English cricket – watching over him. And when Spendlove took his last breath, England were still ahead.

ACKNOWLEDGEMENTS

We couldn't write a book about sport, especially one with an entire chapter about teamwork, without acknowledging the backroom staff and teammates who have done so much to assist, allowing us to simply stand on the goal line and tap the ball into the back of the net.

First of all, thanks to Fred Baty, without whose brilliant editing this book would have been full of tortured metaphors like the one in that last paragraph. From the beginning, we've known we can depend on his excellent judgement and honest advice to improve on our work. There wouldn't be a book if it weren't for Hannah Knowles and Laura Hassan, who between them managed everything at the Faber end, turning our idea into a reality and remaining relaxed, encouraging and good-humoured throughout. And we're hugely grateful to everyone else at Faber – Sara Cheraghlou, Ian Bahrami, Sophie Clarke, Anne Owen and the rest – who worked tirelessly to transform our words into this actual real-life object.

Our friends at QI have also provided invaluable help along the way. Tara Dorrell and Coco Lloyd's eagle-eyed checking no doubt saved us much embarrassment. Jack Chambers' picture research uncovered some truly fascinating and funny images to compliment the text. Alex Bell's influence can be seen in all parts of the design. And the rest of the QI family, too numerous to mention, have been consistently supportive, as well as picking up the work we couldn't do because we were off writing about sports.

As for our *No Such Thing As A Fish* family, Dan Schreiber and Andrew Hunter Murray, thanks for any facts in here that are pilfered from your original podcast research, and thanks in advance for letting us constantly mention the book on the podcast. And in terms of other publicity, no one outside of QI and Faber would know we'd written this if it weren't for Gaby Jerrard and Ruth Killick, who have both been brilliant at helping us spread the word; and James Rawson, who has kept the masses on social media well informed.

James would like to thank: my wife Polina, who always feigned interest when I told her *yet another* fact about darts. My daughter Angèle, who learned 'ball' as one of her first words, and still gleefully shouts whenever she sees one. And my wider family, who got me interested in sport in the first place; especially Eugene, whom we sadly lost while I was writing this book, but who would always support me when I played football growing up, and who taught me to play golf.

Anna would like to thank: Jamie and Charlie, who chipped in with expert opinions at crucial moments. Jane, whose description of her especially courageous marathon was often revisited as a source of inspiration when writing this book. Ralph, for the many miles we have travelled, the many games we have seen. Matilda, who had the courtesy to wait until the day after we'd finished the first draft before being born. And Bean, for the honest and insightful advice, the extensive knowledge-sharing, the endless patience and, well, everything really.

Finally, we're deeply thankful, as ever, to Sarah and John Lloyd, who supported us unreservedly as this project morphed from the 'QI Book of Balls' – a simple collection of sporting trivia – into the all-consuming beast it became. Sarah always ensured that we had the time and space to research and write it; John provided overarching guidance and wisdom. *A Load of Old Balls* is very much inspired by his mantra that everything is interesting if looked at in the right way.

PHOTO CREDITS

Page 10: Werner Forman/Universal Images Group via Getty Images

Page 17: Historical Views/Alamy Stock Photo

Page 39: Kirby Lee/Getty Images

Page 44: Bettmann/Getty Images

Page 51: Bettmann/Getty Images

Page 59: Bettmann/Getty Images

Page 88: Associated Press/Alamy Stock Photo

Page 96: Wikimedia

Page 111: *Daily Express*/Pictorial Parade/Archive Photos/ Getty Images

Page 117: Underwood Archives/Getty Images

Page 124: Bernard Cahier/Getty Images

Page 131: New York Public Library/Smith Collection/Gado/ Alamy Stock Photo

Page 140: Fairfax Media via Getty Images

Page 146: Michael Runkel/robertharding/Alamy Stock Photo

Page 168: Universal History Archive/Universal Images Group via Getty Images

Page 171: Albert Meyer/The Calne Collection/Popperfoto via Getty Images

• Photo Credits •

Page 182: GL Archive/Alamy Stock Photo

Page 189: World History Archive/Alamy Stock Photo

Page 201: Shizuo Kambayashi/Associated Press/Alamy Stock Photo

Page 219: Carl Iwasaki/The Chronicle Collection/Getty Images

Page 230: Alan Gignoux/Alamy Stock Photo

Page 240: Kiyoshi Ota/Stringer/Getty Images

Page 246: David Madison/Getty Images

Page 256: Popperfoto via Getty Images

Page 283: Bettmann/Getty Images

Page 293: Matthew Ashton – AMA/Getty Images

Page 309: Paul Natkin/Getty Images

Page 324: Wikiart/*Harper's Weekly*

Page 336: Cesc Maymo/Stringer/Getty Images

Page 344: Frontispiece to *Annalia Dubrensia*, 1636

INDEX

· Index ·